Mark

Hope you enjoy the true lawyer stories!!

WIN
SOME
LOSE
SOME

WIN SOME LOSE SOME

THE TRIALS AND TRIBULATIONS IN THE CAREER OF A TRIAL LAWYER

a memoir by

MARK N. STAGEBERG

ISBN 13: 978-1-59298-299-8

Library of Congress Catalog Number: 2012901201

Printed in the United States of America

First Printing: 2012

16 15 14 13 12   5 4 3 2 1

Beaver's Pond Press, Inc.
7108 Ohms Lane
Edina, MN 55439–2129
(952) 829-8818
www.BeaversPondPress.com

To order, visit www.BeaversPondBooks.com
or call (800) 901-3480. Reseller discounts available.

TO MY CHILDREN,
MINDY AND JEFFREY

CONTENTS

CONTENTS

PART III

INTRODUCTION

As I drifted towards and into retirement as a civil trial attorney I reflected back on my career of 45 years of memories of the many trials that I both won and lost for clients. In telling some of these tales to those willing to listen I found both lawyers and non-lawyers usually enjoying these true to life trial stories. In my spare time in the evening I started writing a few chapters of some past lawyer event or trial. Finding the experience of reliving these events most enjoyable, it soon became a regular habit to work on the next chapter. Having a few friends read a chapter or two gave me further encouragement to continue.

As a starting point, I suspect that my legal career was probably much more diverse and interesting than most lawyers. Even the law school days of a summer clerkship on Wall Street in New York and fighting off the Vietnam draft were probably more stimulating events than experienced by most lawyers. Thereafter my trial career was almost evenly divided, first doing defense trial work and then shifting 180 degrees to represent the plaintiff's side. I also had the varied experience of practicing in a large law firm with all of its problems and then finishing my career as a sole practitioner. My experiences have been extremely varied. Not many lawyers have had another lawyer drop dead in front of them in the courtroom. Sometime after keeping track of my win-and-loss record in about 160 jury trials, I lost count of the exact number of completed trials. There probably have been over 175 jury trials, all of them different. Over the years, I handled litigation cases in 15 different states with federal or state court jury trials in eight states. I clearly did not win every trial. Many of those losses will be reported, because just like the wins, there often have been interesting and often humorous aspects of the trials.

Each of the stories that I tell is as factually accurate as possible. If documents or appellate cases are available they will be cited. In some cases I have had to paraphrase the trial questions and answers being asked, but they still are substantially correct in terms of what actually occurred. In most instances I have not used actual names of clients unless the litigation involved became a matter of public record. Similarly, I have not identified particular lawyers by name unless the lawyers are dead and gone, or I can recall with absolute certainty the true events being described. A deceased client or lawyer cannot sue me for libel, and the truth is always an absolute defense to any defamation claim.

It is unknown whether this lifetime history of the excitement of being a trial lawyer will guide a few budding lawyers to give up a boring career of tax work or real estate in favor of the battles of the courtroom. That is not the goal of this work. Rather, it is to hopefully provide readers with some insight and humor into the life of a civil trial lawyer.

PART I

I COMPLETED LAW SCHOOL IN 1969
AND STARTED IN THE PRACTICE OF LAW.
THE EARLY YEARS HAD LOTS OF UPS AND DOWNS
AS I LEARNED HOW TO BE A LAWYER.

CHAPTER 1

BECOMING A LAWYER

Some professionals can look back to their teenage and high school years and say, "I always wanted to be a doctor," or "From day one, my heart told me to become a lawyer." I can honestly say that, for me, the thought of becoming a civil trial lawyer—or any kind of lawyer—never crossed my mind until I had rejected a lot of other careers. My college days started at Concordia College in Moorhead, Minnesota. After the first and second school years I returned home to work on my father's sawmill. On August 8, 1964, a tragedy struck and the whole sawmill operation burned to the ground. Initially, my father and I tried to battle the blaze until we realized the effort was hopeless and we retreated. We stood and watched as the sawmill and many piles of cut lumber were destroyed. With no more financial support from home I transferred to the University of Minnesota, borrowed money, and washed dishes the next two years for my room and board.

As I started my senior year at the U, majoring in economics, I had numerous job opportunities. In 1968 it was a buyer's market

1

for grads with a four-year degree in almost any field, from biology to political science. Hundreds of prospective employers came to the U, interviewing any candidate with a better-than-B grade point average for the position of "management trainee." I could have signed up for dozens of interviews with good, national companies. With my B+ or A– grade point average, a respectable appearance (without three ears or a shaggy hippie haircut), and a modestly personable showing in initial job interviews, I received several job offers. One interview produced an invitation to fly to New York City for a home-office visit with the insurance giant Chubb and Sons, a trip that was memorable in many respects. It was my first flight on a commercial jet plane. As the Boeing 720B rolled down the Minneapolis runway for takeoff on a snowy December morning, I watched the wing tips bounce in and out of the snowdrifts along the runway. I was, frankly, scared stiff, and I was amazed when the huge aircraft left the drifted ground behind. After my first New York taxi ride I landed in a historic hotel in Midtown called the Algonquin, another great experience for a small-town boy from Orr, Minnesota.

The Chubb interview in the Wall Street district was as influential an event as any in my career path—a negative influence, that is. My glad-handing interviewer led me into the main workplace, a massive array of desks and workers in a huge room with hardly any dividers between their cramped spaces. Unlike the office peons in today's cartoon *Dilbert*, these workers did not even have their own cubicles. I recall asking the interviewer, "If I was hired as a management trainee, would this be where I would be working?" He proudly answered, "Yes," but he assured me that by working hard and moving up the ladder I could have my own private office. He showed me the private offices belonging to a few vice presidents, all of whom were gray-haired or bald. These higher-ups must have toiled in the morass of mundane workers for decades. This whole interview was a tremendous turnoff about the whole corporate working world.

My second turnoff interview was with the Big Blue: IBM. I was offered a management trainee position there and went to their Minneapolis office for follow-up interviews. IBM at that time stressed an image of corporate unity, requiring that everyone wear white shirts, gray slacks, and blue blazers. I could not imagine myself blending into that big corporate scene.

So where does a disillusioned student in the fall of his senior year go? I got some help from my older brother, Roger. He had graduated from the U in engineering mathematics, a highly specialized science usually leading to an engineering or other technical career. But he ended up at the U of M law school, a choice that still befuddles me. My brother provided a helpful comment: "If you go to law school you have lots of options." With no better ideas, I signed up for the Law School Admissions Test (LSAT) and completed it with better-than-average results. With that okay LSAT score and my decent grade point average, I qualified for admission to the U of M law school, and in the middle of the winter quarter my application for the Class of 1969 was accepted. I was admitted with no scholarships and no financial help from home. Law school looked like a lot of borrowed money. In March, when winter-quarter grades came out, I had a 4.0 average—straight As on the grade sheet. I took that transcript into the admissions dean at the law school, a great guy named Robert Grabb, and gave him my re-energized pitch for a tuition scholarship. Within a few days Dean Grabb had awarded me a full tuition and books scholarship for all three years of law school.

The first days of freshman year in law school rival those of marines in basic training for stress and tension. The 1973 movie *The Paper Chase,* about law students at Harvard, depicts exactly what U of M law students could expect. Like the students in the film we were told, implicitly or explicitly, "Look to your right and to your left. By the end of the year those two will be gone from your law school class." Gulp. I had a one-in-three chance of success. Two hundred of us registered on Thursday and Friday, with classes to begin Monday morning.

My first Monday class was at 8:15 a.m. along with a hundred of my colleagues. The class was Civil Procedure, taught by J. J. Cound, a stocky, no-nonsense professor with a Marine No. 1 haircut. As we sat, pens and notebooks ready, in a semicircular classroom, Professor Cound surveyed our eager faces from the center podium and, without a word of greeting or introduction, said, "Mr. Erickson, please tell me about the case of Smith versus A.B.C. Corporation. After a stumbling response from Erickson [I do not remember the real name of the unlucky classmate] of, "I'm sorry, I cannot tell you what it is about," Professor Cound looked again at his alphabetical seating chart and asked, "Mr. Jones [another forgotten victim], can you tell me about the case of Smith versus A.B.C. Corporation?" Again, the same reply: "I cannot, sir." J. J. Cound then said, "Did any of you read the assignment that I put on the bulletin board last Friday in preparation for today's class?" If any one of the stunned members of the Class of 1969 had seen the assignment and come prepared for Cound's first session, there was no way on God's green earth that he or she would have spoken up at that terrifying moment. Seeing no hands and hearing no response, J. J. Cound gathered his papers and said, "Class dismissed." One hundred of us sat stunned, not knowing what to say or do. I recall a few of the boisterous class members expounding, "This is bullshit." I remember quietly slithering off to reflect on what I had gotten myself into.

Fortunately, law school got better. Most of the professors were scholars and really were trying to train us to become successful lawyers. One exception was our first-year Legal Process class. The then-dean of the law school was Carl Auerbach. He might have been a good administrator, but he was a lousy teacher. The class he taught supposedly covered the different aspects of law, such as statutes, ordinances, court decisions, and constitutional provisions, and their interplay in the legal system. But Auerbach never explained this purpose, so for weeks we had no clue why we were taking this class. With no pleasantness in his confrontation of bewildered students, Auerbach repeatedly exposed our ignorance before our classmates. Every day we walked out of class shaking our heads, saying, "What is this all about?" But by the end of the semester I had somehow garnered enough to get a B on the final exam.

Law school exams are like nothing else. First-year classes covered the full school year, with the grade in each course depending on a year-end score on a three-to four-hour essay test. Throughout the first year it was both overtly and subtly impressed on us that first-year grades were of prime importance in determining our legal careers. If your first-year grades were good enough, you might be invited to join the law review and would have the opportunity to interview in the fall of your second year for a summer clerkship. You got the impression that, if you did not get good first-year grades, you would struggle for your whole legal career. In actuality this stratification was far from accurate. Some of those in the bottom of my class became highly successful lawyers and judges. With that kind of pressure, though, we first-year students studied our asses off. As much as you wanted to engage in group studying and sharing ideas, there always loomed the competitive admonition that two out of three of us would not be back for our second year. I do not remember ever being so psyched up for any event as I was for the first-year finals. The ugly little blue books were passed out with a sheet of hypothetical facts, as though a client had relayed them to you in a law office. You then had to write, based on what nine months of class had taught you, an analysis of the issues in the client's hypothetical problem and how you would reach the correct solution. The grading of these lengthy, handwritten essays was in the hands of the professors who assigned grades based on how many correct points had been suggested in the essays.

Finishing the first-year exams was a tremendous relief. Classmates scattered, looking for work of any kind. With few legal skills as yet, we didn't have much of a shot at the few summer clerkships available for first-year students, especially since grades did not come out until midsummer. Several of us sought whatever summer work was available. Someone suggested driving for Yellow Cab, where you could work for sixty days as a provisional driver without joining the union. Finding nothing better, I signed up and qualified as a driver. Cab driving is a competitive business; every driver is competing for fares, not only against other cab companies, but against fellow drivers. After a few days of work I found that by outsmarting most of the other drivers I could usually have a full cab and earn over twelve dollars an hour for my work. Not bad for a summer job in 1967. I joined several other law school cab drivers in a network on the radios.

In mid-July the word came out that the first-year grades had been posted in the law school. I remember vividly the pounding of my heart as I drove my yellow cab toward the law school to check my grades. With my mind far from careful driving, I rear-ended a car on my way there. Getting out, I found a foreigner in the driver's seat; seeing little visible damage, I buffaloed that innocent accident victim, convincing him that no damage meant no injury. Lucky for me, he apparently did not get the cab's license number as I sped away. I screeched to a halt in front of the law school and ran up the steps to retrieve my grades. To my great relief, I got As and Bs, calculating out to a 13.2 GPA on a 15-point scale. I was in the top 10 percent of the class!

Having good first-year grades did open a whole world of future lawyering prospects for me. I was invited to join law review, which is a positive on your résumé throughout your whole legal career. The following fall, interviewing for second-year summer clerkships was wide open. Being adventuresome, I interviewed with several Wall Street firms. One partner, Howard Orr, was interviewing for the prominent New York firm Milbank, Tweed, Hadley & McCloy. Being from Orr, Minnesota, I hit it off well with him, and he invited me to New York for further interviews, as did a second Wall Street firm. The New York interview trip was most enjoyable, as I was well-entertained by the firms' interviewing partners. I accepted a summer clerkship with Milbank, Tweed at what I thought was a very generous salary. Later that spring, during my second year, Milbank advised me that starting lawyer and law clerk salaries had substantially risen in NYC. My upcoming summer salary had therefore been doubled. Not bad for someone who had never worked a day as a lawyer or law clerk.

The summer of 1968 in New York was most enjoyable, but also eventful. I had just gotten married. As my wife Roxanne and I drove our 1966 Mustang across the country to our rented apartment in Brooklyn, the radio reported that Robert Kennedy had just been shot in Los Angeles. For the rest of the trip we stayed constantly tuned to the radio, and we mourned with the nation his unwarranted death.

We had planned to spend two days in Washington, DC, on our way to New York. When we arrived at our nice hotel, a few blocks from the Capitol, we took most of our belongings inside, but I left my two suits and ties in the Mustang overnight. The next morning the car window was broken and the suits and ties were gone. Those two seventy-dollar suits from Nate's must have looked awfully good to someone who apparently needed them more than me. This story comes with a postscript, too. Two of my law school classmates also took summer clerkships in New York. One fellow and his wife parked outside an upper Manhattan brownstone and went in to check on an apartment. Upon returning a few minutes later they found their VW had been broken into and most of their belongings stolen. The third class-mate's car was broken into later in the summer, and his wife's only copy of her master's thesis was taken. We Minnesotans were three for three in learning the facts of life in the big city.

I could hardly walk into the prestigious Milbank, Tweed law firm without a suit and tie. Fortunately, Mr. Orr excused me the first morning with advice about a discount clothing store in lower Manhattan, much like Nate's in Minneapolis, to replenish my wardrobe. At about seventy dollars a suit and five dollars a tie, I was soon decked out in New York's finest cuts for $200.

The Milbank summer was great in every respect. There were fourteen of us summer clerks. Even with several highbrow hotshots there from Yale and Harvard, I was able to hold my own in my cheap suits. Milbank worked to make the summer clerks happy: The firm didn't work us very hard and tried to convince us to return as associate lawyers after our third year. The firm could then work the tar out of us. We clerks were shuffled around to different departments, doing minor projects and never having to work hard or long hours. We were not expected to arrive early, and the associates and young partners regularly had a 9:30 iced-tea break. Several times a week partners or associates took us out to lunch on the firm. I especially remember leisurely walks down to the Fulton Fish Market and great lunches at Sloppy Louie's. When out entertaining the summer clerks, none of the firm lawyers seemed too concerned about getting back to work.

One of my fond memories was playing on the Milbank summer softball team. My Yale and Harvard colleagues exhib-ited little competitive athletic prowess, while I quickly proved my ability and became the team shortstop. Once a week we would gather somewhere in Manhattan on a vacant lot, often without a grass infield, and challenge a team from another New York law firm. We were pretty good, winning most of our games, and we happily drank a lot of beer in celebration.

In contrast to my easy-going summer at Milbank, my two classmates had quite different experiences at other New York firms. Those firms worked the summer clerks hard to make them prove their worth. One classmate pulled at least one all-nighter on a firm project. I found it interesting that the Milbank firm culture made it quite apparent to me which of the firm associates would make partner and which would not. Making partner in a New York firm, and in fact any firm, is the goal of any associate and justifies hard, long hours and the sacrifice of family and outside activities. The Milbank partners were impressive and hard-working, coming in early and staying late. I could tell that several of my softball-playing, beer-drinking buddies were not going to make it. It was another good lesson learned on how to succeed—and how not to succeed—in the legal business. At the conclusion of the summer all fourteen of us Milbank summer clerks were told how great a job we had done (having actually accomplished very little), and all of us were offered full-time jobs upon graduation. My U of M classmates at the other firms also earned job offers for their long hours.

After earning good first- and second- year grades, I found that the pressure was off during the third and final year. The big challenge was getting elected to the board of editors on the law review. During the second year I had written two law review articles, both of which had been published, and that was unusual for a second-year student. I thought I was a shoo-in for an editor position. But the committee of past editors and faculty members left me off the editorial board. I remember the shocking disappointment of that rejection. It was the first time that I had not obtained what I had sought and felt I deserved.

As it turned out, the Class of 1969 was exceptional. Over the years, my classmates' successes as judges and senior partners in prominent firms seemed to pile up faster than those of any other U of M law class. We also really enjoyed ourselves. In the spring of our first year we arranged a pre-finals fling and chartered two buses to the Twins home opener in April. We stocked the buses with kegs of beer, so we were well watered by the time the game started. Our class organized the law school's basketball and softball leagues. For basketball, the formal player draft was organized and well-attended. My team, called Green's Giants, named after Bruno Green, the head of the law library, was a group of great guys and good basketball players. Several of our games were on the Williams Arena court where the Gophers played. It was as fun as any basketball I ever played. Perhaps the most memorable event of our law school years was the stag party thrown for a third-year classmate who was soon to be married. The party was held in a downtown hotel (since torn down) and was attended by most of the in-crowd. Booze flowed and stag movies were played on a large screen. A couple of professional hookers appeared, and one of them took it all off as she danced to loud music. After a lot of raucous cheering and encouragement, the action slowed down. Just then two policemen appeared at the party-room door with a complaint from other hotel residents about excessive noise. By that point everyone was fully dressed, and we all assured the officers that the party would quiet down. We have since reminisced about that moment, when the majority of our third-year class was just a few minutes from being arrested and spending the night in jail.

In 1969, there were numerous employment opportunities for anyone seeking a legal job, whether at a law firm, in government, or in business. Perhaps it was because the economy was booming during the Vietnam war years, or because the number of law graduates was being depleted by the draft and its unpleasant alternatives. Dozens of firms came to the law school for interviews. Anyone with decent grades was invited for follow-up interviews. After December interviews, I was invited to travel to California for interviews with two San Francisco firms and two

Los Angeles firms. The invitations also included a ticket for my wife. I was particularly impressed by the largest firm in Los Angeles, O'Melveny & Myers, which had just moved into the top five floors of the tallest new building in downtown L.A. One big selling point there was that every seven years the partners could take a full year of sabbatical at full salary for vacationing, teaching, writing, or whatever they wished—even just goofing off. Young O'Melveny lawyers entertained us with a spread of wine, shrimp, and lobster at a gourmet restaurant in the Hollywood Hills. After three days of 75 degrees and no L.A. smog, life in California looked absolutely fabulous. I don't remember if I got job offers from all the firms. An offer did come from the O'Melveny firm. Thus, with six months of law school remaining, I had job offers in New York and Los Angeles. Unfortunately, neither of the great job offers could be accepted and the last six months of law school was to be quite traumatic.

CHAPTER 2

VIETNAM—A MAJOR DISTRACTION

For those of us who lived through the late 1960s, the time has special significance. The so-called undeclared Vietnam war was reaching its heights. By 1968 more than five hundred thousand American troops had been committed to Vietnam, with no end to the war in sight. The military draft was in full force. It was not until 1970 that the lottery draft went into effect—unfortunately a year late for me and my fellow law students. In 1966 we students had been granted a student deferment to finish our three years of law school. But that deferment was gradually running out. At one time, just being a student who was married had qualified you for a deferment. Then, as the war got bloodier and fewer draft candidates were available, a deferment required being married with one child. During our third year of law school, a deferment required being married with two children. I remember joking during our third year that some of our fellow classmates were trying so hard to get a second child that they were shooting blanks and never would succeed.

The reality of the war came home during our third year. A law-school grad in the class ahead of us, who I believe was in the top 10 percent of his class, died in a helicopter crash while serving in Vietnam. It was a sobering prospect indeed for law students and families. The Class of 1969 had few options. If you wanted to protest the war as a conscientious objector, you could go to Canada, avoid the draft, and probably never again practice law in the United States. You could join a volunteer agency and commit two years of your life to some unknown place in the world with VISTA or the Peace Corps. Those positions were in high demand. The military branches had jacked up the time commitments for becoming a military lawyer in JAG to four and a half to five years. Voluntarily enlistment was another option, and with our education we were assured of officer training for a three-year commitment. But it was well known that, after completing officer candidate school (OCS), the new second lieutenants were almost assured of going directly to Vietnam to lead a fifty-man platoon on search-and-destroy missions in the jungle. A guy who chose none of the above would be drafted and serve two years as an enlisted man, most probably carrying a rifle and a seventy-five-pound pack in the jungles of Vietnam. The one legitimate alternative was to find and enlist in a National Guard or U.S. Army Reserve unit.

We were told that we could complete the bar exam in July before we would be drafted. In April of our third year we received notice to appear for our Army physicals. Like many of my classmates, I prepared a medical résumé seeking a 4F draft classification to convince the Army medical personnel of mental or physical disability. Presenting my medical records, I contended that five concussions from high-school athletics had left me vulnerable to serious, disabling head trauma. The Army doctor scoffed at my protestations and doctor's letters and said, "You're in law school, aren't you? Get out of here!" After a fifteen-minute physical I was declared to be 1A and fit for combat.

Sometime during our third year word spread throughout the class that a medical reserve unit out at Fort Snelling was taking new recruits. I, along with twenty or so of my classmates, appeared at the reserve headquarters at three o'clock in the morning along with about three hundred other applicants. Several of my classmates were admitted to the unit, but I was not so lucky. Those reservists did not finish law school with our class because of the six-month active-duty commitment, but they did return the next year to finish school with the Class of 1970.

As May and June approached, my situation was getting desperate. I was married but had no children. I generally supported the administration on the war, so I was not going to Canada. A five-year commitment to JAG seemed an excessive time away from private practice, so I was considering the OCS three-year enlistment. Then good fortune shone on me. One of my fraternity brothers, Terry Starr, bless his soul, was the son of Gordon Starr, bless his soul, who was a good friend of Colonel Bill Harrison, bless his soul, who commanded a thirteen-person legal reserve unit at Fort Snelling. Terry and Gordon secured for me an introduction to Colonel Harrison. Bill Harrison took pity on me and through some unknown manipulation added me as "over-strength" to the reserve unit. Before the bar exam in July I was sworn in as a clerk typist with the 214th JAG Unit. This military commitment required six months of active-duty training, which I did from November 1969 through April 1970, and then five more years as a JAG reserve lawyer. Shortly after completing the basic training, I received an automatic commission as a first lieutenant, and a year later I was a captain.

Back to the lawyer job search. The big East and West-Coast law firms would not hold their job offers open for two to three years while a young lawyer served his country, so those plum positions evaporated while I struggled with the draft issues.

Before graduation I did start clerking part-time with the Minneapolis litigation firm of Meagher, Geer, Markham & Anderson. They offered me a job with the understanding that I still had the six months of active duty with the JAG reserve unit ahead of me.

After graduation in June, my full-time job was studying for the mid-July bar exam. The bar exam was conducted over two eight-hour days. It consisted of sixteen one-hour essay questions—that is, sixteen blue books filled with our analyses of hypothetical legal cases. One interesting aspect of our class's bar exam was that we had a fairly high percentage of failures. Most of my colleagues had paid about $500 for the bar review course taught by local Minnesota lawyers. I didn't have the money and did not feel I needed to take the course. As it turned out, I was lucky. The course instructors had told the students that the bar questions had never included two areas of law, one of which I remember was securities law. So they taught nothing on these subjects, and the students didn't bother to study them. As it turned out, both subjects were part of the exam. One guy in the top 20 percent of our class was among the bar failures that summer.

Remarkably, the night before the first day of my bar exam was the night that astronaut Neil Armstrong made his first step onto the moon. How could anyone go to bed and miss that historic event? As I had given up cramming earlier that day, I went to bed at about 2:00 a.m. believing the universe was in good hands.

Bar results come out in October. Again, a very traumatic time. The results are either pass or fail. I am happy to say that I passed the first time. But my legal career was still going to be stalled by six months as I commenced my Army reserve active duty.

My luck held, and I was sent to Fort Ord, which was situated on the California coast, just north of Carmel and Monterey and an hour and a half south of San Francisco. Not a bad place to spend the winter! Knowing that my active Army time was a maximum of six months, I settled in to actually enjoy the experience. At that time my physical condition was as good as any recruit's, and I found the physical stuff to my liking. In the final physical training (PT) test of eight events I scored the maximum points and was rewarded with a free six-pack from our drill sergeant.

From the moment of our arrival at Fort Ord, the pressure to make recruits into Army clones and killers was intense. The first trip to the barbershop was something. Everyone gets the same No. 1 haircut, which is about five sweeps over the head with the clippers, leaving less than a millimeter of hair. While standing in line I calculated that it took a barber sixteen seconds per haircut, and we had to pay him a dollar each. Recruits with long or stylish locks often found the haircut emotional. One fellow named Twigg-Smith, or Twiggy as we called him, had long blond hair to his shoulders. He lost it all in a pile in sixteen seconds.

After several days of in-processing we were loaded into cattle trucks for the ride up to "the hill." The sergeant barked at us, "When you get to the hill you will start running and never stop until you are fucking trained killers." I was assigned to a two-hundred-man basic training company called B-2-3. There were six of us in the company who were reserve or National Guard, all white guys. The rest were draftees, most of whom were seventeen or eighteen years old, with over half of them black or Latino guys. Faced with the probable prospect of going directly to fight in Vietnam, those young men were scared stiff of the upcoming training. I found the psychological propaganda the officers and sergeants used on these recruits to be most interesting, especially since I would be home in six months and not crawling through the jungle in Vietnam.

There were some humorous times during basic. Every company had a chant for its slogan, which you would shout out on demand from the sergeants. Ours was "B-2-3, we're the best, the hell with the rest, this man's Army is all right." After a few weeks of figuring out what we could get away with, we often changed the slogan to "B-2-3, we're the best, the hell with the rest, this man's Army is all fucked." This always resulted in the sergeants screaming at us to "give me fifty [push-ups]."

I learned that, for some reason, the Army dislikes the term "gun." It is a serious no-no to refer to a rifle or a weapon as a gun. When an erring recruit committed this blunder, the sergeant would glare into his face and shout, pointing alternately to the rifle and to his crotch, "This is a rifle, this is a gun, this is for killing, this is for fun, give me twenty-five!"

Our rifle ranges were a two-mile walk (or run) from the barracks and were located between Highway 1 and the ocean. We would shoot towards the ocean, as there were high sand dunes behind the targets. Having grown up in a hunting family, the shooting was a real pleasure for me. My family never had money for a lot of extra rifle bullets. In basic training there was an inexhaustible supply of bullets to burn as the Army tried to convert every shooting novice into a trained killer. To insure that no one got shot, the training procedure of *load, lock, aim, and shoot* was carefully controlled by sergeants yelling out commands. One day, as about twenty-five of us were lying prone, firing repetitive rounds, a jackrabbit appeared on the sand dunes behind the targets. I believe that I was the first to shoot at the rabbit. But within moments everyone was blasting away as the rabbit galloped across the whole range from end to end. No one hit the rabbit. But the sergeants screamed, "Cease fire, cease fire, you dumb shits! Put those weapons down and give me fifty!" When we all got up, laughing, even the sergeants were grinning as we started our push-ups.

Getting your rifle sighted in for accuracy was very important. I had my M14 perfectly sighted in so that I could consistently hit a human silhouette target at three hundred yards. I fully expected to complete the final shooting test as an expert marksman and earn a medal. But on the way to rifle range on the day of the final shooting test I must have banged my front sight on something on the cattle truck in which we rode to the range. As I started shooting at targets, even the closest at fifty yards, I found I was completely missing the targets. I was shocked. When I finally figured out that my sights were way off, I found I could hit the targets by aiming about two feet to one side. Hampered as I was by that adjustment, I still scored highly enough to be designated a sharpshooter, the second-highest level.

After eight weeks of basic training, we spent the next eight weeks in advanced individual training, or AIT. This was specialized training towards your chosen or assigned military occupational specialty, or MOS. Most of the two hundred draftees had infantry or artillery specialties, and AIT was further preparation for a direct ticket to Vietnam. My MOS from the Minneapolis JAG reserve unit was as clerk typist. The Army needs a lot of clerk typists to fill out all of its many forms and orders. AIT for clerk typists started with teaching people to type, because not many draftees knew how, and then training in how to fill out standard forms and write Army letters and orders. This was scheduled to take eight full weeks. The course was set up to allow progress at your own speed. As an incentive, a three-day weekend pass was offered to anyone finishing early. Well, typing was no problem for me, as I had typed my own papers throughout college and law school. The rest of the course was taught at about the eighth-grade level. I completed the whole course in three days, to the amazement of the other students and the instructor, who said it was the record for completing the course. As I was getting ready to leave for San Francisco on my three-day pass, I was cornered by several black guys calling me a smart-ass, clearly ready to knock me around. It took some fast talking and promises to help some of them with the course to get out of that one.

I spent the rest of my AIT in a regular Army company office with a company commander who was seldom there and two sergeants who were pretty good guys. I typed up forms and never worked too hard. Since one of the sergeants liked to play golf, he and I would head to the Fort Ord golf course a couple times each week. Kind of sounds like Sergeant Bilko's Army, right? AIT ended, and I returned home to finally start my legal career.

CHAPTER 3

FIRST JOB, FIRST TRIALS,
BAD ENDING

From early on in law school I found real estate, corporations, tax, and estate planning courses to be uninteresting and certainly not areas I wanted to pursue as a career. I suspect that developing an interest in a given area of law relies more on the quality of the instructor than on the content. On the one hand, my first-year torts professor was a fun guy named Dan Dobbs, a visiting instructor from North Carolina. He made the course interesting. On the other hand, civil procedure—a big part of trial work—was taught by our first-day tormentor J. J. Cound, who could not crack a smile even under compulsion. Law school does not offer a lot of exposure to real trial work. You learn the tort core concepts of negligence, intentional torts, nuisance, and product liability, but you never really learn much about how to run a trial. So the title of litigator or trial lawyer is really a misnomer for a new lawyer at a litigation firm. Coming out of law school you know very little about trying a lawsuit. You learn to be a trial lawyer by taking your lumps in the real world or, better yet, by trial and error (usually with many early errors) in the courtroom.

After the bar exam I began work at the Meagher, Geer, Markham & Anderson firm in Minneapolis. Six of the seven partners in the firm were well-respected trial lawyers doing almost exclusively insurance defense work. I had hoped to spend time with these lawyers, watching and learning from their experience by going to depositions with them and second-chairing their trials. Unfortunately, the partners made no effort to teach anything to us young lawyers. In my two years there I got no one-on-one training at all from any experienced trial lawyer in the firm. Somehow they believed that trial experience would be infused by osmosis into the young lawyers, or perhaps ingested during after-hours drinking with the partners at their favorite bars. Those two years were wasted. If young lawyers at this firm wanted to become trial lawyers, they had to do it on their own.

During my tenure I tried three small jury trials with no help from anyone. None of them went very well. Two of the three were insurance subrogation cases. In order to get the insurance defense business the firm had to take cases from insurance companies that were trying to recoup from third parties the moneys paid to their insureds. Many of these claims were small and hardly worth pursuing, and they were therefore handed down to the firm's young lawyers. My first case was for about a thousand dollars paid by the insurance company for a property damage car accident. The trial was to be in a rural county in southern Minnesota. I don't remember who I was suing, but it was a full jury trial with an attorney representing the defendant. Even though my case was strong, there was a surprise ending. In its deliberations, the jury looked at the pictures of the damage and drew some totally inaccurate conclusions about prior damage to the car. The jury awarded me much less than the thousand dollars. Lesson learned: Juries go off on tangents, so make sure pictures are fully explained.

The second case involved about $3,500 dollars in insurance money for smoke damage in a nursing home kitchen in Alexandria, Minnesota. The insurance company had hired an engineer from Twin City Testing who traveled to Alexandria and searched for the cause of the fire. He found a switch manufactured by Robert Shaw Controls, tested it, and concluded that a faulty switch was the cause. Thus, my lawsuit was against this huge manufacturer. With no settlement offer from a rough, tough defense lawyer, I went to Alexandria to try the lawsuit. In preparing for trial, I found out that the inspecting engineer had left the company and was now working in Europe. With no assistance or advice from anybody, I decided to retain another Twin City Testing engineer, who examined the switch and came to the same conclusion. During the second morning of trial, after the jury had been selected and I had no doubt given a sterling opening statement, we lawyers were in chambers with the judge when I had to reveal that I had used a replacement expert. Both the defense lawyer and the judge were all over me, because I could not prove that the switch examined was the same one that the first engineer had removed from the nursing home kitchen. I remember Judge Saetre's comment: "If you can't prove that, young man, you will have to dismiss your case." I drove home mad and with tears in my eyes at this defeat. Lesson learned: Experts need clear foundation for their testimony. Do not try to finesse an experienced lawyer and judge.

The third case was a fiasco. This case had been around the office for some time and had been worked on by several associates. It involved the theft of grain from a country grain elevator by the elevator operator and a claim by farmers against the insurance company that had provided a $20,000 fidelity bond insuring against dishonesty and theft by the operator. A partner came down and handed me the file a week before trial and said, "This case is a sure winner, so go try it." When I inquired of other associates about the case I was told, contrary to the partner's view, that it was a real loser. When I reviewed the file I could not see why the insurance company had even challenged the claim, especially since the total loss was much greater than $20,000. The trial was a disaster. A good plaintiff's lawyer brought in several farmers who testified that they had lost many thousands because of the theft. The insurance company's defense was really weak, and the representative I put on the stand looked and sounded like a real schmuck. The end result was predictable: Total award for the plaintiff. One funny thing I remember is that there was on our jury a very attractive young lady who sat in the middle of the front row and often smiled at me. I believed that she would be in my corner during deliberations. The jury was sent out to deliberate late one afternoon. They returned in about ten minutes, before I even had my coat on to leave the courtroom. As the judge read their verdict awarding the full $20,000 amount, the little cutie in the front row just kept on smiling at me. Lesson learned: Don't take loser cases to trial, settle them. Also, trying to read what a jury is thinking is very difficult.

My first law firm was far from a great experience. First, the firm's location was marginal. The offices were on two floors of the Title Insurance Building at Fourth Street and Second Avenue, a full four blocks away from all of the action in downtown Minneapolis. That third-rate building was one of perhaps two office buildings that still had manually operated elevators, with an attendant who felt you were incompetent to hit the button needed to get you to your floor. The offices upstairs looked no better than the elevators and the antiquated lobby.

The culture of the firm was something else. The partners exemplified the fading era of hard-drinking and hard-fighting lawyers of decades past. Historically, trial lawyers would fight hard in court during the day and then retire to the local bar with the opposing lawyer to drink until late hours. It was not unusual to get up bleary-eyed to proceed with trial the next day. Several of the firm's partners and senior associates spent one or two days a week at long lunches at the Court Bar, returning to the office in a loud, obnoxious manner to disrupt those of us plodding along in the trenches. No one ever seemed to criticize the liquid lunches.

Not only was the drinking rampant among the partners, but they brought us young associates into the fold. Around the corner from the office was Schieks bar, which at the time (before it became a strip joint) had an afternoon two-for-one happy hour. Several times one of the drinking partners would prevail on me to go down for happy hour, and hardly could I, as a naïve young law firm associate, turn down a partner who was promising to buy the drinks. Two occasions I distinctly remember. On one night at Schieks, the partner was buying me two-for-one Manhattans (strong pours of whiskey and sweet vermouth). Soon there were not three, but six drinks in front of me. I still do not know how I drove home that night.

Another after-work evening at Schieks really revealed to me what I was dealing with at this firm. One of the senior partners was Mark Brennan. I don't hesitate to reveal his true name because the following was absolutely true. At Schieks, when he was very intoxicated, he came up to two of us young associates and said to us, "You young worthless lawyers aren't worth a fuck, and all you want to do is suck the money away from us partners." I was sober enough that night to file this in my mind and never forget it. It was very hard to ever again have respect for Mark Brennan.

My little office was a floor above the firm's main lawyers (maybe I was relegated to this losers' area from the start), and I was located next to firm partner Art Nelson. This unforgettable fellow was one of those personalities that helped make my first two years of law practice somewhat interesting, or at least tolerable. After gaining a level of experience I realized he was in no manner a competent trial lawyer and maintained his modicum of success by bullshitting judges and opposing lawyers and entertaining client insurance adjusters with lots of drinks and dinners at fine restaurants. With such priming, it was no wonder that the low-level insurance people kept sending Art their simple car-accident cases. His office demeanor was incredible. The women's lib movement wasn't yet in vogue for the legal business in the early 1970s. Dirty and offensive jokes were the norm and not discouraged. One day Art came into my office and looked out onto the sidewalk below and said, "Look at all of those cunts walking along down there just waiting to be fucked." As a first-year associate back then, what did you do other than laugh with the law firm partner?

The best Art Nelson story involved a medical malpractice case that had been tried by partner Burr Markham. Some fellow up in central Minnesota had claimed malpractice against a doctor who had allegedly injured the fellow's penis, contending that he had some lack of function and an inability to enjoy sexual intercourse with his wife. Testimony at the trial indicated the claimant was still able to have sex with his wife, but he claimed it was painful. One exhibit in the trial was a large rubber dildo that someone had purchased at a sex shop. After Mr. Markham's trial, Art had gotten the rubber dildo. After some of his liquid lunches he would return to the office and pull out the trial exhibit and terrorize the women in the office. I remember him stuffing this dildo in his pants, leaving the end sticking out above his belt, and parading around the office with a big grin on his face. Other times he would walk up to a secretary's office and slap the dildo down on the desk next to her. As she screamed and fled her desk, he would laugh hilariously so everyone could hear. Never was there a sexual harassment lawsuit against this firm.

I did get fired by this firm. I don't want to trivialize being fired. It was a real shock to my ego. But, looking back, I can see the progression of events quite clearly. I spent six months of my first year at the law firm doing my Army reserve duty. The firm accepted this disruption. When I came back I let my hair grow longer than usual, almost to the Beatles's 1969 style. This did not go over well with the conservative senior partners.

Then, that summer, there was the annual firm retreat at Madden's resort and golf club in Brainerd. The golf tournament was a serious matter for partners and associates alike. The heavy wagering on the three-day golf tournament was the subject of planning and talk year-round. With my typical competitive attitude, I made serious preparations for the golf tournament. I got up at 5:00 a.m. and went out to a nearby public golf course to play a fast-walk eighteen holes and still get to work by 8:30. My golf game came together. The night before the tournament opened involved a lot of drinking and betting. Those of us without handicaps had to predict what score we would shoot. As a new lawyer, I was a nonentity in the betting. On the first day of the golf tournament I shot the best score of my limited golf career, finishing with an eighty-two for eighteen holes, probably ten strokes better than what I had predicted. I totally disrupted the partners' bets. I was not a popular person at dinner and drinks that night—the term *sandbagger* came up more than once. Out of the blue, Burr Markham came up to me and said, with no friendliness, "You will get a haircut." Later, I realized there were six mixed drinks sitting in front of me at the bar as they tried to get me too stoned to hit the ball the next day. I didn't take them up on the hangover, but out of discretion for my future I purposely missed a few putts over the next two days and let someone else make the betting money. Not that it did much good—afterward I was not favored by any partner.

In my dismissal session I sat with a partner, Clyde Anderson, who said to me, "We don't like your attitude and don't think you can become a trial lawyer." Never had I ever thought of being fired from a job. But here was this senior partner saying that he thought I would never make it. That was a hard one to explain to friends and family. That comment really stuck with me. I vowed to prove him wrong and work hard to become a top-notch trial lawyer. I further vowed to try lawsuits against each of those seven old farts and beat them. And before they retired or died, I tried and beat Bill Flaskamp in two cases and Clyde Anderson for $1.6 million in a wrongful death case.

Fortunately, I soon landed a new job that gave me the opportunity to try many lawsuits and gain the trial experience I wanted and needed. The older partner in a two-person firm had just died, leaving the younger partner, Dick Allen, with a lot of insurance defense cases to try. I worked there for five years and tried between ten and fifteen jury cases a year. I earned a pretty good salary, but Dick was not interested in making me a partner. After I had worked there for about four years, we were very busy and hired a smart new lawyer named Mike. The two of us became quite good friends, as I was mentoring him to become a trial lawyer—exactly the help I had wished for in my first position. Even though I was getting the heavy trial experience that I wanted, it was becoming apparent that there was no future as a partner with Dick. After I accepted a position with Lommen & Cole, I went into Dick's office and announced that I was leaving. Then I went to Mike's office to tell him. He started laughing and said, "You won't believe this, but last evening I also gave Dick my resignation. I'm taking a teaching job at Hamline Law School." It was a double whammy for someone not interested in making partners. Again, a lesson learned: Good lawyers expect to be advanced and rewarded in their careers, and if they are not, they will leave for greener pastures.

CHAPTER 4

THE FABLED PARTNERSHIP TRACK

The newly graduated young lawyer, with good grades and a busy schedule of job interviews, mistakenly believes he or she can conquer the world with legal acumen instantly upon crossing the threshold into the chosen law firm. This newcomer arrives with the belief that he or she was chosen not just as a future law firm star, but as one capable of immediately accomplishing world-shattering legal successes. The first shocking lesson for the new lawyer is being assigned a cubbyhole office, usually within the bowels of the office and without an outside window—clearly not the spacious partner office in which this star was interviewed and enticed to join the prestigious firm.

This is only the first of the hard lessons for aspiring conquerors of the legal world. After an initial orientation, given not by the senior interviewing partner, but rather by some nerdy associate, they sit at 1950s-era laminated desks, empty save for a phone, pencils, and the ever-present time sheet. The manner of completion of the time sheet had merited the lengthiest explanation during orientation, with special emphasis on a yearly minimum of 2,200 "expected associate hours" and a strong admonition that most associates who were "on the partnership track" far exceeded that hourly production. Never has a more intimidating career expectation been laid on ambitious world conquerors than the term "partnership track." In addition to the firm's standards for partnership, new lawyers soon find themselves competing one-on-one against the other associates in the firm. New friends and confidants soon become vicious, reclusive competitors for the golden ring of partnership. New associates soon learn the historical law firm mathematics. Not every associate attorney hired will be offered partnership, even after seven, eight, or even ten years of indentured labor. The young lawyer soon discovers that the chosen few are no more than one or two out of four or more qualified and deserving partnership candidates.

Think for a moment of toiling six and seven days a week for ten years and not being chosen as a new partner in this mighty institution. Too often, numbers are the only factor in partnership invitations. If the firm is partner-heavy, self-interest dictates that few or even no new partners can be added, no matter how many deserving candidates are up for promotion. Don't divide the pie into too many pieces! Whatever the reason for the partner rejection, it is always a crushing blow to the lawyer ego. What then is the future for the rejected prospect? Failure to make partner in a big firm is hardly a scarlet letter, although the associate might initially feel that way. At every job interview thereafter, that associate will be asked, "Why did that happen?" Fortunately, the law field is replete with lawyers who have rebounded in dramatic fashion, often far surpassing the status and income of the partners who previously rejected them.

I have often wondered what percentage of lawyers start and end their careers with the same law firm or position. With all of the moves lawyers make, the majority must have worked at two or more positions. It took me seven years and three firms to find a satisfactory fit. By that time I had tried perhaps forty or fifty lawsuits, winning most of them, and I was developing a reputation as a hard-nosed trial lawyer. In 1977 I was offered a position with two very experienced trial lawyers, John Lommen and Phil Cole, and soon the firm name changed to Lommen, Cole & Stageberg. I had arrived as a named partner.

CHAPTER 5

PAUL AND OLLIE

It is a good plan for a young lawyer to sample a variety of areas of law before choosing a career specialty. My clerkship at Milbank, Tweed had exposed me to many of the different specialties in the field of law. By the time I escaped law school and started my career I was pretty well convinced that trial work was where I wanted to be, as no other area had so piqued my interest. But starting out, as the low man on the totem pole, I also got some exposure to two areas of law that I soon wanted to forget.

One of the senior associates at my first firm was handling a divorce where the husband had been very abusive to the wife. When the wife reported to her lawyer that the husband had been pounding on her apartment door and threatening to kill her with a gun, I assisted in preparing an Order to Show Cause why the husband should be kept away from the scared wife. I was assigned to go find this guy and physically serve the paper upon him. I remember thinking as I tried to track the guy down, "Is this why I spent three years in law school?" I quietly slid the paper under the guy's door and reported to my assigning lawyer that I could not locate him. My effort was clearly not proper service on the guy, but at that point I did not care. After that experience I was convinced that no way was I going to work in family law.

Early on I also was assigned some minor criminal cases. I never did feel comfortable going down to the county jail to spend time, under the close scrutiny of husky guards, in a small room with fellows I personally disliked who had been charged with some crime against their fellow man. Even though these guys inevitably professed their innocence, it was usually clear that most were guilty and would go down hard if they went to trial. I never liked trying to convince some guy claiming innocence that he had better cop a plea and serve his time rather than going to trial. I viewed the prosecution side of the criminal equation as almost as bleak as the defense side. It took only a few of these criminal law exposures to convince me that was not to be my career choice.

After two years in practice I got involved in a series of cases that were challenging and a lot of fun. These were quasi-trial and business-type cases. I have labeled them the Paul and Ollie cases. My firm represented the largest painting contractor in the Twin Cities. At that time, in the early 1970s, there was a construction boom in large apartment and townhouse complexes. One of the biggest developers was a company run by two brothers, Paul and Ollie Ogdahl, operating as Ogdahl Brothers Construction. Paul and Ollie hired our client, the painting contractor, to paint their large complexes, a job that should have been very profitable. But Paul and Ollie had a regular system of running out of money before their projects were completed. Since our painters were usually at the tail end of the projects, they were routinely fighting to get paid for their work.

The legal system has developed a way to protect construction contractors and subcontractors who don't get paid by the owners who hire them. After confirming that payment for completed work is not being received in a timely manner, a contractor can serve and file a set of papers called a mechanic's lien. This lien attaches to the title of the land and can create a cloud on title or a problem for the property owner as well as notice to any prospective purchaser of the problem of obtaining clear title to the property. If the property owner does not settle the debt in order to remove the lien on the property, the contractor can commence in court a procedure to enforce the lien and actually force sale of the property by the county sheriff in order to pay off the debt. Seldom does a mechanic's lien action get this far, as most matters are settled long before any property sale is ordered.

I don't remember how many times Paul and Ollie forced our painting client to come to us to serve the mechanic's lien papers. There were at least five cases, probably more, that progressed into the lien-enforcement lawsuits in court. In each case our painting contractor was not the only unpaid subcontractor. Paul and Ollie were usually trying to screw ten or more subcontractors that had loyally done work on their projects. Each of the unpaid laborers and material suppliers involved their own lawyers, who would each file their mechanic's liens as I was doing for my painters. One of these lawyers would start the lien foreclosure lawsuit, naming all of the other mechanic's lien holders as parties to the lawsuit as well as Ogdahl Brothers. Usually the party starting the enforcement lawsuit was owed a large debt by Paul and Ollie. As my painters were one of the last contractors on the job, our unpaid balance was usually one of the largest in the group of lien holders. After being involved in a couple of these cases, I usually took charge of drafting the lawsuit papers and stood as lead attorney in the action against Paul and Ollie. Every court hearing on the case would involve lawyers for each claimant. Usually the same group of lawyers would show up; soon we created a fairly close-knit group of Paul and Ollie haters.

Paul and Ollie were represented by a lawyer named Charlie Cox. I use his actual name because he has been a friend for many years, and I have long admired the very clever way he represented his clients in these lien foreclosure actions. Since few, if any, of the unpaid contractors really wanted to go to trial to force the dragged-out sale of the property, they usually settled before the lawsuit or before the case was called for trial. Through tough negotiation Charlie Cox would knock off the lien holders one after another with agreements to settle for some substantially reduced amount, like thirty cents on a dollar, for the unpaid labor or material. I quickly recognized that these lien holders and their lawyers were taking a beating because they were scared to proceed to trial. In almost every instance I would hang tough for my painters, boisterously vowing to go to trial. Several times we were the last lien holder left in the case. Eventually, to avoid trial, Charlie Cox would pay us a much higher percentage settlement than those that had settled earlier.

These mechanic's lien cases taught me a good lesson that I carried throughout my career. In any type of litigation you have to bargain from strength, not weakness. If you are scared to go to trial, and the opposition senses that, you will never get a favorable settlement. In my early years of handling trials I purposely presented an arrogant posture in negotiation, indicating that if the settlement was not right for my client I would gladly go to trial. Of course, that forced me to follow through and try a lot of tough cases that could have settled. But, by taking that aggressive position I was creating a reputation to mean what I said: That the case would go to trial unless *favorably* settled.

CHAPTER 6

BECOMING A TRIAL LAWYER
THE HARD WAY

Law students, law students' families, and unfortunately many in the general public hold the misconception that spending three years in an accredited law school magically turns loose a cadre of legal scholars capable of addressing and solving personal, business, and international problems. Unfortunately, this is far from reality. Newly graduated lawyers may know some general legal principles and where in the law library to search out answers, but the new lawyer is hardly ready to render thoughtful and consistently correct advice to clients in need of solutions. Seasoning—not just sprinkles on gourmet creations, but rather molding over time by experience—is what creates a worthwhile and trustworthy counselor capable of addressing a client's concerns. There is one shortcut around the laborious five to ten years of conditioning needed to become an effective lawyer, but that requires the unusual good fortune of finding a true, experienced, and concerned mentor in the legal profession.

For the first seven years out of law school, I had no mentor to guide me through the hard realities of becoming a trial lawyer. Some thoughtful lawyer in my past had opined that it took four to five years of hard knocks in the courtroom to become a competent trial lawyer. Without question, my best teachers in those first years were the experienced opponents who beat me up in the courtroom, often exposing my ineptitude and humiliating me in front of judge and jury.

I date my true arrival as a trial attorney to about five years into my practice. Until this trial I had lacked confidence in the courtroom; afterward I felt I could tackle any trial situation thrown at me. I was defending Emcasco Insurance Company in a case involving a serious injury to a child. A rear car door on a vehicle insured by my client had swung open as the vehicle turned a corner, and an infant child of the driver, not seat-belted or in a car seat, had fallen out of the vehicle, sustaining serious injuries. The injury claim against the insured driver, for reasons I cannot now recall, had not been reported to Emcasco for several years. Based on insurance policy language requiring notice of a claim within a "reasonable time," Emcasco had denied liability coverage for the driver of the car from which the injured child was ejected. Among the many defenses that insurers can raise to injury claims, lack of timely notice is at the far deep end. With a $50,000 policy limit and potential damages to the child far above that limit, the only issue that proceeded to trial was the lack of timely notice of the claim.

Representing the sympathetic parents of the injured child was the notorious Minneapolis personal injury attorney, Irving Schermer. I use his real name here out of respect, for Irv was one of the most resourceful trial attorneys I encountered. In later battles with Irv, it was astounding how he could turn a routine $10,000 whiplash rear-end accident into a brain-injury claim worth policy limits of $50,000 or $100,000. With the help of a friendly University of Minnesota neurologist, "questionable EEG brain studies," and his courtroom reputation, Irv could convince many insurance adjusters and defense attorneys to pay his settlement demands.

The Emcasco case was to be tried before an experienced trial judge who openly called my opponent, his well-respected legal colleague, by his first name. All of the in-chambers conferences with the judge demonstrated his deference to and tolerance of Irv and his sarcasm. The judge listened politely to my protestations and usually rejected my arguments. Before the judge, Irv was absolutely demeaning in his behavior towards me. In front of the jury, he called me "the young insurance company lawyer." My repeated objections to Irv's antics were seldom sustained, and the judge never reprimanded Irv before the jury. In my mind, my protests seemed only to increase the jury's displeasure with the insurance company lawyer interfering with the progress of the case. During the four days of this trial I did not sleep while fretting over the beating I was taking.

But no matter how sympathetic was Irv's case, there was logic in the policy requirement for timely notice, which gives an insurer the opportunity to arrange a thorough case investigation. Because of the notice delay, we could not locate a critical witness, and other avenues of investigation had been lost. Faced with Irv's emotional plea for the permanently injured child against the rich and obstinate insurance company, I tried to spell out in my closing argument a logical illustration of the prejudice to Emcasco by the late notice. Leaving the courtroom after a battle like this, I felt like a limp dishrag; I wanted nothing more than a stiff scotch and heavy relaxation.

For whatever reason, this jury returned its verdict for Emcasco, finding against Irv and his injured child. Two significant epilogues followed that verdict. The next day, Irv taught me something about being a real trial lawyer. He called me up and congratulated me. "You are going to be a good trial lawyer," he said. From that day forward, in every trial that I lost, it was my absolute rule to call and congratulate my opposing lawyer, no matter how bitter the in-court battle might have been. Secondly, following this victory over one of the best, I knew that no matter what opposing counsel or an obstinate judge threw at me, I could handle it without trepidation. I felt that I had arrived as a trial lawyer.

PART II

I BECAME A PARTNER IN 1977 IN THE SMALL
ATTORNEY FIRM OF LOMMEN COLE & STAGEBERG.
IT GREW THROUGH HIRING AND MERGERS INTO
THE FORTY-TWO ATTORNEY FIRM OF LOMMEN,
NELSON, COLE & STAGEBERG, WHICH OCCUPIED
TWO FLOORS OF THE IDS BUILDING IN DOWN-
TOWN MINNEAPOLIS. FROM AN INITIAL PRACTICE
HEAVY INTO INSURANCE DEFENSE TRIAL WORK,
THE FIRM EXPANDED INTO OTHER AREAS, AND
I MOVED INTO TRYING LARGE PERSONAL INJURY
AND WRONGFUL DEATH CASES FOR PLAINTIFFS.

CHAPTER 7

LOSING OR
WINNING A MILLION DOLLARS

Throughout this personal history I will laud the intellect, savvy, and charm of my senior partner, John Lommen. He was my mentor, the one who taught me a lot about trial work as well as how to progress through a career as a trial lawyer. John was a great trial lawyer. His position at the top of the heap was recognized by his contemporaries, who regularly tried lawsuits against him for over four decades. Not only did I follow his guidance in my career, I also loved this man as a person and a personal friend.

One Johnism, as we used to call his words of wisdom, was as follows: "You never become a real trial lawyer until you have either won or lost a million-dollar case." Back in the 1960s, when I started practice, there had not been more than perhaps a half a dozen jury trial verdicts in excess of one million dollars. In most of the routine trials we handled, the amount at risk was an insurance policy limit of $30,000 or $50,000, or in the rare case $100,000. As defense lawyers, we would battle to the end to protect the amount of insurance available for our client. This was probably one of my big problems in doing insurance defense work. I would work my buns off doing a great trial job, but for what? To save some multibillion-dollar insurance company a few thousands on a liability insurance policy. Often I would conclude that the injured person really deserved the $30,000 or $50,000, but I had out-lawyered the opposing attorney to win the case. Could this make you really feel good about winning? I had just screwed some deserving injured person out of a recovery because I was a better, more persuasive lawyer than the incompetent he or she had hired. This was one of those fuming ethical confrontations that eventually drove me to take only cases for injured plaintiffs.

By the time I got serious about John's million-dollar admonition, he had already lost several million-dollar lawsuits. My first opportunity came in 1983, as a result of my being considered the office's workers' compensation specialist. If a workers' comp insurance company pays a lot in benefits to an injured worker, that insurance company has a so-called subrogation interest in retrieving some of the amount paid to the injured worker from any recovery the worker may receive from a third party. Frequently, lawyers will tell you that a subrogation interest "fucks up a good lawsuit." By both federal and state law the insurance company that paid benefits to an injured worker can either get actively involved in the lawsuit or sit back and let the plaintiff's lawyer try the suit and at the end make its claim for its share of the winnings. Any amount recovered by settlement or trial is divided up according to a complex formula dictated by the state statutes. This convoluted system gave me my first opportunity to prove to John that I had arrived as a trial lawyer by winning a million-dollar verdict.

Glen was a truck driver who delivered cement blocks for his employer, an insured of one of our large workers' compensation insurance companies. Glen had sustained a horrendous electrical burn when the boom on his truck came into contact with a 7,200-volt power line. Glen survived the injury but, after lengthy hospitalization, remained severely disabled and scarred by the burns. As he had been working for his employer at the time of injury, he received many thousands of dollars in workers' compensation benefits, creating a large potential subrogation interest for the insurance company. Glen had retained a general practitioner attorney in the small town of Benson in western Minnesota. This lawyer had no clue how to proceed in a product liability lawsuit of any type, or even how to prepare and present his client's very severe burn injury case. After some discussion with me regarding the several hundred thousand dollars of the insurer's subrogation interest, the lawyer allowed me to be lead counsel in the product liability lawsuit against DICO, the manufacturer of the cement block hoist. The case was not going to be easy to put together, much less to try to a conclusion. In a pretrial in Swift County District Court in rural Benson, Minnesota, the trial judge informed us that there had never been a big plaintiff's verdict ever from a jury in this "conservative county." This was not the kind of encouragement I needed before starting the trial!

But whether you call it fortuity or just plain dumb luck, Glen's case launched my career as a big-case plaintiff's lawyer. I put together Glen's product liability case with help from a smart mechanical engineer expert from New York, a sixty-nine-year-old engineering professor from NYU who had previously been involved in several similar DICO injury cases. This old codger was great, and I probably owe him credit for some part of my future career as well. He determined that the DICO cement block hoist had an electronic relay that had malfunctioned, resulting in the boom hoist unexpectedly rising into the 7,200-volt power line as Glen manipulated the switches on the control box. The expert found that a small condenser had been installed backwards by someone at the manufacturing plant. His testing of the impact of a reversed polarity condenser was not all that great, but it was sufficient to support his opinion that the reversed condenser would cause the control-box electronics to act radically and sometimes not allow the operator to stop the rising boom.

One fascinating part of trial work is evaluating the pretrial settlement offers and demands of the parties. Every case has some settlement value, whether close to the plaintiff's expectations or to the defendant's conservative evaluation. What defendants and their insurance companies want is to evaluate the risk of winning and losing and then offer just enough money in settlement to force the plaintiff and his attorney to forgo the risk of a trial and a possible total loss and accept the amount offered. From the standpoint of the injured party, as settlement offers increase it gets tougher and tougher to advise the client to go for it, to try the case and leave a large sum of money on the table. Any trial, of course, leaves the plaintiff's fate in the hands of six or seven unknown jurors who must first allow you to win and then somehow provide a bigger verdict in damages than the settlement offer.

Since this was my first big plaintiff's case, I had no real experience as a lead plaintiff's attorney in evaluating offers and advising a client on whether or not to reject an insurance company settlement offer and go to trial. Fortunately, in Glen's case it was easy to evaluate and advise the client that we must proceed to trial. The primary defendant, the manufacturer of the boom hoist, offered a maximum settlement offer of $100,000. As I learned in many major cases thereafter, it was comforting to my psyche when the final offer was so low that advising the client to gamble and try the case was an easy decision. With Glen's severe burns and disabilities, the offer was so minimal that trial was the only realistic option. After two weeks of tough trial in rural Benson County, Minnesota, the jury found the hoist manufacturer liable, with Glen 30 percent at fault, and awarded $2.4 million in damages to Glen. Not bad, compared to a settlement offer of only $100,000.

One part of Glen's trial is implanted in my mind. Because of Glen's severe injuries, his marriage fell apart. His wife divorced him mid-lawsuit, leaving social services to care for his serious injuries. When I contacted Glen's wife, she turned out to be a delightful lady who openly confessed that she just could not handle the severity of her husband's injuries and disabilities. Empathy for Glen bubbled out from this woman. She agreed to appear at trial as one of our damage witnesses. On the stand this devoted wife testified that she went daily to visit Glen in the hospital, but eventually she could no longer tolerate the stench of his rotting, burned flesh. Wow! The courtroom was very quiet at she wept on the witness stand. No doubt her testimony had a major impact on the jury. The appellate opinion affirming the trial result is found at *Dahlbeck v. Dico*, 355 N.W.2d 157 (Minn. App. 1984).

Thus, according to my mentor's criteria, I arrived as a trial lawyer in 1983. Before boasting further about this trial accomplishment, I must relate how I met that goal a second time in the same year. Unfortunately, this second big lawsuit put me on the other side of that million-dollar mark—the losing side.

While still predominantly doing defense work, I was involved in a paraplegic injury case in western Minnesota. The spine of a twenty-five-year-old worker had been severed while he was trying to transport a portable grain elevator with his company tractor. His lawyer, a prominent attorney from Minneapolis, sued the manufacturer of the grain elevator. The defendant manufacturer brought in as a third-party defendant the injured worker's employer; I represented that employer. After all of the usual trial preparation we went to trial in Madison, Minnesota, a town nine miles from the South Dakota border. Coincidentally, the Stageberg family tree had roots in Madison for at least three generations before me. Midway through the trial I located a long-lost family relative, a second or third uncle, and I spent an enjoyable evening learning of family history.

But back to the trial. This was clearly the biggest injury trial ever held in Madison. The young paraplegic with no hope of future employment as a laborer was seeking millions of dollars in damages. In preparing the defense case, we always did a jury evaluation to find out what we could expect from the jury in the trial venue. We found out that Madison and the surrounding county was probably one of the conservative Lutheran capitals of the United States. When I drove to Madison to find a motel for two weeks, I found no fewer than three Lutheran churches located around the town square. How could a defense lawyer find a better venue in which to try a personal injury case, on a weak product liability case, than this very conservative, very religious county? When the jury was selected it was comprised of six women, including the wife of a local Lutheran minister. On paper it was a defense lawyer's dream: A conservative jury reluctant to go crazy on a damage award. Furthermore, as the trial testimony developed, this badly injured twenty-five-year-old was seen to have become the town drunk who daily wheeled himself downtown and consumed a multitude of beers at the local pubs. The product liability theory advanced by the plaintiff's lawyer was remarkably weak, though it had the support of one of the best University of Minnesota engineering professors. Fully anticipating that this conservative jury would find in our favor, we received a massive surprise when the manufacturer of the grain elevator was found negligent for inadequate warnings on the grain elevator, and the jury awarded the drunk paraplegic $2.2 million in damages. Well, again, a lesson learned. Don't try to prejudge a jury based on stereotypes. If your case is not good enough you will lose, and often lose big, no matter who is sitting in the jury box.

I still marvel at that Madison, Minnesota, result, and I shared frequent laughs with the other attorneys involved in the case. But despite the sting of failure, for the second time I had arrived as a trial lawyer in John Lommen's view. In fact, I had the dubious distinction of having both won and lost a million dollars in the same year. And now I could say thanks, John Lommen, for making me a trial lawyer.

CHAPTER 8

TRYING CASES ON DA RANGE

I grew up in northeastern Minnesota, about fifty-five miles south of the Canadian border on the northern fringe of the Mesabi Iron Range. For those who have long forgotten the details of American history, one of our nation's great mineral finds was the discovery in the late 1800s of vast quantities of iron ore in north-eastern Minnesota. European immigrants flocked to the area's ore mines to take work at decent wages. Predominant among the immigrant population were Finns, Poles, Croatians, Czechs, and Serbs, many of whom arrived with past mining experience. The Iron Range, known more commonly there as "Da Range," developed into a unique melting-pot community with one very common goal of extracting iron ore from the ground and ship-ping it east to the steel mills of Illinois, Indiana, and Ohio. Until the high-grade ore started to peter out in the 1960s, Rangers were a proud group of middle-class Americans.

My hometown had only three hundred residents and was, ironically, called Orr, Minnesota. The town was actually named after one of the area's first prominent residents, Billy Orr, and not the iron ore being mined nearby. Although my father was in the logging and sawmill business, many Orr residents were miners on Da Range, commuting forty to fifty miles morning and night to their places of employment.

After I started to defend insurance cases, I found myself trying many lawsuits on Da Range. The practice of law in the Hibbing and Virginia state courts of St. Louis County was as unique as the Range itself. One of our firm's major insurance clients had developed a low-premium insurance liability policy that sold like hotcakes to municipalities throughout the state. Almost every town on the Range was insured by our client, the Home Insurance Company. For several years, until The Home, as we called it, began losing its shirt (that is, when claims paid out exceeded premiums taken in) and cancelled the municipal policies, we defended many claims brought against the towns on the Range.

A frequent claim against the Home-insured municipalities that I was defending involved sewer backups from the city sewer systems. Every town had both a sanitary sewer system and a stormwater system. In most towns these systems were fifty or more years old, antiquated, leaky, and in most cases overloaded by expanding residential and commercial development. The towns seldom had resources and tax money to modernize and expand their sewer systems to keep up with development. When there was substantial rain or heavy snowmelt, the leaky stormwater systems added more water to the already overcharged sanitary systems. With no place to flow to, the systems backed up into the basements of the residents with the lowest-level sanitary sewer connections. If homeowners were lucky enough to have a one-way flow valve on their sewer system, the backup went to the next-lowest neighbor who lacked such a valve. As we used to joke, can you imagine waking up to find two feet of shit in your finished basement? Sounds pretty ugly, right? And who do you blame? The city, of course. Especially when the homeowners discovered that their homeowner's insurance policies did not cover sewer-backup losses.

Homeowners and their local lawyers were not a happy bunch, looking hard for some insurance dollars to pay for cleanup and to replace carpeting and basement paneling soaked with water and worse. My legal research soon disclosed that a municipality was not automatically liable for a sewer backup from its system. The claimant had to prove that the city was somehow negligent in allowing this to happen. Once the homeowners' lawyers realized that my position was correct, they tried a variety of tactics and arguments to show negligence on the part of city officials. Said officials, usually the mayor and city manager, would simply throw up their hands and say things like, "We know our system is outdated and overloaded, but unless we heavily tax our city residents we can do nothing to solve this problem." This was not negligence, and the sewer-backup claims had to be denied and defended through trial if necessary.

With a variety of claims on the court dockets, I was soon making frequent trips to appear before local judges in Hibbing and Virginia. In my first appearance before any judge, I always brought up the fact that I was a local boy from Orr (a mere forty-five miles away) and should be treated like one of the Range lawyers and not some smart-aleck big-time insurance lawyer from the Cities. This worked well, and soon I was part of the local judge-lawyer fraternity on the Range. If my presence was required in court around lunchtime, I would join the judge and lawyers involved in walking two blocks to dine at the Coates Hotel in Virginia or the Androy Hotel in Hibbing. If there ever was a good old boys' roundtable, this was it. Usually there was a lot of laughter and kidding, but sometimes we discussed and even resolved pending cases over lunch. I don't remember but a single time joining that group for drinks after a day of trial, but no doubt I did, and frequently. My consistent defense position on the sewer claims was becoming well known and accepted by the judges and the claimants' lawyers. Even though I could have become the hated insurance lawyer, I instead developed a favorable reputation in the Iron Range legal community.

Over the years I tried several jury cases (other than the shit-in-the-basement cases) to conclusion on Da Range. Politics are important in the region. With the iron-mining industry dominant and with heavy union involvement, northeast Minnesota is strongly supportive of its Democratic Farmer Labor Party candidates. Any DFL-nominated candidate was a shoo-in for state or federal elections. When trying jury cases on the Range, one had always to be cognizant that the jury would be primarily comprised of citizens with strong union ties and a dependence on the American steel industry. Seldom did one see on the streets of Hibbing or Virginia a Japanese or German automobile. At the time I was driving around Minneapolis in either a Toyota or an Audi, so when I traveled to the Range for a court hearing or trial I traded cars with an office lawyer or secretary and drove up in a Ford or Chevy. During jury selection I would openly state to the prospective jurors, "I should make a disclosure to you, that I grew up in Orr and my father had a sawmill and lumberyard there. I know he sold a lot of lumber here on the Range, and I need to ask you prospective jurors if anyone had any business dealings with my father, Haven Stageberg?" Suddenly this trial lawyer, initially introduced as "Mark Stageberg, from Minneapolis," was just another Ranger, and obviously a good guy.

One very funny Range story, told to me by a Hibbing court reporter, involved a huge jury verdict won by a good Hibbing attorney named Ed Matonich. Ed represented a client who became a paraplegic while operating a front-end loader in one of the mines. The loader tipped over, pinning the operator and damaging his spine. Ed's product liability theory against the loader manufacturer, the Clark Equipment Company, was that the loader should have been manufactured with built-in roll-over protective structures, or ROPS. This product design theory was being advanced around the country, but it was tough to prove. Defendant Clark was initially represented by a very experienced, gray-haired Duluth attorney who obviously knew how to try a case on the Range. But Clark and its liability insurer decided they needed a real heavyweight trial lawyer to defend this case. They brought in a forty-five-year-old Jewish lady from Chicago to be lead trial lawyer in Hibbing. My court reporter friend just chuckled over the jury selection on this case. The defense always goes first in directing questions to the jury. The prospective jury members, all with difficult Finnish or Slovenian names, were totally turned off as the big-time Chicago lawyer butchered their names during the questioning. Local boy Ed then went forward with his questioning and quickly ingratiated himself with the jury. It was all downhill from there. The jury ruled against Clark Equipment Company, coming back with the largest injury and punitive damage award to date in Minnesota.

One fun case I tried in Virginia involved a personal injury sustained during a collision between two trucks on a road construction project on the Range. My insured client was a local boy from Orr named Jimmy Howard. Jimmy was a real nice fellow, about fifteen years my senior, and a truck driver who was hauling gravel on the construction site. Jimmy's truck had somehow collided with the injured guy's truck, and the questions were, which driver had the right of way and who was more negligent. Our investigation found an eyewitness to the collision who had been operating a road compactor nearby. Before trial, I visited this witness at his home and found him to be about fifty years old, with a typical Finnish name. The story that he relayed to me was totally in Jimmy's favor on the accident facts. This fellow, however, had a serious stutter. It took quite a while for him to relay his observations to me. He agreed to come to court and "try" to tell his story. As I left his meager home that evening, I had a big grin on my face. As I had anticipated, this Finnish fellow was the greatest witness I have ever placed on the stand. As he stumbled through his story, every juror moved to the edge of their chairs, nodding their heads and encouraging this fellow to get the words out. As he finally finished his story, there was almost a gasp of relief from everyone in the courtroom, including yours truly. There was no way his story was not totally believable and no way the opposing lawyer could cross examine him. The jury found in our favor, a fact that Jimmy broadcast loudly in Orr, boasting about his great trial lawyer.

Another interesting case on the Range involved my good Chippewa/Ojibwe friend Harold Goodsky. Growing up in Orr introduced me to many American Indians from the Nett Lake Ojibwe tribe. About 20 percent of our little high school came from Nett Lake. Some of my best lifetime friends were the Indians that I hunted and fished with as a youngster. Every one of these guys had a nickname. My friends included Whiz, Skunko, Jap, Rip, Peg, Fidgity, and, for Harold, Dayshun. Two sons were born to Dayshun, Rodney and Harvey. Rodney, at about age twenty-five, died in a motorcycle accident. Dayshun asked me to help in the case. It seems that Rodney and a friend were riding a motorcycle one night when it went off the road, throwing both off the bike, killing Rodney and injuring the other fellow. There was a $30,000 liability policy on the motorcycle protecting the operator for negligent operation resulting in death or injury to the passenger. The other fellow, seeing $30,000 to his benefit if Rodney was the operator, claimed Rodney had wanted to drive his bike, so they stopped, the bike owner exchanged places with Rodney, and then Rodney drove off the road. With Rodney dead we had little to contradict this story. Dayshun, however, stated that Rodney was scared of motorcycles and never would have driven the bike at night. He convinced me that Rodney was the passenger and that Dayshun, as his father, was entitled to the $30,000. The other fellow was represented by another Range lawyer, one whom I knew well. We agreed that instead of a jury trial we would do a binding arbitration, with the winner getting the $30,000. We chose an experienced Duluth attorney as our neutral arbitrator and had a half-day hearing. In tracing the police investigation of the accident we found some indication that Rodney was the passenger. But moreso, in the ambulance record, and the Duluth hospital record for the other fellow, there were some critical admissions that he was "operating" the motorcycle when it left the road. With Dayshun's strong testimony that Rodney never would have driven the motorcycle at night, the arbitrator found in our favor. A great win for a good friend.

I do not remember how this last Range case came to me, but it turned out to be not only a good victory but changed workers' compensation law in Minnesota as well. The client was a thirty-five-year-old laborer at the Eveleth Taconite Company. In the mid-1960s, as high-grade iron ore was running out in the Mesabi range, the steel companies built huge taconite plants to process the lower grade iron ore. The mammoth plants, constructed with Minnesota legislative tax breaks, produced marble-sized taconite pellets that went to the smelting mills on the east end of the Great Lakes. For the lagging iron ore industry, taconite was a boon to the Iron Range. Somehow I was referred to the laborer, Michael, who had suffered severe burns at the Eveleth Taconite plant. Investigation showed that Michael had been ordered by a supervisor to clean out one of the processing machines in preparation for a scheduled plant shutdown. The processing machinery was stopped, and Michael had taken a garden hose to wash out the interior of one of the large machines. As he crawled into the trapdoor of the machine with his hose, spraying to clean out debris, some water hit remaining red-hot taconite material remaining in the chamber, resulting in clouds of steam blowing back onto him while he remained trapped inside the machine. Imagine the fright to someone being scalded from high-temperature steam with only a narrow, backward avenue of escape to back away from it. Michael sustained serious second- and third-degree burns over much of his body.

The injury case was straightforward, but the legal issue involved was important. Since Michael was on the job at the time of his injury, he received workers' compensation benefits for medical expenses and lost time from work. Normally in Minnesota law, as in every other state, once an employer and the employer's insurance company pays workers' compensation benefits, the employer is immune (no matter how negligent) from a civil lawsuit by the employee. However, at that time in Minnesota law there was a seldom-used exception: If a supervisor of the injured employee was found to be individually negligent, it would circumvent the immunity rule and subject the employer to additional liability beyond the workers' compensation paid. In Michael's case I advanced the theory that his supervisor was negligent for directing Michael into the machine without confirming that the material inside had appropriately cooled. As expected, with a strongly union-oriented jury, a finding of negligence on the supervisor resulted in a fine verdict for Michael.

This was to be the last case allowing a negligence recovery against a coworker supervisor. At its next legislative session, the Minnesota legislature amended the workers' compensation law to require proof of gross negligence, not just simple negligence, to hold a fellow employee or supervisor liable for a worker's injury. In Michael's case, in no way could we have met a burden of proving gross negligence on the part of his supervisor. Again, probably due more to lucky timing than my great lawyering, I recorded a good win for a deserving client. But, as happened a few other times in my career, a win in one of my cases resulted in bad law for other litigants in future cases.

CHAPTER 9

PRO BONO WORK,
OR A LOT OF WORK FOR NO PAY

Long ago, members of the legal profession made a very astute observation: Many of our citizens need serious legal help with their problems but do not have the wherewithal to hire a lawyer. Social welfare stepped in and created the public defender system for criminal problems and legal aid societies for the rest of the legal woes. Without question, government funding for these programs has never been adequate, so too few lawyers were usually trying to help too many clients and doing a mediocre to totally lousy job of client representation as a result. We did get some socially spirited direction in law school suggesting that part of our function as lawyers was to contribute voluntary legal services to those in need. But for most young lawyers, working many overtime hours while fighting to get established in a career left little time and energy for pro bono (free) legal services. Fortunately, many of the large, established law firms were altruistic enough to allow their young lawyers to contribute some volunteer hours without a reduction in their salary or status.

For many years I participated in the Legal Advice Clinic. One night a month I would sit at a desk in a street office in some low-income area and give several hours of free legal advice to walk-in clients. Most problems could be resolved with advice or one or two letters and a little follow-up. But some cases required more time and office work. I remember hearing so many sad tales from ladies in need of a divorce to leave abusive relationships. But I could not help them because by that time I had firmly committed myself to doing no divorce work. I thus guiltily handed these sorrowful clients off to other clinic lawyers. I have often looked back on that decision with regret because of the real help I could have provided to many people.

What is interesting about pro bono legal work is that many of a lawyer's promising cases can turn into unintended pro bono work. I don't know how many cases I agreed to pursue after hearing a real sob story in the first interview with the client. With the common use of contingent fees (where the attorney agrees to be paid some percentage of the amount recovered for the client), we lawyers too often take a flier on a client's case for all of the wrong reasons. If you are going to gamble your legal time—and usually your money in client advances as well—you want the case to have a good chance of succeeding in the end so you can divide the spoils with the client. One of the real truisms of the law practice is that a case seldom gets any better than it seems during that first interview. But many woebegone clients enticed me to pursue their questionable injury claims on a contingent fee basis. Too often I developed serious regrets about agreeing to pursue a questionable case that turned out to be an unintended pro bono and a waste of a lot of legal time and money.

Having grown up in northern Minnesota with lots of American Indians as friends and acquaintances, I knew that many of them relied on pro bono services for help. My first real court experience was an attempt to be a criminal defense lawyer for two of my Orr High School classmates. Within months of my passing the bar exam, I learned that two Ojibwe twins named Mike and Ike Leecy were in jail in Minneapolis for a vicious assault on a fellow while they were intoxicated. I vividly recall my first criminal court appearance with Mike and Ike for their arraignment on the assault charge. I appeared in court before Judge Crane Winton along with many other lawyers and probably twenty to thirty defendant/clients in orange jail suits. I planned to watch the other criminal lawyers do their thing and then copy them. But, as luck had it, Mike and Ike's case was called as the very first one, and I had no idea where to stand or what to say. Somehow, with Judge Winton's help, we got through it with a not-guilty plea for both of my clients. Neither Mike nor Ike, then about twenty-two years old, had a prior criminal record, so even with an aggravated assault charge my hope was to avoid heavy jail time for them. With help from my brother, Roger, we arranged for the twin who had finished high school to get enrolled in general college at the university. The other agreed to a commitment to return to high school to get his diploma. In negotiation with the prosecutor and Judge Winton, this looked like an acceptable resolution with no further jail time. Unfortunately pro bono work for unpredictable clients doesn't always work out. The day we appeared before Judge Winton for the agreed-upon lenient sentencing, one of the brothers appeared with a beat-up, bandaged face from involvement in another fistfight. With no hesitation Judge Winton rejected our plea agreement and sent our one battered client immediately to five years in the state prison in St. Cloud. The other twin got probation on the condition of starting at the university. He started, but sadly it did not last.

The story of Mike and Ike had a tragic end. Several years later, one of the twins—I believe it was Mike—got into a fight outside of the Orr municipal liquor store. When the local sheriff tried to intervene, Mike attacked him. In what was called self-defense, the sheriff pulled his gun and shot Mike in the groin. Mike survived the shooting but was charged and convicted of felony attempted murder and sentenced to twenty years in prison. Several years later, Ike was found in the ditch south of Orr with a bullet in his head; the authorities said it looked like an execution. The shooter was never apprehended. Perhaps if we would have succeeded in that initial defense effort, there might have been a different ending for Mike and Ike.

Many other Indian friends have requested legal assistance over the years. Several had decent personal injury claims that I pursued on a contingent fee basis and actually made a few dollars. One family called me when their cute twelve-year-old daughter was bitten by a neighbor's dog on the reservation. The little girl had been at the neighbor's door soliciting something for school when the screen door opened and the dog lunged out and bit her right in the pubic area. Quite to my surprise, the dog owner did have a homeowner's insurance policy to cover the dog's assault. Without a lot of effort I worked out a good settlement, setting up an annuity to pay for four years of college expenses for the girl when she reached age eighteen.

Most cases in American Indian communities don't end up that easy. Let me describe my failed efforts for Frank, a fellow I played basketball with in high school. Frank had a good job as a road-grader driver on the reservation. At about age fifty-five he was at the casino in Tower, Minnesota, when a casino bouncer decided Frank was being unruly and physically hauled him outside and assaulted him. The result was a serious back injury that prevented Frank from continuing his work. Before coming to me, Frank had hired someone he called "a pale-face lawyer" in Virginia, Minnesota, who sued the casino and bouncer in Minnesota state court. After that lawyer fooled around for a year or so with the case, a state court judge dismissed it, saying it should be in tribal court since it was Indian-against-Indian business and the state court had no jurisdiction.

Having gotten nowhere with his injury case, Frank came to me for help. Not having been in tribal court before, I started by educating myself on a new legal system. There were few procedural rules, and the right to pursue a typical injury case was nowhere defined. Blundering along, I managed to get the case before a female tribal judge, from Bemidji, Minnesota. But here is where things got crazy. Long ago, when the federal government rounded up the American Indians and confined them to reservations, those reservations became sovereign nations. As such they could claim immunity to liability in U.S. courts of law. In preparation for the case, I researched a couple of past injury claims brought by non-Native Americans against the Indian casinos. In each case the casino denied liability because it was protected by sovereign immunity. State and federal courts in several cases had supported this rejection of typical injury lawsuits.

But logically sovereign immunity should have had no effect on Frank's case, right? A tribe member suing a tribal business would clearly be under the jurisdiction of the tribal court. Well, it was not so. For some reason, in the midst of Frank's case the Tribal Council, the governing body of the reservation, passed a resolution that sovereign immunity could be raised as a defense by an Indian entity against an injury claim by another tribal member. Perhaps for some reason unknown to me the council needed to punish Frank. This absurd resolution essentially negated any type of injury claim, no matter how severe, by one tribe member against another. Frank and I did get a hearing before the reservation tribal judge. I prepared a strong legal brief explaining that the ridiculous resolution, even under Indian law, could not deprive Frank of his rights. We did not prevail. In a short written opinion the tribal judge explained that she felt obligated to follow the dictates of the reservation council. The end result was a seriously injured fellow with no legal avenue for relief in any court.

CHAPTER 10

THE PARTNER RETREAT

One of the personality traits that makes lawyers successful and separates the cream of the crop from the mediocre mass is self-aggrandizement—or, as the psychologists might define it, ego strength or high self-worth. The timid, unassertive lawyer facing up to the barracuda-type litigator will usually lose, especially in trial, not through lack of legal skill, but rather the inability to convey to the judge or jury an impression of incomparable correctness on any dubious position. This trait serves the experienced and successful trial lawyer well in the courtroom, but not in interpersonal relations, whether at home or in a legal partnership of supposed equals. The ego of the trial lawyer is a tough animal to contain. This conviction of legal and professional superiority does not work very well in a so-called democratic partnership meeting. Minor issues quickly become confrontations between partners, and the trial lawyers usually lead the arguments for the issues they champion.

Which brings me to collegiality, an enviable quality, but one that is difficult to foster in any legal partnership, especially in a mixed bag of trial lawyers and practitioners of the "lesser specialties." How does one foster collegiality and goodwill amongst a diverse mix of self-important, bull-headed, narcissistic lawyers? Many firms never deal directly with the issue, letting divisive partner issues become personal battles that never get resolved. Confronted with these issues, the Lommen Nelson firm chose two routes: The partner retreat, and, as discussed in a later chapter, the law firm consultant.

When our six-lawyer firm merged with an eight-lawyer firm, it resulted in eight voting partners of diverse backgrounds, capabilities, and interests. It was my idea to have a partner retreat to get to know each other better and develop some of that mysterious collegiality. I floated the idea to the partners as a business expense important for the success of the new firm; it was initially greeted with skepticism, but also a mutual willingness to give it a try. Since the idea was mine, it was my task to research reasonably priced options and report back. I was not above satisfying my personal interests in fishing and golfing, so my chosen retreat was a golf resort in eastern Wisconsin that offered a charter-boat service for king salmon fishing on Lake Michigan. Pitched to four partners interested in fishing and four who were avid golfers, my proposal (and its reasonable projected budget) met with modest enthusiasm. Lest this be a complete boondoggle, I created an agenda for a long-term planning meeting for the firm. Reports were to be prepared and become part of the official retreat notebook.

Before describing the memorable events of the first partner retreat, I will leap ahead to report years of successful, happy retreats that usually generated the desired collegiality, and often a lot more. In subsequent years, retreats went twice to Keystone, Colorado; to the Broadmoor in Colorado Springs; the Cordillera Lodge in Colorado; Williamsburg, Virginia; LaCosta, California;

and Lake Tahoe, California. Year-round talk embellished the fun and benefits of the retreats. Senior associates jostled for the plum perk of an invitation to the partner retreat, with its unlimited food and drink at the firm's expense. Without violating the sworn secrecy of partner memories, I'll recall some highlights from retreat events. No one will forget walking down the cliff to Black's nude beach in California with the partners too timid to join the crowd. Who could forget the girls' softball team at Keystone? No one had a camera to capture partner Al wading waist-deep in a pond at the Vail golf course to retrieve balls. One night long to remember occurred at a honky-tonk bar near Keystone to which we had gravitated after our dinner meeting. There, a flirtatious, voluptuous gal in a short skirt and bare midriff was clearly enjoying her evening out. Proudly flaunting her attributes, she drew many favorable comments from the partners, particularly from my senior partner, Owen. After a bit, a local bar gal next to me, upon seeing my partners' adulation, informed me, "She's got a dick!" Having never encountered a real transvestite before, I bought her/him a drink and enjoyed half an hour of enlightened conversation about the life of a transvestite. Of course, Owen and my partners thought I really had something going with the babe of the bar. When I revealed her/his true identity, I'll never forget the look on Owen's face.

But back to partner retreat number one. To plan the Lake Michigan fishing expedition, I called and lined up two charter boats for 6:30 a.m. When I asked, "Will we catch salmon?" the captain replied, "No, it's too late in the year, but we will catch lake trout." Not having caught many lake trout in many years of fishing, I decided this was an acceptable alternative. At 6:30 a.m. everyone was up and enthusiastic as we departed the dock, four partners in each boat with a captain and first mate. Needless to say, those small charter boats are not ocean liners; they bounce up and down rather energetically in the Lake Michigan swells.

Before even reaching the fishing waters, one senior partner on my boat, John Lommen, became unusually quiet. John was an experienced boater with a fifty-one-foot houseboat on the Mississippi River. Even though his stable houseboat never caused him seasickness, poor John was sick the whole four-hour trip and never attempted to catch a fish.

Did we catch fish, you ask? Every few minutes the captain or first mate would yell, "Fish on!" With lots of shouting and excitement we took turns cranking in the fighting silver lake trout. Before long our boat had our limit of twelve lake trout, ranging from four to seventeen pounds each, with most of the fish over ten pounds. Back at the dock we found that our colleagues in the other boat had equal success. We joyously headed off for the golf course, leaving the first mate to clean and freeze our fish to be picked up after the next morning's fishing.

The non-fishing part of the retreat met or exceeded expectations. Golf, dinner meetings, lots of drinking, and completing most of the business agenda proved enjoyable to all involved. We all came away with optimism for the firm's future and feeling some of that collegiality, with the impression that we were all pulling the same plow through the field.

Now, back to fishing. On the second morning, John wanted no part of fishing and Lake Michigan. Three other partners also opted out, leaving four of us fishermen in one boat to again chase lake trout. With little skill or effort on our part we returned with twelve more large fish. Now it gets interesting. We were 450 miles from Minneapolis, and we had somewhere between 250 and 300 pounds of lake trout, some of it frozen and some freshly caught. The local supermarket had gigantic Styrofoam coolers about 6 feet by 2 feet by 2 feet. Our lake trout, packed in ice, almost completely filled three coolers. We taped the coolers shut and somehow got them into cars and airplanes for the trip home. Upon returning home on Sunday afternoon I, as the retreat organizer, found myself with three full coolers of fish sitting on my front lawn.

Four partners refused to take any fish. The other three partners each took a few small fish, not wanting any of the fifteen-pounders. It was now my task, late on a summer Sunday afternoon, to do something with over two hundred pounds of fish. Fresh, unfrozen lake trout is delicious grilled or fried. Unfortunately, lake trout is a very oily fish and does not freeze well. Within a month or two the oil turns rancid and the fish become almost inedible. The bigger the fish, the worse the problem. Scouring the yellow pages, I found a south Minneapolis meat market, open that afternoon, with the capability to smoke a hundred and fifty pounds of lake trout. At that point, cost was not a factor.

Smoked lake trout can be very tasty, but in small doses. I dutifully picked up over a hundred pounds of smoked fish from the meat market. Though it was packaged in plastic and brown paper bags, some of the fish oil seeped through the paper onto my rear car seat before I got home. Forcing a few partners to fulfill their commitment to take their share, I carried to the office a few paper bags of smoked fish and placed them in the lunchroom refrigerator, ready to be taken home at the end of the workday. The paper and plastic bags were no barrier to the fish oil. By lunchtime there was almost open rebellion amongst the staff as the stench of the smoked fish not only permeated any lunches kept in the refrigerator, but also wafted throughout the office.

Being a sportsman of the belief that you eat what you kill, I persevered for months, frying, grilling, and poaching the lake trout, driving my family out of the house in favor of fast food as I stoically tried to eat my oversized share of the smelly fish. No one questioned the partners about how much of the fish they consumed. Hopefully, like me, they were kind to their garbage men and passed it through the disposal rather than into the garbage cans.

CHAPTER 11

TAKE THAT, CHARTER COMPANY

Everyone at some time has felt like the underdog, the one at the mercy of the big guy and the system, with no remedy or way to fight back. In most cases, the little guy just does not have enough at stake to hire a lawyer to prove that he was right all along. Lawyers sometimes donate their legal time and expertise, but pro bono clients are often impoverished and can get legal assistance in no other way. For the middle and upper classes of society there is no free lunch when it comes to legal services. If your feelings and principles are strong enough and you are willing to pay, lawyers will be happy to help your cause and to soothe your damaged ego—at $300 to $400 per hour. Between the wealthy and the impoverished stands a huge block of citizens who are often wronged and damaged, who have justifiable legal claims, but who have no reasonably economical way to pursue them. Conciliation court does work up to a claim of $7,500, but most people don't know it exists and never use it to resolve their disputes.

I will tell you a tale of how I helped a whole planeload of middle-class citizens to get justice. It all started with Minnesotans wishing to make their annual winter pilgrimage south to Florida, Arizona, and beyond to escape the blizzards and subzero temperatures for a few days. Most are happy to return with a royal sunburn. As we had done a few times before, my wife and I and another couple signed up for a budget-priced charter flight and hotel package trip for seven days in Cancun, Mexico. The flight was to leave the Minneapolis charter terminal at 6:00 a.m., with the requirement that we check in at the terminal two hours early, requiring arising at 3:00 a.m. Together with about 150 other sleepy-looking fun-lovers, we congregated at the charter check-in with bags, sunscreen, straw hats, and golf clubs.

Then the problems began. The check-in folks had little to tell us except that there would be a delay. They didn't know how long, but they kept advising people to stay calm and relax. Sometime past 6:00 a.m. some of us pressured the check-in folks for the truth about what was really going on. We heard that the plane hired by the charter company had major mechanical trouble out east and was not coming; they were scrambling to find another plane to lease and bring to Minneapolis for the trip. With that information now public, the charter company recommended that we all depart and return at four o'clock in the afternoon, when the new plane would arrive. At this point there was no choice but to try and make the best of it. We departed, had a good brunch, and went home. Many of the disgusted passengers, especially those from out of town, hung around the airport instead. Checking by phone in the early afternoon, I learned that the four o'clock departure was a myth and they now projected departure at ten o'clock that evening. We were wondering what kind of an operation we were dealing with. Even if they could find a plane, would it be safe?

Arriving again at the charter terminal, we found a jet plane at our gate with a planned departure around 10:00 p.m. And depart it did, with many apologies from the flight attendants, who were trying to quickly serve drinks and food to weary passengers who mainly wanted to sleep. Before dozing off I processed what had just happened. On this plane were 150 people on a one-week trip, all of whom had just lost a complete day of their vacation. They would be losing one seventh of their hotel commitment and would now arrive, dead tired, at their hotel in Cancun at about 4:00 a.m. on the second vacation day. I thought, *It just is not right for people to be treated so poorly.* But how could these 150 people with their justified but really quite minor losses get some satisfaction? When I tell the rest of this story, most people wonder how I got away with what I did.

I went to the front of the passenger cabin and asked the lead flight attendant if I could use the microphone to speak to the passengers. No one offered any great resistance, so I said the following: "We all just had a horrible experience. We all lost one or more days of our vacation and incurred a lot of unnecessary expense. I am an attorney, and I am going to pass among you passengers a yellow pad. Please write down your name, address, phone number, and how many people are traveling with you. Get the yellow pad back to me, and when we get home I will see what I can do to get some kind of refund for everyone." Those who were still awake gave some cheers and way-to-goes. My yellow pad did return, with what looked like all of the folks having followed my instructions.

As predicted, our 4:00 a.m. arrival at a Cancun hotel required half a day's sleep before anyone recovered enough to begin enjoying the vacation. As I recall, the remainder of the stay in Cancun was just fine, and the charter flight home was on time and without incident.

Now, as a junior partner in a large Minneapolis law firm, what do you do with 140 to 150 new clients with individual claims worth at most a few hundred dollars? Oh well, justice needed to be done. Thank goodness for a good secretary and modern word processing. We started by transferring all of the yellow-pad names and addresses onto the computer. A class action was not really possible, as all of these folks had very different damage claims. So a combined lawsuit on behalf of 140 to 150 individual plaintiffs was the only solution. I mailed each of the contacts a letter confirming my intent to sue and asking each of them to do the following: (1) Sign and return a simple one-third contingent fee agreement retaining me as their lawyer; (2) Calculate all out-of-pocket expenses caused by the delay; (3) Send me receipts and other verification of their losses; and (4) Identify any other personal problems they encountered due to the delayed flight. I advised that I would try and make some type of money recovery on their behalf from the charter company.

The responses flooded in from Iowa, North and South Dakota, and all parts of Minnesota. Almost everyone responded with their expenses and back-up receipts. There were many encouraging comments like "Go get 'em!" Again, with the help of a good secretary and a computer, the client info was soon appropriately organized. I cranked out a lawsuit against the charter company, naming every confirmed client as a plaintiff and asking for compensatory damages as well as punitive damages. The defense attorney who appeared for the charter business's insurance company was a lawyer I had known for many years. Our first discussion about the case was humorous as I related my first-hand experience on the trip and my knowledge of the grief and expense caused by his charter company's negligence. I remember him hitting on the biggest problem with my lawsuit: "If you go to trial, how are you going to present the evidence of the claims of all of your clients? Each one, from North or South Dakota, or wherever, will have to appear for a trial in Minneapolis to collect two hundred dollars."

We answered the defense attorney's interrogatories on behalf of all of our clients, disclosing our calculation of their individual damages. Not to be outdone, I sent a heavy-duty set of interrogatories and document demands on to the charter company. I wanted to know how much money they made on this trip, all about their airplane lease agreements, everything they had done that morning to avoid the delay, and the names of everyone involved in the trip for the charter company. The defense attorney could not help but read this as a threat, as he could tell this was a serious effort to pursue punitive damages against his client.

Settlement discussions quickly followed. Quite clearly my bluster was far louder than my real intent to pursue the issue to a finish for my many clients. My response to the settlement overture was a single and non-negotiable demand: You will pay 100 percent of everyone's out-of-pocket expenses, plus you will pay $150 to each passenger, whether adult or child, for their inconvenience. With little further by-play or negotiation, the defense lawyer and his insurance company agreed to my demand. Not wanting any objection to the terms from my mail-order clients, I wrote to them, explaining that each would be getting all of their expenses back, plus $150, and they would owe me $50 per person as my attorney's fee. I strongly urged that no one object to the settlement. Fortunately, no one disagreed. A check for all damages arrived and was deposited in our trust account, subject to distribution to all of the clients. Getting all of their expenses back plus $100 a person (including $100 per child) made everyone happy, if not quite satisfied. Many clients passed along thanks and good words.

Hardly can this be called a pro bono effort for the poor! I actually made about six thousand dollars on the fifty-dollar contingent fee agreement. This might have worked out to about thirty dollars an hour for my time. I did assume that sometime in the future one or more of these satisfied clients would call back and become a real money-making client. Unfortunately, it did not happen. Nonetheless, I remember the case for something far more significant. It holds a very special place in my career as an example of how the little guy can recover from a trampling by the system with the help of a creative lawyer.

CHAPTER 12

TWO BIG ONES IN FEDERAL COURT

It is amazing what a big plaintiff's win will do for your level of confidence in yourself as a trial lawyer. After the $2 million win in Glen's electrocution case in Benson, Minnesota, I remember looking around for more big plaintiff's injury and death cases to try. I had proved to myself that not only were these serious plaintiffs' cases fun and challenging, but also that I was pretty darn good at winning them. Within the next couple of years I had the opportunity to try two more major injury cases in the Minnesota federal courts.

Since our firm's merger with the Coulter, Nelson firm, we had an older workers' compensation lawyer named Lyle in the office. Somehow, Lyle had taken on as clients two widows whose husbands had been killed in an electrical explosion at the Twin Cities Army Ammunition Plant in Arden Hills. The case had been sitting around for a couple of years with little progress, as Lyle did not know how pursue it. I remember the Coulter, Nelson partners describing the case as being very difficult and in need of a lot of work. After the merger, Lyle had John Lommen, as senior partner, look at the case. After sitting on the case for another several months, John likewise advised Lyle the case was too tough to win and he did not want to handle it. Knowing that we had to do something with the case or get rid of it, I volunteered to do a full review. With my then zealous approach to plaintiffs' cases, I disagreed with my partners and described the case as not only winnable but also as having great damage potential.

Here are the facts. Two electricians, Welter and Kapaun, were doing contract work on a large electrical buss duct running throughout the arsenal building near the ceiling. The buss duct looked like a rectangular sheet-metal vent pipe surrounding the high-voltage cables running inside. On the top of the duct was a small entrance panel that could be unscrewed to give access to the cables inside. On the day of the accident, Welter and Kapaun were standing on stepladders, working close to the entrance panel. One of them unscrewed the panel and accidentally dropped a screwdriver into the opening, shorting out the cables inside and causing a massive explosion. Both electricians suffered fatal burns as they were blown off their ladders. What scared the lawyers who had evaluated the case was the potential negligence on the men, not only in dropping the screwdriver and causing the short, but also in failing to cut the power on the buss duct before working on it. As I got involved, I found that these and several other issues in the case had hardly even been explored.

I initially obtained the complete electrical plans for the building back to the time of its construction. I took those plans to two electrical experts, and we made some major discoveries. First, there was no way for the electricians to shut off power to the buss duct without shutting off power to the whole huge building. That would have required shutting down production of ammunition for the federal government, a totally unreasonable possibility. The experts further found from the plans that upstream from the buss duct in the whole electrical system there was no safety shutoff or circuit breaker (essentially a fuse). The electrical code required such a safety shutoff, and yet it clearly had not been installed. The experts were strongly of the opinion that had there been such a interrupter in the system when the screwdriver was dropped, causing the short, the high-voltage current would have been instantly cut off before it could cause any serious damage to the workers.

With these opinions in hand, I felt highly energized (pun intended!) and sued the case out in federal court against the government designers of the electrical system, the building architects, parts supplier General Electric, and the electrical contractor who installed the system. In the depositions, key people for these defendants all had to admit that the electrical code did require the installation of a circuit breaker and that the system should have had it. Thus, by their own admissions, every defendant from the designers to the installers of the system could be found negligent for violations of the electrical code. The defendants all disputed our claim that activation of such a breaker would have saved the electricians' lives. They further argued that the dropped screwdriver would result in a finding of greater negligence on the men than on any defendants.

With nominal settlement offers, the case went to trial. Because of potential conflicts as to which of the men dropped the screwdriver, we had to refer out the smaller of the two cases to another experienced trial lawyer. As it turned out during the case, I did 95 percent of the work, and co-counsel basically gave moral support.

After two tough weeks of trial the case was ready for the jury. I argued first to the judge and then the jury an interesting view of the defense's claim of negligence for the men in dropping the screwdriver. Since there were no eyewitnesses, it was impossible to know whether Welter or Kapaun had dropped the screwdriver.

Thus, as it was total speculation to say that either one did it, there could be no finding of negligence against either because of lack of proof. The jury obviously liked my argument, because on November 21, 1983, the verdict was returned, finding no negligence on either Welter or Kaupan and finding negligence on the defendants as follows: Federal government (55 percent), architects (30 percent), electrical contractor (10 percent), and General Electric (5 percent). Welter's family was awarded $600,000 in damages, and my clients, the Kapaun family, were awarded $1,400,000. In 1983 these were huge verdicts and were written up on the front page of the morning paper.

What was particularly sweet about the win was beating the lawyer for the architect. Remember Clyde Anderson, the guy who fired me from my first job with the statement that he and his partners thought I would not become a trial lawyer? From the day of the firing I had sworn that someday I would beat every one of those Meagher, Geer partners in a trial. This was my chance against Anderson. During the process of this whole case he had tried to act superior to me, belittling many of my efforts. Then, during my closing argument, he moved his chair away from the defense counsel table and toward the jury box so as to be in my line of sight as I argued to the jury. He then feigned being so bored and disinterested in what I was saying as to have fallen asleep. What a complete asshole! Well, he had to go back and tell his client that they must pay $600,000 towards a case that I am sure he had promised that he would win. Oh, sweet justice!

The next big case was also fascinating. Like the case of Glen's electrocution, this case originated in my representation of a large workers' compensation subrogation interest paid by one of our insurance clients. A small-town Iowa lawyer, who represented the client, had called me for assistance in pursuit of the wrongful death case in Minnesota federal court. Seeing another big plaintiff's case thrown at me, I was happy to take over as lead counsel.

The client, Sandy Mielke, was a delightful lady. Her husband, Randy, had been killed outside of the unloading dock of the Red Owl warehouse in Hopkins, Minnesota. Randy had driven an eighteen-wheel tanker truck loaded with corn syrup from Iowa to the Red Owl warehouse. He had backed into his warehouse dock and begun unloading when a garbage truck owned by Container Services, Inc., backed in next to him to drag onto its hoist a large commercial dumpster. As Randy remained by his trailer, supervising the unloading, the dumpster was dragged onto the truck hoist. When the dumpster had been dragged most of the way onto the hoist, it toppled off, crushing Randy to death.

My lawsuit was against Red Owl for an inadequate unloading area, Container Services and their driver for negligent operation, and Dempster Systems, Inc., the manufacturer of the hoist that had been installed on the garbage truck. After the usual go-round of depositions and other discovery, we reached a settlement with Red Owl and Container Services together paying $650,000. The case was going to continue against Dempster Systems. This product liability claim was fun to put together. With help from my mechanical engineering expert we developed arguments of two serious design flaws in the Dempster hoist. The guide rails on which the dumpster slid up onto the hoist were only two inches high, allowing the dumpster to jump off track as it was being elevated. Secondly, this hoist design required the operator to sit inside the truck cab to operate the controls. With the hoist running behind the operator's back, and with major parts of the hydraulics and the hoist obstructing the view, the operator had very limited visibility of the progress of the lifting operation.

One nice summer day, my expert and I flew down to Chicago to attend the national garbage haulers' equipment show at McCormick Place. We found Dempster equipment on display along with the equipment of perhaps ten or twelve of its competitors. We found that most hoists had guide rails built three to four

76

inches high. Also, most competitors had the hoist controls on the outside of the cab or offered two sets of controls, one inside and one outside. We took many pictures to illustrate the much better designs on competitors' equipment. These were great exhibits in the trial.

Under Minnesota law, when one or more of several defendants in a lawsuit settle, the case still goes to trial and the negligence or fault of the settling party or parties is still decided by the jury, along with the fault of the remaining defendant. The plaintiff never has to give back the money already received from the settling parties, but in order for the plaintiff to come out ahead there must be a finding of large damages and a finding of a high percentage of fault for the defendant still going to trial. For instance, if the jury here awarded one million dollars in damages and found the garbage company 100 percent at fault, we would have made a bad deal to settle for the $650,000, having given up $350,000. On the other hand, if the jury found Dempster 100 percent at fault, we would get to keep our $650,000 and collect an additional $1,000,000 from Dempster. With the nice settlement amount securely in bank, going to trial against Dempster was a good gamble.

Once again, it was to be an unforgettable trial experience. Our federal judge was my law school classmate, James Rosenbaum. He had been on the bench only a short time before this trial. We revealed our law school relationship quite openly to defense counsel, who did not object to the judge handling the case. The judge and I have since frequently laughed about this case and its outcome.

My liability case went in very smoothly, with the jury being quite impressed with our Chicago pictures. My expert's opinions were that the two design defects caused the accident: First, with only inside controls the truck driver could not see the dumpster sliding off track as he elevated the hoist, and second, had the hoist had rails higher than two inches, the dumpster would not have jumped off track. He further rendered opinions that the truck driver was not at fault because Dempster's design had forced him to operate the lift with limited visibility.

My damage presentation was one I will never forget. Sandy and Randy had three boys, around the ages of thirteen, eleven, and nine at the time of trial. Two of them had red hair. I spent considerable time with the boys working on how we would present their testimony in court. I suggested that after some preliminaries, such as their grade in school, I would ask only two questions: First, "Tell the jury what things you and your dad liked to do before he died." Second, "Now tell the jury how things are different since Dad died." Each of the boys had prepared a list of good answers to both questions, and they assured me they could do the job.

As it turned out, the whole damage phase of the trial took about one hour. I first put the family minister on the stand to talk about the family in general. Then Sandy did a good, but not very emotional, job of describing Randy and the losses she and her children had suffered. I next called the redheaded thirteen-year-old to the stand. We did just fine with the preliminaries and the first question about the past relationship with his dad. Then, as I finished the second question about how things had changed, the boy stumbled on a couple of words and then broke down sobbing. I looked at the jury and to a person they were crying. I was crying, and for perhaps for half a minute I could not utter a word. I don't know if the judge was crying, but I suspect so. Finally, I blubbered out, "Judge, that's all I have for this witness, and plaintiff rests her case." The boy continued to sob as I helped him back to his seat with his mother and brothers. Judge Rosenbaum later told me, and I am sure many other lawyers, that this was the best "underselling" of a damage case he had ever seen.

Now, if you are the defense attorney, and plaintiff has rested his or her case with that kind of emotion in the courtroom, it will be no fun to start putting on defense witnesses. After I rested our case, the judge took a recess and asked to see the lawyers in chambers to discuss settlement. He strongly recommended that the case settle right away. He asked what I was demanding, and I said I wanted $350,000 from Dempster. (I was fixated on getting this figure to give my clients a total of one million dollars). The defense lawyer said he had only $250,000 to offer but would call the insurance claim manager in New York. He came back and said his final offer was $300,000. Irritated, the judge called the claims manager directly from his chambers. He reported back that he could get nothing further from New York: $300,000 was it. I met alone with him at that point, and we talked like old law school buddies. He strongly encouraged me to take the $300,000. I responded that our defective design case was very strong, and their defense case would not turn it around. I did agree to go talk to Sandy one last time.

After explaining to her that we were only $50,000 off and already had $650,000 in the bank, I asked her, "Sandy, do you like to play poker?" She said, "Yes I do." I explained how many good "cards" we were holding and that we had the chance for a really big win. Furthermore, with the money in the bank, the gamble was not all or nothing. Sandy agreed that we would tell the judge and defense lawyer to forget it and let the jury decide. Although the judge expressed his disappointment, we went back into the courtroom to start the defense evidence. As I predicted, there was nothing outstanding from the defense evidence and it certainly did not seem to turn the case around. Final arguments were set for Monday morning.

Meanwhile, some quite distracting events were going on in my life. My father was dying of prostrate cancer and was in a hospice in Virginia, Minnesota. I spent the weekend with him, working off hours in a motel preparing a closing argument. Back in the courtroom on Monday morning, just before arguments began, I saw my wife enter the back of the courtroom looking very sad. Without asking I knew that my father had just died. That was April, 28, 1987. But I absolutely had to put thoughts of my family out of my mind as I finished the trial without major problems.

What a verdict! Decedent Randy was found not at fault; Dempster was found 80 percent at fault; the three settling parties combined 20 percent at fault. Total damages awarded to Sandy and her children were $1,401,250. Dempster's 80 percent of that number was $1,121,000. When this was added to the settled amount, the total recovery was $1,771,000. It is awfully nice when a gamble pays off. Maybe I should have played poker in Las Vegas.

CHAPTER 13

TRUCKING IN NORTH DAKOTA

In one year, two of our major insurance clients, Excalibur and Iowa National, went into non-voluntary insolvencies imposed by their state insurance departments. We (now Lommen, Nelson, Cole & Stageberg) did a lot of defense business for Excalibur and Iowa National over the years until they went insolvent. With Iowa National we were left high and dry, with over $200,000 of unpaid defense bills incurred by the firm; none of that was ever recovered, so we wrote it off as a bad loss. But with Excalibur, John Lommen had such a good relationship with the company vice president that he received a call a couple of days before the commissioner's takeover of Excalibur, telling John to FedEx down our bills and the VP would get them paid. It worked, and we received about half of the $150,000 owing in unpaid attorneys' fees. That is one of the downsides of representing insurance companies on defense cases. Needless to say, our bottom line suffered that year.

Backtracking a bit, I will relate a memorable defense case for

Excalibur. This insurer had cornered a major portion of the insurance for the interstate trucking industry. To get that much business they were probably undercutting the market on insurance rates, which is fine for the truckers but will catch up to the insurer when the liability claims start coming in and premiums are insufficient to cover the losses and defense costs. (That was one obvious reason for Excalibur's demise.)

I was called by Excalibur to defend a small interstate trucking company based in Ohio. They had dispatched a load for a leased driver (meaning he owned his own truck and hauled under contract the loads on the trailers of the dispatched interstate carrier). This load was sent from someplace in Ohio up to central North Dakota. The driver, Stan, was to deliver his load to a power plant under construction. After unloading, Stan contacted his dispatcher to obtain a load to haul back toward Ohio. He was dispatched to pick up a load some sixty miles further west in North Dakota. To get there Stan traveled with his empty trailer along rural roads. This led to his downfall and eventually a lot of trial work for me.

Stan was covering ground across the North Dakota prairie at most likely well above the speed limit. As Stan came to a long downhill slope he saw a pickup truck on the upslope ahead of him, slowing in his lane, left turn signal flashing for a turn into a driveway on the left. Stan thought that rather than slowing behind the pickup to allow it to clear the lane, he would instead swing onto the right shoulder and breeze past the pickup without slowing. Well, in those few critical seconds, the pretty young housewife in the pickup, while signaling for the left turn into her ranch, looked into her rearview mirror and saw the large grill of the rapidly approaching diesel semi behind her. Fearing a rear-end collision, she pulled suddenly onto the right shoulder and stopped. Approaching at high speed, Stan observed all of this ahead of him and, as he later testified, reflexively swerved to the left, across the center line, to avoid colliding with the pickup.

Stan's reflexes were good, and it was a good emergency move to make if you didn't want to slow down. Unfortunately, approaching at that moment from the opposite direction was a vacationing family from St. Paul in a station wagon. As Stan crossed into the oncoming lane he hit the station wagon head-on. I don't quite remember how many were in the station wagon, but it was a dad, a mom, and at least two kids. Mom was killed instantly. Dad had serious injuries, and the hood of the station wagon was driven back through the windshield, striking one daughter in the forehead at the base of her hairline, essentially scalping the poor teenager.

My defense efforts on behalf of Stan and the Ohio trucking company resulted in three trials and a major trip to the U.S. Court of Appeals for the Eighth Circuit. Perhaps the most convenient aspect of the case's timing was that it occurred during the time when I piloted private aircraft. Minneapolis to Bismarck was perfect for private flying, and I logged many flight hours on this case.

My truck-driving client, Stan, was a fat, slovenly, middle-aged fellow who maintained he was a "professional driver" who did everything right in this crash. That may sell in the smoky back room of a teamsters bar in Ohio, but not in central North Dakota. I personally disliked my client, but I was being paid well to defend him and the trucking company. Trial number one in Bismarck was to determine the relative fault between the woman driving the pickup, the driver of the station wagon, and my client. On the witness stand, Stan came across as even more arrogant than he had in our earlier discussions. He maintained that, as an experienced professional driver, he was always looking for his escape route and did nothing wrong in trying to avoid the pickup suddenly darting to the shoulder before him. I knew this wasn't selling to the jury. The twenty-two-year-old Sweet Polly Purebread was clearly the victim in front of this jury. With little deliberation the jury found Stan 100 percent at fault in causing the collision. With that decided, we now had to resolve all of the damage cases.

The lesser injury cases and the mom's death case were settled. The major injury case of the scalped girl went for trial in Bismarck. Being from St. Paul, the surviving family members hired a young lawyer from their hometown to handle all of the cases. He claimed to be a trial lawyer and tried to act the part, but he clearly had no real experience. Excalibur was somewhat happy, as we thought the lawyer had undersold the settlement value on the death and minor injury cases. But he was bound and determined to reap a gigantic verdict on the injured girl's case. Most of the girl's medical and rehabilitation treatment occurred in St. Paul. In preparation for the Bismarck trial the lawyer took somewhere around ten long and tedious videotape depositions from the girl's medical providers. For the defense I had a trusted, elderly, defense-oriented doctor evaluate the girl and her disabilities and provide me with a favorable set of opinions on her condition and lifetime disabilities. With that preparation, we proceeded to trial in Bismarck. My St. Paul opponent bored the jury to death with his interminable videotapes of damage witnesses. I flew my seasoned defense doctor up to Bismarck to appear live at trial, and he convincingly portrayed the girl as having a great recovery with few ongoing disabilities. In the end, the jury awarded the girl far less than the attorney had demanded and less than we had offered in settlement. From a defense standpoint, we call that a clear win. More appropriately, it was a tactical outsmarting of an incompetent attorney.

The litigation was not done. With somewhere over two million in damages already paid, there remained a dispute between Excalibur, as the trucking company's insurer, and the company that had insured Stan's truck. This developed into a major precedent-setting case on the respective liabilities of the insurers for a lessor and a lessee of over-the-road truck equipment. The third Bismarck trial dealt with which insurer was primarily liable. Now, I don't remember how it came out and whether we won or not, but the resulting appeal from the decision from the federal district court in North Dakota to the Eighth Circuit Court of Appeals was interesting.

It was to be my second oral argument in St. Louis before the appellate court. The first one had not been a pleasant experience. But I was cocky and confident that I could handle those appellate judges. I don't remember whether I or my opponent stepped to the podium to argue first. During my turn, the chief justice of the court, Donald Lay, began pushing me with aggressive questions. I fielded his questions for a while and held my own until I was forced to flatly disagree with him. I finally said, "Your Honor, I cannot agree with you, as I think you are wrong." The great Donald Lay then swiveled his chair around, turning his back to me, and remained that way through the remainder of my oral argument. There have not been too many times where my confidence has been seriously shaken, but that was one of them. I returned home and advised client and colleagues that we were going to lose the appeal.

Well, impressions can be misleading. The circuit court opinion found totally in our favor, with Judge Lay also ruling in our favor. The other insurer was required to pay most if not all of the damages.

About once a year after this episode, I ran into Judge Lay (a Minneapolis resident) at bar association events. He would look at my name tag and greet me warmly with, "Hello, Mark, it's good to see you again." I was usually cordial, but inside I wanted to punch his lights out. I would have probably been disbarred for doing so, but it sure would have felt good.

CHAPTER 14

JUDGES—AN INTERESTING BREED

A common misperception among the general public is that our judges have some level of superior legal knowledge that justified their appointment as the final arbitrators of our unsolvable disputes. These judges and magistrates somehow appear to be legal geniuses, clothed in Darth Vader robes and an aura of infallibility. In reality, however, judges have no more legal education or expertise than Joe Average Lawyer and, in fact, they are seldom chosen from among the top scholars in their graduating classes. Most judges are selected because of political connections unrelated to their experience, expertise, or intellect. The cream of every law school class garners the top law firm positions. After a few years of toil as associates, those high achievers are making more money than the judges in state or federal courts. By the time these smart lawyers reach a level of legal seasoning suitable for judicial consideration they are law firm partners, with status, prestige, and substantial financial well-being. To then become a judge would require major sacrifices that most partners would never accept. Thus, the typical state court judge comes from the group of lesser scholars and less financially successful legal practitioners.

Who, then, are our state and federal judges? The vast majority of judges are appointed rather than elected, so judicial positions are filled primarily by the age-old system of political patronage. The state governor has plenty of latitude to award old law school chums, firm cronies, or major campaign contributors with judgeships. The honored appointees do not even need to have civil or criminal trial experience—or indeed any significant legal experience—as long as they have a law degree and the requisite political connections. One of the worst appointments I recall was of the son of the speaker of the Minnesota House of Representatives. This young lawyer, with no real legal experience, was in treatment for manic depression and also suffered from narcolepsy. During one malpractice case I tried before this judge he had to take a twenty-minute break every forty-five minutes and would lock the door to his chambers to calm himself.

In another civil trial, this one in Anoka County District Court, I appeared before a newly appointed trial judge who, even after obviously studying her judicial handbook, did not even know whether the plaintiff or defendant went first in jury selection.

A very interesting group of judicial appointments came from Minnesota governor Rudy Perpich, a former dentist from the Iron Range who served three terms as governor. He thus had ample time to appoint a major percentage of Minnesota trial and appellate judges. Perpich maintained that the judiciary lacked gender and racial diversity—a fact well supported by statistics in the 1970s and decades before. The vast majority of law-school graduates and most practicing lawyers were white, male Anglo Saxons. It was not until the 1980s that law schools enrolled significant percentages of women and minorities. While Perpich's diversity goals were noble, he had a small pool of qualified women and minorities to choose from for his appointments. The lack of talented lawyers did not deter the governor. Appointment after appointment passed up qualified candidates vying for a judgeship in favor of poorly qualified candidates, all to meet the governor's requirements for judicial diversity. I clearly remember one female judicial appointment who had worked a couple of years in the Office of the Revisor of Statutes at the state legislature. Is that any qualification for a district court judge? The quality of the trial bench in Minnesota during the Perpich years really suffered. Some of those appointed did become competent and impartial judges after a few years of seasoning. But the whole process made a mockery of the idea that the governor would appoint the best qualified candidate available.

State judges must run for reelection every six years—another joke in the judicial process. Seldom in state history has an incumbent judge lost an election. On every ballot on the second Tuesday in November, right behind the judge's name on the ballot form, is the word "Incumbent." Voters receive little information about either incumbent or challenger. Incumbents do somehow obtain endorsements from groups of lawyers. In the days before every election the newspapers are full of official-looking advertisements bearing long lists of lawyers endorsing the incumbent judges. How can the average voter ever make a knowledgeable choice? To an uninformed electorate with little understanding of judges' or challengers' real qualifications and legal abilities, that single word "Incumbent" on the ballot kills the challenger's chances. To those outside the daily business of law, the label seems to have been bestowed because of merit and judicial talent, not patronage appointment.

Occasionally, a judicial vacancy requires an election from new candidates. One memorable election comes to my mind. A very bright Harvard Law graduate, one with ten years or more of solid trial experience with a major law firm, filed for an open judgeship and won the primary. He received glowing and well-deserved endorsements from many lawyers. His opponent was a female law graduate who had worked for two years as a law clerk for another district court judge. Lacking any significant practical experience, and without much to show in the way of academic achievement, she received not one endorsement from the bar. But in the general election, the unknowing electorate gave her the judgeship by a wide margin. Statistics later showed that something like 80 percent of female voters voted for the female candidate regardless of qualifications.

The national procedure for the very important federal judgeship positions is equally goofy. The three levels of federal judges—district court, court of appeals, and the Supreme Court—are all appointed by the president with the advice and consent of the Senate. Neither political party has ever blushed at the open practice of political patronage in federal judicial appointments. No potential candidate for one of the lifetime appointments, no matter how qualified, would stand a chance if he or she were not a member of the sitting president's political party and did not share the president's judicial philosophy. Impartiality thus takes a back seat to political philosophy. This politically motivated judiciary, at the highest level of our judicial system, has routinely affected major issues in the lives of citizens. The federal system will never change, but fortunately neither political party has remained in the White House so long as to stack the court totally to the left or right.

Every trial lawyer no doubt has a wealth of interesting judge stories. I will relay here some of mine. I have encountered two sleeping judges. My very first attempt at a jury trial—first described in Chapter 3—was the $3,500 insurance subrogation claim from the kitchen fire in Alexandria, tried before the elderly Judge Gaylord Saetre. This being my first jury trial, I had prepared a lengthy series of potent questions for my voir dire questioning of the jury. I was, no doubt, boring and tedious. As I grilled the jurors, a familiar, rhythmic sound emanated from the judge's bench behind me. Judge Saetre was sound asleep, peacefully snoring and oblivious to the courtroom happenings. Needless to say, once I realized this, I brought my jury questioning quickly to an end.

My second experience with a judicial nap happened in Hennepin County District Court before a gruff, cigar-smoking, hard-drinking judge named Chester Durda. Never a great legal scholar, Judge Durda was generally disliked by defense lawyers because of his reputation for favoring the plaintiff's side in injury cases. While doing defense work I tried before Judge Durda the case of a thirty-five-year-old mentally and physically disabled Native American woman who lived in an assisted living residence along Portland Avenue, just south of downtown Minneapolis. This lady, who ran with a wobbly, shuffling gait, had darted out between two parked cars onto the one-way street directly into the path of a seventeen-year-old-girl driving an old Chevy. The lady was hit by the right front corner of the car, then rolled up onto the hood, and when the girl stopped the woman rolled hard onto the pavement in front of the car. The impact left the woman as a wheelchair paraplegic in addition to her previous disabilities.

My task was defending the seventeen-year-old driver. Her insurance company, with only a $60,000 liability limit, decided that the case was defensible and directed me to prepare the case for trial. Part of my case was to present the testimony of the best accident-reconstruction expert in the state, who had calculated that my client had not been speeding and had less than two seconds to react and avoid hitting the lady entering the street. Considering that the badly injured plaintiff would be very sympathetic before a jury, my idea—shared by my partners, whom I had consulted—was that we would be better off with a court trial before the liberal Judge Durda than in a jury trial. To my surprise, the plaintiff's lawyer agreed.

In my mind this was a case the defense should clearly win, especially with the unopposed reconstruction testimony of my expert. My expert took the stand in Judge Durda's courtroom after the lunch break. Now, although I had never witnessed it, Judge Durda had a reputation for liquid lunches, even during his jury trials. As I methodically proceeded through my expert's critical testimony, my focus, for some reason, went from my witness to the judge. He was sound asleep and probably had been for some time. Thinking that his inattention was only momentary, I raised my volume as I asked the next couple questions. No response. I then looked at the judge's clerk, Pat, whom I knew quite well, and gave her a hands-up look of "What do we do now?" Pat took a sheet of paper, wrote something on it, and went up and tapped the judge on the shoulder, placing the note in front of him. Although now awake, His Honor's attention to my expert's remaining testimony was bleary-eyed and not of sufficient intensity to merit his taking notes in his judicial diary.

Judge Durda's decision at the close of the case was remarkable, finding in favor of the plaintiff, assigning 49 percent negligence to plaintiff and 51 percent negligence to my client, and awarding $660,000 in damages to the plaintiff. A big win for the plaintiff, but there existed only the $60,000 of insurance coverage. Following the next logical step, the plaintiff's lawyer filed a bad-faith claim against my insurance company to try and collect the full judgment amount from the insurer. Faced with the bad-faith claim, we decided to appeal with the primary issue that we did not have a fair trial because our judge fell asleep and missed the critical testimony of the defense expert witness. Sounds like a good issue on appeal, right? In preparation for the appeal, I tried to obtain an affidavit from Pat as to the events surrounding the judge's nap. Being loyal to her judge, she refused.

I next tried to subpoena the judge's trial diary to show the gap in his notes during my expert's testimony. Again, it was denied because of judiciary immunity. With my affidavit and affidavits from my client and my expert, we processed the appeal. The appellate court affirmed the decision and criticized me in its opinion, suggesting that I should have taken more affirmative steps to wake the judge and ensure that he was paying attention to the testimony. Imagine if you will my chances in a court trial before Judge Durda if I had embarrassed the trial judge by awakening him and placing on the record my objections to his lack of attention!

Probably my most interesting civil defense trial involves another interesting judge story. A thirty-five-year-old Minneapolis businessman had a head-on collision while vacationing in a national park in South Dakota. Although it was a low-speed impact, he had struck his head on the visor above the windshield. Several months later he developed the first symptoms of multiple sclerosis (MS). His condition progressed rapidly to total disability and confinement in a wheelchair. This clearly had the potential to become a huge damage case if the car accident precipitated the MS. I assumed the defense of the case with a $300,000 liability policy protecting the defendant driver. Having researched the causes of MS, I found that the best researchers in the world on the subject were at the University of Arizona in Tucson. With comprehensive retrospective and prospective studies of the relationship of trauma to the development of MS, the experts' well-supported conclusions were that there was no relationship. I lined up the key researcher as my expert witness to come to Minneapolis for trial. In response to my efforts, the plaintiff's attorney sought out the world's leading advocate of a connection between trauma and the development of MS. This seventy-year-old Harvard professor had been advancing for years, and testifying frequently, that traumatic disruption to the blood-brain barrier initiated the destruction of the myelin sheathes on the nerves in the spinal cord, resulting in MS. My expert scoffed at this opinion as having absolutely no scientific support.

The jury trial of this case came before a newly appointed Hennepin County judge, a lawyer I had known for years and considered to be a legal lightweight. His career had been handling low-level criminal cases and DUI defense work. Tennis and partying with the good old boys were his primary interests. If this was not his first civil trial, it was clearly the most significant civil case he had encountered either as a trial lawyer or as a judge. My opposing counsel and I brought before this judge the two leading experts on the very controversial issue of whether a minor trauma could initiate the onset of MS. Never have I had two experts of this quality and with these credentials in the same courtroom, dueling over a major legal-medical issue. At one point during my expert's critical testimony, we lawyers had to approach the bench (as lawyers frequently must ask and receive permission to do) to discuss some issue about the expert testimony I was offering. As I stood before the bench and peered over the judge's diary book, I observed that he was occupying his time during my expert's critical testimony with an issue of *Sports Illustrated* carefully hidden in his diary book. I guarantee that this judge, throughout his time on the bench, would never have had a more intellectually stimulating and interesting case than this one. But *Sports Illustrated* won out.

The end of the story. Judicial ineptitude did not alter the results of the case. The jury deliberated four days longer than any civil jury in my career. They eventually came back with an obvious compromise verdict finding the necessary causation allowing the plaintiff to recover and awarding a quite small award of $200,000 in damages. A loss, but I saved $100,000 on the insurance policy.

I cannot discuss judges without commenting on the most

prominent and impressive jurist I have ever appeared before. I had the privilege of trying three cases over the years before U.S. District Judge Edward Devitt in the latter years of his career. Judge Devitt had been on the federal bench for over twenty-five years and had coauthored the prominent federal jury instruction guide used throughout the entire federal judicial system. Judge Devitt, at that time, well into his seventies, had a head of long white hair and a judicial demeanor that immediately commanded total respect from anyone in his massive courtroom. Especially impressive was the stuffed bald eagle ready to launch into flight from the room's corner. (I once knew the story of where this protected national symbol came from and how it ended up in his courtroom, but that I cannot now recall.)

The most memorable of those three cases was a business litigation case for a small Minnesota corporation that had developed and sold a new prototype fluorescent lightbulb to market giant Phillips Lighting. Our allegation was that Phillips had taken our client's technology without agreed compensation and misappropriated it for its own use. The case, scheduled before Judge Devitt in St. Paul federal court, was defended by a big-time litigator from the large Faegre & Benson law firm.

Judge Devitt called a pretrial conference in mid-December for all of the many cases scheduled on his calendar. Perhaps thirty or more lawyers gathered in his courtroom. As with each case, when ours was called, he politely directed us to a particular conference room to "get together" and settle the case and then report back to him in an hour. As defense counsel and I had long before exhausted our settlement attempts, we sat around making small talk for an hour before returning to Judge Devitt's courtroom and reporting our unsuccessful settlement efforts. Judge Devitt then courteously asked us how long the case would take to try. We responded with our agreed-upon seven or eight trial days. Judge Devitt, in his quiet and resonant voice, advised us that we would try this case in four days, starting on December 20th. The pre-Christmas date did not bother me, as I had no holiday plans. My prominent defense counsel, however, pleaded to the judge, "Your Honor, I would request a different trial date as I have a two-week holiday vacation planned in [some Caribbean island, as I recall], and my young associate is scheduled to spend the holidays in California with her aunt who is dying of cancer." Without hesitation, the esteemed jurist responded, "I think you fellows can work out those problems." With that, I sat back smugly, thinking that my opponents were really up against the wall. But then the good judge added, "I think what we will do is bifurcate and only try the liability issue on December 20th." Now my jaw dropped and I was speechless, because for a plaintiff's lawyer, separating the damage aspects from a liability trial eliminates all of the sympathetic "help the little guy" aspects of the lawsuit. But I was hardly in any position to argue with Judge Devitt. His Honor had ruled, and that was it.

Trying a case before Judge Devitt was a remarkable experience. After he set the outside time limit to try the case, both sides simplified and chopped and channeled their presentations and cross-examinations. During the trial Judge Devitt's mannerisms dominated the courtroom. If you paused for a few seconds in questioning, the judge looked down and said, "Counsel, do you have any more questions for this witness?" One day my scheduled witnesses came out twenty minutes short of the 4:30 end of the day. The judge implored me, "Counsel, do you have another witness for me?" When I replied that we were done for the day and did not have another witness ready, the judge turned to the jury and said, "Folks, I am truly sorry, but the lawyers do not have another witness for us. We will have to go home and hope that the lawyers will have a full day for us tomorrow. Good night to you."

Again, the end of the story is of interest. During the trial I produced before the jury probably the best smoking-gun piece of evidence in my career. In the midst of boxes of documents I had reviewed in Phillips's home base in Boston I had found a document identifying a five-year future projection of thousands of sales of the new Phillips lightbulb (which used my client's design and technology). Contrary to Phillips's contention that my client's lightbulb design was never utilized, this one critical document proved it had fully adopted it and were lying in their testimony. At the conclusion of the four-day liability trial the jury returned its verdict, finding that Phillips Lighting had breached its contract and had committed fraudulent misrepresentations in its dealing with my Minnesota developer.

With the liability trial concluded before Christmas, Judge Devitt immediately scheduled the damage phase of the trial to commence between Christmas and New Year's. My defense colleague returned from a shortened one-week vacation to the Caribbean with a good case of tourista and clearly uninterested in proceeding with the damage trial. We settled the damages for a nice amount of $500,000 for my client.

CHAPTER 15

THE CHINESE MURDER CASE

Most civil trial lawyers view the criminal process and its criminal lawyers as a poor second sister. Most of the criminal lawyers serving as county attorneys or taking public defender positions on the defense side were not the top scholars in their law school classes and took those jobs because nothing better had been offered. Prosecuting attorneys have the police, or the FBI and U.S. attorneys in the federal system, to do all of the workup on the cases. The prosecuting attorney has only to present the evidence to the jury and argue that they have met the burden of proof. Similarly, the defense seldom has to prove much of anything and instead sits back and picks away at the prosecution's witnesses, arguing strenuously that they have not met their burden to prove the defendant guilty beyond a reasonable doubt. Seldom does a civil lawyer have the opportunity to play one of these roles in the criminal process, as the Chinese murder case allowed me to do in a most interesting lawsuit.

Living near the East Hennepin area of Minneapolis during

college and law school, I occasionally got take out or sat in for low-budget dinners at the Hoy Toy Café, located in a strip mall on East Hennepin Avenue. Nothing ever seemed out of the ordinary there, where the elderly couple who owned the place and their teenaged Chinese workers served up chow mein and egg rolls. Well, so much for tranquility.

The case came into our office from one of our insurance companies in connection with a wrongful death claim. Having been given the defense case, I found the claims and underlying facts fascinating. The children of the owners of the Hoy Toy Café were suing their mother for wrongful death of their father, the sole owner of the restaurant. Every homeowner's insurance policy has an exclusion avoiding coverage for any intentional act by the named insured or a member of the insured's family. In order to hook a homeowner's insurance policy into covering the mother in the death of father, the claimants alleged that the wife was insane at the time she killed her husband and thus could not have formed an intent to murder, therefore avoiding the policy exclusion for intentional acts. A bit of legal research confirmed that this argument had been accepted in prior cases. Thus, my task in trying to save the insurance client its policy limit of coverage was to prove that the wife was not insane, but rather had known what she was doing and had intentionally killed her husband.

The criminal case against the wife had been handled in summary fashion, with a prominent Hennepin County District Court judge accepting the defense that she was criminally insane at the time of the homicide and therefore not responsible. The judge had sentenced the woman to the mental-health facility in St. Cloud for an indeterminate term. We found out that she served about a year before being found by the powers that be to be totally recovered and subject to release as rehabilitated. The family's lawyer then commenced the wrongful death lawsuit by the children against the mother for negligently causing the death of the father. Note that I mention "negligently causing" the death, because if the mother had intentionally killed her husband, then no insurance coverage would protect the mother's act.

A good plaintiff's lawyer named Gene Adkins represented the children in the wrongful death claim against their mother. I liked his tenacious attitude, and later, after he had been appointed to the district court as a judge in Scott County, I had a good relationship with him. At this trial, Adkins sought to show that for decades, dating back to the couple's life in China, the husband had abused opium and had subjected his wife to such brutal treatment that the SOB deserved to die. An interpreter translated lots of Chinese history, which was interesting to me but hardly relevant. Adkins's intent was to convince the jury that the wife had been mentally abused to the degree that she murdered her husband without really knowing what she was doing—i.e., the act was not intentional, but negligent, and was thus covered under the insurance policy. For my side I sought to show that the homicide was an intentional act rather than some insane fantasy. I prepared and presented the defense case just as a criminal prosecutor would have done in a capital murder case.

The evidence in the investigation file was most revealing. The wife claimed that she had a delusion in the middle of the night that her husband was fleeing out of the bedroom window with his young lover and that they were stealing her chest of antique Chinese coins. To stop this thievery, she claimed, she reached for her pistol, which was kept in her night stand, and wildly shot across the room. Only then did she wake up to find that she had shot and killed her husband. Somehow this alibi had convinced the first trial judge that the woman was temporarily insane and in need of treatment rather than incarceration. After reviewing the investigation file and interviewing the investigating officers, I recommended that no settlement of the civil case be attempted. The trial was a real circus.

Throughout the trial, the woman and her attractive daughters attended the proceedings dressed to kill in fancy, expensive clothes and elegantly coiffured hair. Attorney Adkins utilized a Chinese interpreter to present several family witnesses (who claimed to not speak much English) to establish the supposed history of family abuse that precipitated the shooting. I put the investigating officers on the stand with the pictures of the scene. One picture showed the deceased husband lying on his side in the family bed. The officers had shaved the top of his head, exposing six small, black holes in a circle about five inches diameter in the back of his skull—the work of the wife's .22-caliber revolver. When I presented this picture to the jury, I almost laughed at the wife's delusional assertion that she was randomly shooting at her fleeing husband. This picture of six well-placed bullets clearly showed intentional homicide. This jury took very little time to find that this was an intentional killing and not covered by the liability policy. I remember our trial judge marveling at how the first, experienced judge had bought the woman's story of being insane at the time of the shooting. In retrospect, I thought that the wife-beating, opium-smoking husband probably got just what he deserved. And until it closed, I still went occasionally for Chinese food at the Hoy Toy Café.

CHAPTER 16

BATTLING THE MIGHTY MAYO CLINIC

As trial lawyers we always hope to have a level playing field for a lawsuit. In theory at least, neither plaintiff nor defendant should start out with an advantage before a jury. Undue influence on a jury, whether overt or subtle and unspoken by jurors in the courtroom can lead to a trial outcome not justified by the law and evidence and out of the trial lawyer's control. The burden of proof required of the plaintiff attorney to win requires only that the evidence favor the plaintiff by the slightest margin or by the greater weight of evidence. When the deck is stacked against the plaintiff by some unknown underlying bias, that burden of proof requires, as in a criminal case, proof beyond a reasonable doubt—frankly, a burden usually impossible to meet no matter how strong and convincing the case may be.

Suing the mighty Mayo Clinic or one of its doctors for malpractice presents such a challenge. The Mayo Clinic has a favorable reputation with laypeople that is probably unmatched in Minnesota and beyond. Most Minnesotans with a serious medical condition will consider the Mayo Clinic as the first choice for treatment. The clinic, with its hundreds of doctor specialists, is centered in Rochester, a city of 75,000 in southeastern Minnesota. With the many high-paid doctors residing in the city, Rochester has one of the highest standards of living in the country. Many nonmedical persons in Rochester and throughout the surrounding Olmstead County are economically dependent on the Mayo Clinic directly as an employer or indirectly through other financial connections.

It is a basic rule of venue that a defendant has a right to be tried in his or her county of residence or primary place of doing business. Consequently, the Mayo Clinic and its resident doctors routinely can only be sued in Olmstead County. A Minnesota resident claiming medical malpractice against a Mayo doctor has no choice but to commence and pursue the malpractice case in the home court of the Mayo Clinic. The only exception is if the plaintiff should be a resident of another state and can then proceed in Minnesota federal court because of diversity of citizenship. There is no branch of the federal court in Rochester, so federal trials are held in St. Paul. A number of years ago, we trial lawyers believed that the Mayo Clinic had never lost a malpractice case that had been tried in Rochester. This may still be true today, as I am aware of no successful malpractice verdicts coming out of Olmstead County. A few years ago a Minnesota plaintiff's lawyer sought to prove the built-in bias facing a medical malpractice lawsuit against the clinic in Olmstead County. He hired an expensive investigation firm to survey county residents to find out what percentage were medically or economically dependent on the Mayo Clinic. The results were astounding. Something like 75 percent of the county's residents were patients or in some manner economically tied to the clinic. With that evidence the lawyer went before the Olmstead County judge demanding a change-of-venue because his client could not get a fair trial from an unbiased jury. The change-of-venue motion was denied, as the judge held that the data did not prove sufficient bias that a plaintiff could not get a fair trial in the home of the Mayo Clinic.

My one effort against the Mayo Clinic fit the same pattern, with a resounding defense verdict in favor of a very negligent Mayo doctor. The following story should convince any plaintiff's lawyer of the futility of suing a Mayo doctor in Rochester. I had the displeasure of making a direct comparison of the same case tried in Olmstead County and also tried before a different jury in a county a hundred miles away.

During my heavy defense-lawyering years I tried several medical malpractice cases for doctors. My track record was very good, with no jury trial loss in half a dozen trials. In this one I was defending a Mankato, Minnesota surgeon in a very serious injury case. A thirty-eight-year-old farmer had been injured when a cement block wall collapsed on him. He had dragged himself to his truck and driven to the hospital in Mankato. X-rays showed a separated pelvis, and he was hospitalized on bed rest. During his hospitalization he was seen by several doctors including my client, a seventy-year-old surgeon. These doctors watched this fellow get sicker and sicker with obvious signs that something was amiss in his abdomen. After eight days of steady decline, with the patient exhibiting a bloated abdomen, high fever, and no bowel sounds, the Mankato doctors finally agreed something was seriously wrong and transferred him by ambulance to the Mayo Clinic.

In the Rochester hospital emergency room the patient was seen by a trauma surgeon by the name of Dr. Mucha. This fellow was not short on self-confidence. As should have been done days earlier by my surgeon in Mankato, Dr. Mucha immediately did an exploratory operation into the abdomen. He found a perforated bowel and an abdominal cavity badly infected with peritonitis, an inflammation of the lining of the abdomen. After cleaning out the infection, Dr. Mucha had two options to repair the bowel. One method, called an anastomosis, required cutting out a section of the bowel around the perforation and then sewing together the two ends of what should be good clean tissue. The alternative is to bring the end of the bowel to the surface of the abdomen and allow the bowel material to flow into a colostomy bag. This favored approach allows the infection to settle down. After a few weeks of healing a second operation can be done to reattach the two ends of the bowel and return to normal function.

We found out from consulting with our surgical experts that with widespread peritonitis, as in this case, the two-step colostomy procedure was clearly the preferred procedure. Dr. Mucha, however, chose the one-step anastomosis surgery on this very sick patient. As could be expected, the anastomosis broke down when the stitches failed in the infected bowel tissue. Thereafter, the patient went through a horrendous recovery. He spent weeks in the Rochester hospital, had thirty-eight different operations and procedures, and left the hospital with his abdomen wide open and packed with sterile gauze. It then took months for the open wound to gradually heal. The patient was totally disabled and could no longer work.

The lawsuit commenced in Mankato against several doctors and the hospital. The patient was represented by attorney Ed Parker, a former Minnesota trial judge who had returned to private practice. He obviously had not handled many medical malpractice cases. After we defense lawyers reviewed the facts, including what happened at Mayo, and consulted with our experts, we were convinced that even though our defendant doctors were in trouble for their lack of attention to obvious signs of abdominal injury, Dr. Mucha was also very negligent in his choice of surgery, which was the primary cause of most of the patient's permanent disability.

One of the basic rules of malpractice defense is that two

defendants do not fight between themselves, which usually will help a plaintiff succeed in the overall case. Cross-claims or third-party lawsuits against other doctors who may be at fault are almost never pursued. In this case, because of the magnitude of the damage potential and our strong belief about Dr. Mucha's negligence, we on the Mankato defense team met with Mayo Clinic lawyers, laid out our case against Dr. Mucha, and requested contribution from Mayo toward a possible settlement of the plaintiff's case. Our efforts were quickly and soundly rejected. With strong urging from our doctor clients and permission from their insurance carriers we commenced a third-party contribution action against Dr. Mucha. The Mayo Clinic retained as their defense attorney James O'Hagen, a senior partner at the large Dorsey & Whitney law firm. O'Hagen had been the clinic's choice for years. (At the end of this chapter you will find the tale of the tragic fate of this fellow, whom we ungraciously called Baldy O'Hagen because of his totally bald top.)

Strategy compelled us to settle with the plaintiff and preserve our claim for contribution towards the settlement against Dr. Mucha and the Mayo Clinic. The plaintiff was paid $1.6 million for his injuries. The contribution case then proceeded to trial in Mankato before an experienced, pleasant, elderly judge. Among the several attorneys representing the Mankato hospital and doctors I was nominated as the lead to pursue the contribution case against Dr. Mucha. The trial lasted five weeks, which made it the longest single trial of my career.

I have to digress here and relate a fascinating story about one of the expert witnesses originally hired by the plaintiff's attorney. This expert, a well-credentialed gastroenterologist named Dr. Eisenberg, was formerly associated with the University of Minnesota but had relocated to a big hospital in Brooklyn, New York. When the plaintiff settled, Attorney O'Hagen took on Dr. Eisenberg as Mayo's expert witness. Dr. Eisenberg had rendered strong opinions in a pretrial report that the Mayo doctor was not at fault and the group of Mankato doctors were very negligent. Prior to trial, we defense attorneys went to Brooklyn to take his deposition. Arriving the afternoon before the deposition, four of us enjoyed a great Manhattan dinner and then saw the Broadway play *A Chorus Line.* The next morning we cabbed to Brooklyn for the deposition. We had quite a greeting. The hospital was surrounded by a police security line, large cement barricades, and several hundred hospital employees and nurses on strike, loudly protesting some unknown issues. As we threaded into the hospital through the yelling picket lines, we were called some not-too-pleasant names.

Prior to the expert's deposition we had requested that he produce all of the documents provided to him by counsel. He produced a ten-inch stack of documents. While another defense attorney began questioning the doctor, I reviewed the pile of paper. It contained some amazing disclosures, including a preliminary draft of a report the expert had sent to the first attorney, along with the attorney's unedited comments on the report. The expert's preliminary comments differed greatly from his final report and included his first opinions that some of our Mankato doctors were not negligent. At the first break in the questioning, I advised my fellow defense attorneys that this guy's file contained, as I still remember saying, "fucking dynamite." We correctly decided not to use the documents to question him that day, but to save them instead for trial.

My encounter with Dr. Eisenberg on the witness stand in Mankato was one of the high points of my career. His draft opinions in writing, which had been rejected by the first lawyer, significantly contradicted the opinions he gave under oath on the Mankato witness stand. With that kind of ammunition, I destroyed the hotshot's credibility in front of the jury. As he walked out of the courtroom with his tail between his legs, I went up to him, shook his hand, and said, "I presume I will see you again in another case."

The follow-up on Dr. Eisenberg was indeed interesting. A couple years later, on a somewhat similar serious medical malpractice case that I had been assigned to defend, I talked to the plaintiff's attorney, a friend for years. He related that he had contacted Dr. Eisenberg in New York to be an expert in his case. Before accepting the assignment, the good doctor asked who the defense attorneys were on the case. When he learned that Stageberg was on the case, he refused to get involved because of how he had been beaten up in the Mankato case. That one really felt good.

Back to Mankato. After five weeks of hard-fought trial, the jury's verdict found the group of Mankato doctors 60 percent at fault and Dr. Mucha 40 percent at fault. This meant Dr. Mucha and the Mayo clinic would be contributing 40 percent of the $1.6 million dollars, or $640,000, toward the settlement. The jury had accepted my argument that nearly half of this badly damaged farmer's problems related to the inappropriate choice of reconstructive surgery by Dr. Mucha. This looked like a great win for me and the Mankato doctors.

Unfortunately, the story does not end there. The Mayo Clinic and its lawyers do not like to be beaten in malpractice cases. They processed an appeal to the Minnesota Court of Appeals claiming errors in some of the trial judge's quite insignificant trial rulings on the admission of evidence. Remarkably, the appeal worked and the appellate court reversed the verdict and ordered a new trial. We don't know why it happened, but we speculated that the plaintiff's initial attorney, who had been recently elevated to the court of appeals, exerted some influence. Not only did the court reverse our verdict, but it also concluded that since this was just a contribution case among defendants it should be retried in Olmstead County rather than a hundred miles away in Mankato.

We knew we did not stand a chance on the retrial in Rochester. Picking the jury got no honest answers as juror after juror assured us they could treat the conduct of a Mayo doctor the same as that of the Mankato doctors. The good news was that we completed this second version of the same case in two weeks rather than the five weeks of the first trial. As expected, the Rochester jury came back in a short time, finding the Mankato doctors totally at fault and relieving Dr. Mucha of all responsibility. The good news is that during this long case scenario I was being paid by the hour by the insurance company rather than on a contingent fee basis.

The epilogue to this chapter is the fall of Baldy O'Hagen. Within a year or two of the end of my case, O'Hagen was on the front page of the newspapers due to criminal charges of falsifying documents and defrauding his favorite client, the Mayo Clinic, out of several million dollars. On malpractice cases like ours, O'Hagen would settle with plaintiffs for one amount and then advise the Mayo that the settlement was for a higher amount. The balance went into O'Hagen's greedy pocket. He not only lost his ticket to practice law but also spent considerable time behind bars for his indiscretions. Boy, even now it really hurts my ego to have been beaten by that kind of guy.

CHAPTER 17

ARGUMENTS BEFORE THE APPELLATE COURTS

...lawyer has this image of standing before ...ces of the United States Supreme Court ...ase of nationwide importance. In law ...s, including the oral argument before ...ted to a status far beyond what is justi- ...a few years, those lawyers who toil in ...cts and ignorant trial judges to reach ...ome the real architects of dramatic ...But somehow, those few who elevate ...pellate lawyer garner the laurels as ...cisions. The appellate practice is a ...e practice of law. As the following ...ade a wise decision when I followed

...my résumé find numerous exam- ...f record on some major appellate decisions establishing principles of law. Two such prominent decisions in Minnesota are the cases commonly known as *Butzer* and *Malmon*. Both cases involved personal injury procedures for maximizing insurance coverage for injured victims. These cases are of such importance that someday, perhaps a hundred years from now, some attorney will review these cases for applicability to their case and say, "Who was Mark Stageberg?" Hey, if a trial lawyer is to leave a legacy, this one isn't too bad!

From early on in my trial lawyer career it was impressed in my mind that the secret to success was 95 percent winning in front of the jury, and I focused on that goal throughout my trial practice. If I could get a favorable jury verdict, we would somehow hang onto that verdict in the appellate process. On both the *Butzer* and *Malmon* cases I was victorious as the trial lawyer and turned the appeal over to one of our appellate specialists.

One of the interesting rules of the appellate process is that the appellate court views certain issues differently. This is called the standard of review on appeal. On the facts of a case submitted to a jury for decision, the decision on those fact issues will seldom be overturned unless so far off-base that justice requires a reversal and new trial. On most issues decided by the trial court, the standard of review requires a change of result only if the trial judge abused his or her discretion in deciding the issue. Usually this is a tough burden for an appealing party to meet. In every complex trial, the trial judge may make dozens of these discretionary rulings. As a trial lawyer I know that I will win some and lose some of these judge's rulings. Unless the trial judge has some undisclosed bias for or against my client or my case, usually these trial court rulings will balance out pretty close to a 50/50 win-and-loss ratio. When I have been on the losing side of a jury verdict, seldom have I ever filed an appeal to challenge the discretion of the trial judge.

Somehow, appellate oral argument has been given far too

much credence as influential in appellate decisions. Appealing parties each file fifty-page appellate briefs with lengthy trial transcripts and exhibits. The appellate judges usually review these briefs and then sit to hear oral argument in four to five cases in a single session. The lawyers in each case generally are allowed fifteen or twenty minutes for oral argument. Usually one of the justices previously assigned to your case will have read the briefs, will be paying attention, and will ask a few questions during the oral argument. The questions will sometimes require a logical answer or a diversion to distract that jurist and totally confuse his colleagues on the bench. The actual decisions are usually researched and written by the law clerks assigned to the justices. The justices might then proofread the clerks' opinions and nod an assent, often not ever fully understanding the issues or the rulings they are approving.

As a younger lawyer I, too, had been of the belief that presenting oral argument before an appellate court was one of the ultimate achievements in a trial lawyer's career. With that in mind, I argued several of my trial results before the appellate courts. I really remember none of these cases, or my oratory or lack thereof, or even whether the justices ruled my way or not. The trial results discussed in this diatribe, rather than a fifteen-minute oral argument before an appellate court, are far more memorable and hopefully more interesting to the reader.

My experience with the Eighth Circuit Court of Appeals merits some comment. In Chapter 11, I have already described my unpleasant experience with Justice Lay. To those uninformed, the U.S. Constitution set up a federal court system in addition to the state court judicial systems established in each of the fifty states. Some cases gravitate to the federal system for reasons hard to explain to those who are not scholars of our Constitutional federal system of government. Some of my litigation cases have tediously plowed through the federal court system, ending up on appeal before the mighty Eighth Circuit Court of Appeals in St. Louis, Missouri.

My first case before the Eighth Circuit was an embarrassing disaster. This was a complex insurance coverage case that a small-town lawyer in western Minnesota had won on summary judgment. My client, the losing insurance company, wanted to appeal the result. Despite my advice that we could not win on appeal, we were being paid by the hour, so what the heck, let's do it. Down in St. Louis before the three judges of the mighty Eighth Circuit, my oral argument was greeted with obvious skepticism. I floundered over repeated tough questions from one of the judges. By the time I finished, it was apparent to me and anyone else present that my appeal was already lost. When my country lawyer opponent stood up to argue, the head judge said, "Sir, do you think you really need to say anything?" He wisely sat down with a polite "No, Your Honor." By the time I had traveled from St. Louis back to Minneapolis, the decision of the Eighth Circuit, in the form of a short three-page opinion denying my appeal, was waiting on my desk. This panel of distinguished justices had obviously decided the case on the briefs and finalized the written opinion before a word of oral argument began. So much for the importance of oral argument!

At the large Lommen, Nelson, Cole & Stageberg firm, with designated appellate specialists, I was more than happy to pass my trial cases, both winners and losers, to these specialists to handle any appeals.

CHAPTER 18

COMPANY CARS

Everyone that I have ever known, including every law partner, wants to minimize their taxes—or, to say it more graphically, to screw the government out of a few bucks. Trial lawyers, although usually not well versed in tax law, have an innate sense that they, as trained legal scholars, can manipulate the system to pad their take-home at the expense of the government. (Perhaps it is because Tax I was a required course in law school.)

Like other macho leaders, successful partners project their image with the automobiles they drive. Can you imagine the loss of prestige inherent in parking your Toyota Corolla outside a prominent courthouse as you try a major lawsuit? How embarrassing if another trial attorney were to see you exit your mundane vehicle and slither past the Cadillacs, Mercedes, and BMWs that somehow always garner the premier parking slots in any parking lot. The lawyer's vehicle is far more than mere transportation. It is the single most important overt symbol of a lawyer's success and status. If you want to look like a successful attorney, you never would be driving a Volkswagen or a Chevrolet, but would always drive up in a Porsche, BMW, or equivalent, even if you never could afford it. As someone has graphically described it, for the modern male, a vehicle is an extension of the penis. (Perhaps a similar physiological metaphor of status applies to the rising group of female trial attorneys, but I cannot generate an appropriate analogy.)

With this far-from-scientific analysis of lawyers' unacknowledged investment in their automobiles, I now turn to one of the most heated debates of law firm management: The company car program. Those few within a law firm's management structure who got beyond Tax I constantly advocate to partners the advantages of a companywide car policy. That is, it is to every partner's tax advantage to have the firm own his or her primary car and bear the cost of investment as well as all insurance, gas, maintenance, and other operating expenses. All looks rosy as the firm bears these vehicle expenses instead of the individual lawyer. Whatever the IRS may require for the division between "business use" and "personal use," the gray areas between the two justify a company car for all who may be eligible. With hardly a thought for ethics, the driver might head out with the kids to a movie on a Friday night or cruise the two hundred miles up north to see grandma, then charge it off as business miles on the company car.

So, if this is one of the great quasi-legitimate tax breaks, why doesn't every law firm, small or mighty, have a company car program? One simple word: Administration. Our thirty-attorney, fifteen-partner law firm illustrates the upsides and downsides of the firm car policy. When we had fewer than ten partners, our car policy was administered by the office manager, with quite loose rules for the partners. The senior partners (the "old farts") controlled the program and, unsurprisingly, decided that senior attorneys required (or, narcissistically, "deserved") expensive transportation. Thus, senior partners John, Owen, Phil, and

Mark (the other Mark), felt totally justified in buying full-size Cadillacs, Lincolns, and Audis at company expense. My respected partners, John and Owen, drove Cadillac Sevilles for years. (Some of us called those ugly battleships "senilles.") But as more young partners arrived, more discussion and even outright controversy arose over the firm's car policy. We argued over what types of vehicle would be appropriate for new, junior partners. If senior partners spent $30,000 on their vehicles, why couldn't the newest partner, buying a $15,000 Toyota, enjoy the same level of firm expenditure as part of their compensation?

Very soon, with an increasing number of new partners expecting the benefit of a company car, administration of the car policy became a nightmare. The rapidly expanding fleet soon forced the office manager to spend an increasing amount of his time handling the buying and selling of vehicles, insurance, maintenance, and the inevitable fender bender. Rehashing the merits and problems of the car policy soon became the number-one agenda item at partner meetings. The alternative was providing partners a "car allowance" of some percentage of salary, which did not favor the senior partners and their status quo of top dogs getting top dog cars. Perhaps no single issue generated more partner debate over the years.

Eventually, a thorough review by the office's competent tax attorney justified the continuance of the existing car policy for partners because of the tax benefit. As a short-term compromise, we agreed that partners could choose either a car allowance based on seniority or use of a company-owned car. It wasn't much of a solution, and it created an even bigger administrative headache for the office manager. When I left the firm, that complicated two-part car policy was still in existence.

But I can hardly complain about the firm's car policy. As a rising young partner with marginal personal finances I had welcomed the perks of a company car. Upon reflection, never

could I have owned a new car of the quality of the vehicle
as part of my law firm compensation. Since no one e
tioned my personal use of the vehicle, I used my com
fully for personal use without hesitation or thought for
consequences. A new car every three years was the
Since my vehicle status rose with my partner status, I
driving my dream cars: A Toyota Supra, an Audi Cou
full-size Audi sedan. Needless to say, I was a strong ad
the company car policy.

My first car as a new partner was an Oldsmobile
nice family car for a father with two young children.
nice car lasted a short time. In February of 1986, I b
had the two biggest consecutive-day snowfalls in Mi
history, dropping something like 17 and 19 inches of
the first day I was to meet my wife at the airport at mid
to Texas for a long weekend vacation. Being a loyal e
went to the office that morning and worked until noon
foot of snow had fallen by the time I entered onto Inters
south from downtown, heading to the airport. As I cr
Lake Street overpass in the left lane I saw numerou
tangled in an accident ahead. Stopping was like bra
skating rink. My emergency plan to avoid the pileup a
to turn left into the cement divider to try and slow the
Cutlass contacted the divider, sustaining only minor d
the front left corner, then swung counterclockwise and
stop well short of the tangled cars ahead. Feeling mo
happy that I was unscathed and secure, I looked back
saw a school bus in my lane, totally out of control a
toward my helpless, stationary Cutlass. That moment
will never forget. I closed my eyes, leaned against the
and wondered how badly I was going to be hurt when
me. The impact was solid, sending my Cutlass and the b
toward the crashed vehicles ahead.

Opening my eyes and finding all body parts basically secure, I sought out the highway patrolman already at the scene. As I claimed no injuries and was driving a company car, the highway patrolman was happy to let me call the firm's office manager and request a tow truck to handle the totaled Cutlass. Among the drivers of the smashed vehicles I found a lady, with a still driveable vehicle, heading for the airport and willing to give me a lift. I still caught the plane to Texas. I never worried about or even saw my Cutlass again. When I returned I went out and bought a new car. Ah, the wonders of a company car and a good office manager!

Whether driving a company or personal car, we all like to be secure in coming and leaving from work. Accordingly, another great partner perk was free parking in the convenient but expensive indoor ramp below our office. But alas, convenience does not always mean security. When we officed in the Twin City Federal building we parked in the TCF ramp below the offices. Senior partner Mark Sullivan and I each had company-owned Audis which we parked on the second floor of the ramp. Mark's Audi was the first to experience a break-in: A smashed window and the extraction of the Audi's Blaupunkt radio. A few days later I found that a fire extinguisher had been thrown through the driver's window of my Audi. The thief had not only extracted the Blaupunkt radio but also gratuitously jabbed his screwdriver into the one-piece padded dash. Automobile safety glass is a wonderful passenger safety device, but when struck with a solid object it shatters into a million small pieces that seem to hide in every crevice of the vehicle interior.

After hours of cleaning, several days of waiting for replacement parts (imagine where a complete padded dash must come from!), and restoring the Audi to pristine condition with a new Blaupunkt radio, I returned to my normal parking routine at the TCF ramp. But my first stop on that morning was with partner

Mark Sullivan to find out who had installed the new security system in his Audi. Satisfied with Mark's report on his new security system and the $300 of company money he spent on its installation, I scheduled the installation of a similar security system in my car that afternoon. I left the office early, heading for the security company, only to find my Audi once again with its window smashed in and another black hole where the untested Blaupunkt radio had resided. The anger of having my personal property again violated by some worthless punk sent me stomping around the parking ramp with my briefcase in hand, ready to beat to a pulp the bastard who had vandalized my company car. After several minutes of posturing I realized that the thief could be physically my superior (I had not engaged in fisticuffs since age ten, after all) and might wield a gun, knife, or at least a screwdriver.

Logic dictated my retreat to the office manager to file another insurance claim.

Several months later, probably after extracting innumerable German radios from parked vehicles, a single thief was apprehended. He no doubt served minor jail time or a suspended sentence and then returned to the Blaupunkt underground.

One final anecdote about company cars. When I left the firm in 1994 I decided to keep my company car, an exchange that could be accomplished with an appropriate payment of vehicle value to the firm. At that time I drove a very sporty two-year-old Alfa Romeo coupe, one of few in the area. After I had secured personal financing for my vehicle and confirmed payment for the purchase of the Alfa from the firm, I proceeded home in my now privately owned car. Two blocks from my home, a teenager blew a stop sign and nailed the left front corner of my Alfa. Even before I left my damaged Alfa with its steaming radiator, I began feeling the classic symptoms of a whiplash injury to my neck. Now, despite having handled scores of auto accident cases and giving my clients careful legal advice about appropriate behavior, on this day, with my newly purchased Alfa smashed and whiplash pain in my neck, I completely lost it. I yelled at the kid and called him an idiot. By the time the police arrived I had settled down somewhat, and the kid and I had exchanged information. The officer's first question was, "Is anyone hurt?" I replied, "I can't believe it, but my neck hurts." The kid immediately responded, "Yeah, and he's a lawyer too." The officer had to restrain me from going after the kid. I arranged for insurance coverage on the Alfa—without the assistance of a patient office manager—and the neck pain eventually disappeared. But wait, there's more!

Within a week or two of the accident, my wife and I went to Sunday services at a Methodist church near downtown Minneapolis. After church we went for brunch at a restaurant on Hennepin Avenue in south Minneapolis. As we entered the restaurant, with me still listing hard to the right and aching with the cervical whiplash injury, I observed that the young fellow who inflicted this pain upon me was working there as a waiter. I wanted to accost him, show him my pain, punch him out, and demand his removal from the premises. Cooler heads prevailed, and I skulked out with my sore neck after grudgingly eating my scrambled eggs and English muffins. Where is retribution when you need it?

CHAPTER 19

HARASSMENT IN THE WORKPLACE

Forty years ago, when I started to practice law, sexual discrimination in the workplace was hardly worth a reprimand, let alone a full-scale lawsuit. Lawsuits based on discrimination against race or religion were finding their way into the courts, but sex discrimination was not yet in vogue. Not that many men weren't being their usual brutish selves, demeaning and abusing women in workplaces that offered unequal pay and promotion opportunities, but women were not asserting themselves because that was the way it had always been.

This kind of boorish male behavior began a dramatic change in the 1960s with Gloria Steinem, women's lib, and Virginia Slims cigarette ads. No longer were women going to be second-rate in the workplace. They began demanding equal treatment, wages, and respect. No longer were groping, dirty jokes, and Playmate centerfolds acceptable in the workplace. As tough as it was for business owners, managers, and senior partners in law firms to accept, sexual discrimination had to end, and these male chauvinists had to reluctantly change their behavior. In theory at least there was to be equal treatment of female and male workers on pay, promotion, respect, and facilities in the workplace. A violation quickly drew a sexual discrimination lawsuit, often producing a significant settlement. This leads to my most interesting sexual harassment lawsuit, which involved the unforgettable Debbie (not her real name).

I had previously done some minor legal work for a small corporation and its president, whom I will call Sam. The president had hired Debbie some two years earlier at the urging of a friend, Bob, who had convinced Sam that this disadvantaged young lady had reformed herself and needed a new chance at respectable employment. As I got involved in this case, I learned more about Debbie's checkered background. She had grown up on a Minnesota Indian reservation and had been married there for a short time before running away to Minneapolis and becoming a stripper. She moved to Iowa at some point and continued in that profession while living with a big-time drug dealer. When the authorities arrested the boyfriend and searched their apartment, Debbie was charged as an accomplice in the drug dealing. Bob, who had known Debbie in some unknown capacity in Minnesota, convinced a prominent Minneapolis criminal lawyer to go to Iowa to defend Debbie in the federal prosecution. Rather than pleading guilty and facing a minimal sentence, Debbie and her hotshot criminal lawyer went to trial, earning for her a resounding conviction and a federal penitentiary sentence of two to five years. Bob had maintained contact with Debbie while she served her time in prison, and upon her release on probation he brought her back to St. Paul. It was at that time that she went to work for Sam as one of his assistants.

Debbie was very attractive, with a sexy look that turned men's heads. It did not take many months before Sam started spending a lot of extra time with Debbie. She soon got promotions and work favors not extended to other female workers. Sam quickly found Debbie to be, as he said, "a soul mate." At the time Sam's wife was struggling with cancer, and Sam's home life was lonely and unhappy. Sam found Debbie to be a wonderful listener with whom he could unload his troubles. The relationship wasn't centered on sex, but it gravitated to occasional episodes in Sam's car and then to motel trysts. Sam related a memorable motel date when Debbie appeared in a sexy, red, see-through negligee. (Later interviews with some of Debbie's other lovers revealed that the red negligee was a well-traveled pair of pajamas.) Sam and others relayed that as sexy as Debbie looked, she was not a great lover, but went through the motions and didn't seem to enjoy sex.

Sam became increasingly dependent on Debbie as a friend and source of emotional support. He began following her home and waiting for hours outside her apartment. Debbie later reported a multitude of unwanted phone calls. Much to my dismay as Sam's defense lawyer, Debbie had kept many of Sam's love notes, cards, and e-mails. She was carefully planning ahead for her lawsuit. When I reviewed these items in Sam's hand-writing, all hope of Sam's denying his aggressive pursuit of Debbie disappeared.

It is amazing that such a high percentage of office romances do not end quietly, but instead erupt into much-publicized lawsuits. Even if the romance is a relationship between two consenting adults, a difference in employment status, particularly if the man holds a superior position, is almost guaranteed to produce a sexual harassment lawsuit. Sam and Debbie's friend-ship, or whatever it was, came to a halt after Sam and his business partner made a legitimate business decision that involved the elimination of Debbie's position and her transfer to a lower-status position at the same salary. Sam explained the situation to a very unhappy Debbie. It took only a few days for Debbie to retain a well-known discrimination lawyer in Minneapolis, and her sexual discrimination lawsuit was to soon follow.

As I got involved in Sam's defense, this crazy story unfolded. Bob disclosed all of Debbie's sordid background as a stripper, drug dealer, and convicted felon. But Sam's position wasn't much better: There was no denying that he, as Debbie's superior, had given her special treatment in exchange for sexual favors. He had also continued to chase her after she tried to cool the relationship. Because of potential conflicts, I remained as Sam's personal lawyer, but Sam's corporation would be defended by another law firm.

I asked to review the general liability insurance policy for Sam's company. After spending years as an insurance defense lawyer, I always determined as the first step in my analysis of a case whether insurance coverage was available. It is amazing how few lawyers forget to explore the availability of an insurance obligation to defend a corporation or individual in a lawsuit and provide insurance coverage for the claims. Several years after Debbie's case I was asked to defend a small corporation and its president in a securities fraud case. As that case evolved, the client disclosed to me a prior lawsuit against his company by a former employee who alleged discrimination. To defend this claim the client had retained as its lawyers one of the big downtown law firms. As is usual for the litigation departments of these big firms, they convinced the client of the need for defense efforts and then spent unlimited time at a high hourly rate. The lawsuit was eventually won on summary judgment, but the law firm had billed the client $225,000. When I learned of this expensive defense effort, I offered two thoughts: I could have defended the same case for under $50,000, and there probably was coverage and a defense obligation by the client's liability policy for this employee lawsuit. A review of the client's insurance policy and consultation with the insurer confirmed that the corporation would have received a free insurance company defense and saved itself

$225,000. Obviously, this big law firm did not know insurance law and how to read insurance policies. I advised the client to sue the law firm for malpractice to recover their outrageous lawyer fees.

Back to Debbie. Before I became Sam's personal defense lawyer, Sam's company had similarly hired one of the big Minneapolis law firms to defend this case. This big firm had, typically, failed to even consider whether the company's liability insurance would be required to provide a defense and coverage for the allegations in the lawsuit. Upon review of Sam's insurance policy, it was readily apparent to me that it provided coverage to the company and officers of the company for harassment claims. I contacted the insurance company, and they agreed to take the lead in the defense but reserved the issue of coverage until later. With this limited commitment from the insurer I stayed involved as Sam's personal defense attorney. With the insurer now involved to pay expenses, we set in motion a full, expensive investigation of Debbie's background. We hoped to locate witnesses to support our defense of her promiscuity and her efforts at swindling her former male partners.

The lawsuit progressed with depositions over several days. You can imagine how tough Sam's deposition with Debbie's lawyer was, given that he had Sam's incriminating love notes and e-mails. Our defense focused more on the consensual relationship element and the legitimate business reason for Debbie's job transfer. Sam held up pretty well on those issues. The memorable part of his deposition was my first face-to-face meeting with Debbie. She appeared in her finest, with perfect makeup, a wild hairdo, and the fashion flair of a high-class hooker. During the questioning by the other lawyers she made frequent flirtatious glances at me across the table. Without sounding egotistical, I later openly said to co-counsel and to Sam that during that deposition, Debbie's body language had suggested quite clearly, "Fuck me, mister."

Next in the case defense was Debbie's deposition. Among the three defense lawyers, I was chosen to question Debbie. For this deposition, her lawyer woke up and had Debbie appear in matronly clothes, with little makeup, and with her hair tied back in a bun: The appearance of the perfect victim of aggressive sexual harassment by a domineering corporate president. With all of the material from our investigation into Debbie's background, my questioning was a lot of fun. She was forced to repeatedly admit to prior affairs, taking money and favors from prior lovers, and seducing several partners, like Sam, with the red see-through negligee. After this deposition you could see the enthusiasm dissipating from Debbie's lawyer.

The end of this case was a mediated settlement, with Debbie getting some money, the amount of which I now cannot remember. To avoid ongoing defense costs, the insurance company paid the majority of the settlement. Part of the settlement was giving Debbie a lake cabin Sam owned but no longer used. After the settlement, I then pursued Sam's insurance company to reimburse Sam's company for all of my defense costs and most of the defense costs charged by the firm's attorneys. I succeeded, so Sam's total cost was his lake cabin and the loss of his so-called soul mate.

I often pondered what would have happened if, after all of the dust settled, I had called Debbie and suggested that we meet at her new lake cabin. Oh, what missed opportunities!

CHAPTER 20

TRIALS WERE VARIED AND INTERESTING

In the civil trial arena, never do you see the same case twice. Each has its own twists, turns, and surprises. Every trial lawyer tries to anticipate and eliminate the unexpected in order to remain reasonably in control of the case. This can be a scary prospect for a young lawyer. But once you get past the fear of the unknown, encountering and dealing with the varied aspects of every trial is truly a lot of fun. I will provide here a short summary of four interesting trials, three winners and one loser.

One of the insurance companies our firm represented insured a Lake Street used-car dealer. For those unfamiliar with the town, Lake Street is not one of Minneapolis's high-rent commercial districts. In fact, "Lake Street used-car dealer" was a classic insult. On this case I was defending one of these infamous salesmen. He had on his lot an old Dodge, just like the Dukes of Hazzard's General Lee. A young man had showed up at the lot, very interested in the Dodge, and lifted the hood and roared the big V8.

My client's salesman told the kid, "It's a good runner." That inno-cent-sounding sales pitch proved to be the decisive element in the case.

The kid paid a few hundred dollars and happily drove out of the lot on his first ride. After going ten blocks south he did a 180 and headed back toward Lake Street. Somewhere along the way, he claimed, the accelerator stuck, propelling the Dodge forward with no way for him to slow down. Of course, an experienced driver would have turned the key to off, put the car into neutral, or applied the emergency brake. Not this young driver. As he careened toward the heavy cross-traffic on Lake Street, desperate to stop his car, he aimed at a large elm tree on the boulevard. He hit it head-on, pushing the engine back into the passenger compartment. Needless to say, he sustained some pretty severe injuries.

Now for the legal part of this case. On used cars it is univer-sally held that there are no warranties unless expressly provided. Once ownership is transferred it is "buyer beware," as the new owner will be responsible for any subsequent problems. The kid's lawyer cleverly claimed that the statement "It's a good runner" created an express warranty, and since the accelerator stuck, there clearly was a breach of warranty.

One part of the case was a real learning experience for me. One of the jurors on the case was the wife of a lawyer I knew. After the jury came in with a big damage award, I called the gal to find out what happened. She described that during the trial my used-car salesman had sat behind me snickering, laughing, and making an ass out of himself well within the view of the jury. Being busy at the counsel table, I had been totally unaware of his antics. The jury was very much aware. She described that this jury just hated my client because of his behavior. She quoted one juror as saying, "I want to put that son-of-a-bitch out of business." A very good lesson learned: Lecture your client and witnesses to refrain from any visible courtroom reaction, no matter how damaging or ridiculous the accusations.

Because of the large verdict we appealed to the Court of Appeals. Not only did we lose there, we also created a horrible precedent for Minnesota used-car dealers. The court affirmed the verdict, agreeing that the phrase "It's a good runner" created an express warranty. The decision is found at 384 N.W.2d 562 (Minn. App. 1986).

Another fun defense case involved the personal injury claim of one of the city's rising hotshot criminal defense lawyers, whom I will call Derrick. On a snowy winter day, after working out at a club, he was a passenger in another lawyer's car heading downtown around the city lakes. As a city snowplow approached in the oncoming lane, the car skidded across the centerline and collided with the snowplow. I ended up defending the driver and his insurance company against Derrick's injury claim. Derrick had flown forward, striking his chest on the dashboard. As I recall, he had a couple of broken ribs. Even after the ribs healed, his injury claim expanded. Derrick claimed that because he had not been able to work out regularly due to his injuries, he became depressed, could not work full-time, and neglected his clients, resulting in a business loss of over $200,000. In the case I defended, Derrick hired one of the better personal injury lawyers in the city to present his case. He must have owed Derrick a big favor.

This trial had some great moments. Derrick's testimony was that he had not worked out for several months. I found in the records of his treating doctor, midway through his period of claimed disability, a note saying that "Patient stops in after his workout claiming difficulty doing exercises." At this time in Derrick's successful criminal defense career his annual income was somewhere over $400,000, an amount several times larger than any juror's income. Even so, Derrick and his lawyer put big exhibits in front of the jury showing how in the two years after the crash Derrick's income had declined to something like "only" $300,000 a year.

At one point near the end of the trial I was in the bathroom when one of the male jurors pulled up at a urinal beside me. With absolutely no solicitation from me he said (and I remember his exact words), "What gives with this guy?" I laughed and said, "I'm sorry, I cannot visit with you." The defense verdict shutting out Derrick was in the bag. Since this trial I have seen Derrick frequently and made friendly conversation. He once told me that the reason he did that civil trial was because at the time he had been pursuing some class action civil cases and wanted to see how a civil trial was handled. If he truly focused on how ridiculous his claim was and how I destroyed it, maybe he did learn something.

In another case, a lady and her two kids also in the car, had stopped for a red light in the right-hand lane at an intersection with a major highway. A semi was approaching the intersection on a slight downward slope from the south just as the light turned yellow and then red. The truck driver, believing he could get through, gunned his engine and proceeded into the intersection. The lady had observed the light turning green in her direction and started forward, her view of the fast-approaching semi blocked by the stopped car to her left. One of the dramatic moments of this trial was her eight-year-old son testifying that just before the impact he screamed something like, "Look out, Mom!" The impact was heavy, pushing the car several hundred feet down past the intersection. The two kids sustained relatively minor injuries, but the lady was badly injured.

This trial produced a great example of the untrustworthiness of supposed eyewitness testimony. The uninjured truck driver, of course, claimed that the light changed in his direction with no time for him to stop. The defense identified an elderly couple driving behind the semi who supported the truck driver. On our side was the driver who had been stopped next to our client and who witnessed the whole sequence, as well as another driver who had been approaching the intersection behind our car. With the highway patrolman I went out to take measurements, especially of the length of the right turn lane on the main highway and the distance back to the crest of the hill. The turn lane started a significant distance back from the intersection. I took a series of pictures showing what the truck driver and his eyewitnesses would have seen as they approached the intersection.

At trial I was extremely polite to the elderly couple as I destroyed their eyewitness testimony. Their description of what they saw from about a quarter mile back, at the crest of the hill, was very confused. Then they both said that when the light changed from green to yellow to red the truck had been right at the start of the right-turn lane. At that point the wife had screamed, knowing that there was going to be a collision at the intersection. But according to the measurements of the highway patrolman, this all happened when the truck was more than one hundred yards and six seconds back from the intersection. Clearly, the truck driver could have, and should have, stopped or avoided the collision. The testimony of the elderly couple ended up supporting our case.

The trial was in Wright County, just west of Minneapolis. At a pretrial conference the judge had encouraged settlement by stressing that this was a very conservative county and jurors did not give out big verdicts. He strongly urged me and my client to settle for about $100,000. We did not accept that advice or the defense's offer. At the conclusion of this trial the jury found the truck driver totally at fault and awarded my client $414,000 for her injuries. So much for small verdicts in Wright County!

At another time I became the lawyer for a very nice young farming couple in western Minnesota. The wife had sustained serious injuries while traveling on a through highway when a young girl blew a stop sign and pulled out directly into the lady's lane. The young girl was driving a vehicle owned by her father, who was farming a lot of valuable Minnesota land. He had only $50,000 of liability insurance coverage on the vehicle available to cover his daughter's negligence. As my client's injuries far exceeded that coverage, as well as available underinsured coverage, we started looking at the father's farm assets. That is when it got very interesting.

First, there was a jury trial on the liability and damage issues. We won with a nice jury award of around $200,000, if I remember right—well above the available insurance. After all insurance was paid, we entered the judgment and began pursuing a sheriff's execution of the father's farmland. We soon discovered that the father had transferred all of his land into some kind of trust that had been assisted and drafted by some guy in North Dakota. Further investigation disclosed that the farmer was an active member of the protest group Posse Comitatus. This far, far right dissident group refuses to pay taxes or abide by civil laws, claiming a constitutional right to disobey every aspect of government and authority. Our farmer was a regular attendee at Posse Comitatus meetings in North Dakota, and this type of land transfer into a trust was recommended and frequently accomplished as a protest against the civil justice system.

(To digress just a moment: One day a few years back I sat at a lunch counter in my hometown with a former high-school football colleague, now a local auto mechanic, who began asking me for legal advice. Espousing the same goofy theories, he related that when recently stopped by a highway patrolman he had refused to show his driver's license, claiming that he had an unlimited right to drive without government interference, guaranteed by the Constitution. Obviously, the patrolman had hauled him to jail, and now he needed a lawyer to defend him. After listening to half an hour of his anti-establishment ranting, I declined to be his lawyer.)

Since the farmland had been transferred, legally or not, we first had to pursue a fraudulent conveyance lawsuit to get the property back into the farmer's name. The farmer filed in court a variety of crazy arguments including a challenge to the whole United States monetary system. He further claimed that because of the gold standard, the judgment awarding dollars was invalid and unenforceable. Because this crazy group had a history of violence and violent protests with weapons, the judge ordered extra security in and around the courtroom. I felt particularly ill at ease when sitting at counsel table with the farmer, his relatives, and many supporters seated a few feet behind me. The judge quickly determined that the land transfer was a fraudulent conveyance and ordered the sheriff's sale to satisfy the judgment.

At the sheriff's attachment sale my clients bid in the value of their remaining unpaid judgment and became the fee owner of a portion of the farmer's good land. Since the clients would be farming the land directly adjacent to the farmer's remaining property, my clients and I for several years were constantly concerned that some crazy would attempt to shoot them off their tractor. Fortunately, nothing of that sort ever happened.

CHAPTER 21

ON THE SCENE INVESTIGATIONS

When representing injured plaintiffs, I initiated factual investigations as soon as the client was signed up. In motor vehicle
crashes particularly, getting pictures, taking measurements, and
interviewing witnesses often made the critical difference between
losing and winning. In almost every auto collision case, at some
point before settlement or trial I personally went out to the scene
with camera and tape measure. One case I recall happened at a
rural intersection where the defendant's vehicle collided with my
client's vehicle after the defendant ran a stop sign. The defense
claimed that my driver was significantly negligent for not seeing
the defendant coming, slowing down, and possibly avoiding the
collision. The police report and photographs taken by the officers
showed nothing unusual. When I went to the scene, however, I
discovered in the northeast quadrant of the intersection a large
bank of trees that totally obscured my client's view of any vehicle
approaching the stop sign. My photographs and measurements
eliminated the defense argument.

As a defense lawyer I had some very interesting on-site visits. Three come to mind. At one point when the Minnesota economy was in recession, many struggling businesses mysteriously burned down, resulting in claims against the fire insurance companies. In just one year, three restaurants in the depressed central Minnesota resort area burned to the ground. On two occasions I was summoned by insurance clients, almost before the ashes were cold, to accompany a cause-and-origin fire investigator to the scenes. In all of these fire cases the insurance company suspected arson, usually for good reason. I found it fascinating to dig around the burned-out buildings, looking for burn patterns or other evidence that confirmed suspicions of a torch job rather than an accident. These were not times to wear suit and tie.

Another fun case involved a drugstore in the small, southern Minnesota town of Pine Island. The owner, who was remodeling his drugstore, had somehow gotten talked into installing a new style of flat roof on his building. My client was the local distributor and sales rep for the manufacturer of the supposedly foolproof roofing system. It first required laying down several inches of Styrofoam insulation. Then a synthetic rubberized coating was sprayed on to make the roof waterproof. My client's sales pitch and his advertising literature claimed the rubber surface would withstand temperatures above 150 degrees and lower than 30 degrees below zero. Within the first year, however, the drugstore owner claimed there were leaks in the roof. Several repair attempts had failed, so there came the lawsuit.

My client claimed innocence and tried to blame other construction issues for the problems in the drugstore. Soon after answering the lawsuit I drove down to Pine Island with an extension ladder to do my own inspection. I found the drugstore owner friendly and cooperative, and he helped me up onto the building roof. What I found was astounding. There were numerous cracks in the rubber coating, allowing rainwater and melting snow to seep down into and through the white Styrofoam. I couldn't tell if it was from heat or cold, but the rubber coating was shrinking all over the roof, resulting in the gaping cracks. My pictures confirmed the pictures already taken by the owner. When I went into the drugstore the scene was almost comical. The poor owner had water coming in at several places. He had tried to hang some metal gutters to channel the water towards an open window. Suspended over his merchandise was plastic sheeting that looked like an upside-down parachute. He explained that on one occasion the plastic had become overloaded with water and ruptured, spilling gallons of water onto his Hallmark card display. He was such a nice guy that I felt like sending him a condolence card.

Shortly after this visit we found out that the manufacturer of the rubberized roof system was already out of business. Resolution of the lawsuit was left to my distributor and his insurance company. Upon my strong recommendation, full damages for repairs, damaged merchandise, and even some lost profits were paid by the insurance company to the drugstore owner.

The third defense case involved the alleged failure of a powered barn-cleaning machine. A farmer could turn on this device and watch as the blades of the machine scraped the cow manure out the back of the barn. Obviously, this was a great alternative to the back-breaking work of shoveling the stuff. As I recall, from the start this scraper had not worked properly, requiring repairs and replacement of parts. The lawsuit came against my client, who had sold the machine and whose repairs had failed to make it work. Pictures, blueprints, and sales literature hardly disclosed how this thing was supposed to function. So I made arrangements to travel to the cattle farm in southern Minnesota.

Other than pheasant hunting on a variety of farms over the years, I had never spent any time in a cattle barn, and certainly not one occupied by several dozen smelly cows continuously dumping their waste onto the floor. Of course, farmers are oblivious to the smells; I wanted to gag as we entered the barn. The farmer and his lawyer had on knee-high rubber boots. Seeing that I was wearing loafers, they offered me plastic baggies to put over my shoes and rubber bands to secure the baggies around my ankles. From my first step into the barn I was walking through a sloppy mess of urine and manure. Sometimes I shuffled along through two to three inches of the stuff. Several times my baggies started to slide off, requiring me to dance around on one leg as I tried to readjust my shoe covers.

When the farmer started up the machine, the chain-driven blades did scrape some percentage of muck toward the back door, but there still remained a lot of handwork for the farmer. The lawyer pointed out the many problems with the machine. It was obvious that any repair efforts required the farmer or the repairman to be down on his hands and knees in the middle of this mess. I was being convinced that this barn-scraper was just a lousy product. When I had seen enough I started for the door, anxious to get out of there. My mistake was in walking too fast, causing one of the baggies to totally abandon my shoe. As the farmer and his lawyer laughed, I said, "Oh, what the hell!" and continued baggieless towards the exit.

One can only scrape so much doo-doo off of a shoe. The stink remains. At the first opportunity away from the farm I pitched the shoe into a ditch. This hardly eliminated the smell, as all of my clothes were saturated with the barnyard scent. I drove home with the car windows wide open. The lawsuit settled shortly after this visit. After relaying my manure story to the insurance-claims man, I lobbied for hazardous duty pay. It didn't work; he probably thought I got what I deserved.

CHAPTER 22

FAILED IMPLANTS

Whoever designed the human body of bones, blood, tissue, and so forth no doubt failed to anticipate that human creativity would develop a multitude of artificial replacement parts. Not unlike an automobile that can have all of its parts replaced, most of the human body is now replaceable. Hearts, lungs, livers, kidneys, knees, shoulders, and hips that have worn out can all be replaced. I can personally vouch for implant success. After over thirty years of running, both of my knees needed titanium replacements. Both now work well without significant pain or problems.

Unfortunately, replacement parts have also produced a lot of damaged people and resulting lawsuits. One of the most publicized groups of cases were claimed failures of silicone breast implants. I would never criticize any lady for wanting to enhance her figure. But a fairly significant percentage of the implants leaked silicone into the surrounding tissue with numerous claims of adverse consequences. The breast implant lawsuits came out of the woodwork with claims of all kinds of illnesses caused by the leaking silicone. Few of those cases went anywhere. Contradicting several small research studies, a large, government-sponsored study concluded that none of the claimed maladies could be traced to silicone. A lot of lawyers who spent a lot of time and money on breast implant cases came up totally dry.

A second very interesting group of cases involved failed hip and knee replacement parts manufactured by Sulzer Orthopedics. This major international manufacturer started seeing part failures requiring follow-up replacement surgeries for many hips and knees. The massive class action lawsuit that followed had, if I remember correctly, more than one thousand failed knee implants and more than three hundred failed hips. Both types of implants required the insertion of a metal shaft into the femur bone, expecting that the bone's natural healing would close in and securely affix the implant. Research disclosed that in the implant factory a worker whose job it was to clean the implant parts had been using a solvent that left an invisible film on the shafts. When the shaft was inserted into a bone, the film prevented the bone from securely connecting to the shafts, resulting in loose implants.

I had one case for a relative whose failed knee implant required a do-over. Proving the failed implant was easy. Every implant in a hospital is carefully recorded by serial number in the hospital chart. Knowing the number on the offending part, the operating surgeon was very willing to render an opinion that the required replacement perfectly fit the mold of the class action. After acknowledging fault, Sulzer paid over a billion dollars in total settlements, including not only a nice sum to my client, but also $40,000 to me in attorney fees for what hadn't been a lot of work.

My most interesting implant case involved a company called Vitek, Inc., out of Houston. This company had developed a replacement implant for damaged temporomandibular joints

(TMJ). Common TMJ problems include a clicking noise and deterioration of this joint where the lower jaw connects to the skull. Normally there is a small cartilage cushion between the two bony structures. Tooth-clenching can cause this cartilage to tear or wear out, resulting in a painful jaw joint. Vitek had taken a Dupont-manufactured product called Proplast and widely promoted it among dentists and oral surgeons as a replacement for worn-out TMJ cartilage. Between 1983 and 1988, hundreds and probably thousands of the Vitek implants were surgically placed in TMJ joints.

It did not take very many years for the Proplast failures to start surfacing. It seemed that when implanted the Proplast started a progressive bone degeneration on both bones around the implants. X-rays showed serious degeneration of the condyle of the lower mandible (jaw) where it contacted the Proplast. Lawsuits started popping up all over the country. One of our defense insurance companies had product liability coverage for a period of time that Vitek sold the implants, so we got the defense of all of the cases in Minnesota. Somewhere around twenty-five claims and lawsuits had been filed requiring our defense. As Vitek cases were prosecuted all over the country, we became part of a national defense team. Memos from Vitek, its founder and president Dr. Charles Homsy, and their lead defense counsel claimed the lawsuits were totally defensible. So, under my leadership in the firm, we dove into an aggressive defense effort.

Vitek's Houston office hosted what was to be an almost comical meeting. All defense counsel were invited to meet Dr. Homsy and learn about the Vitek defense strategy. Lead counsel were from Arizona, and they reported that two cases had already been tried before juries. The first resulted in a hung jury (so no result), and the second was a plaintiff's verdict with a small damage award. Arizona counsel and Dr. Homsy were very enthusiastic about defending all of the cases. These sessions reminded me somewhat of a high school pep rally, with the audience cheering and applauding the optimistic messages. It all seemed kind of silly to a bunch of experienced defense lawyers. The highlight of the session was the speech given by Vitek's key defense witness, Dr. Kent, who had tested and retested the Proplast implants at Rice University and written approving articles, based on his research, declaring that the product had met all government regulations. Dr. Kent had testified in both of the completed Vitek trials, and Dr. Homsy's introduction portrayed him as the savior of the company.

As Dr. Kent gave his talk, we defense lawyers exchanged puzzled looks. Dr. Kent was less than confident in his own research and described some of the problems the plaintiff's lawyers could show in his work. His whole attitude was far from enthusiastic about the success of defending the Vitek implants. Following the talk, I remember commenting to some of the gathered defense attorneys, "Is this the guy who is our key witness and who is going to win all of these cases for us?" After all of the prior rah-rah, this was a ridiculous way to send the defense lawyers home.

I don't remember how many weeks after the Houston meeting it was that we received word that Dr. Kent, our key defense witness, had recanted his support of Vitek and essentially conceded that the Proplast implants were causing the bone damage. He would no longer testify for Vitek. That announcement was followed in a few days by Vitek filing for Chapter 7 bankrupcy. There was nothing else to do but submit case dismissals to all of the plaintiff's lawyers. With only a portion of the defense cases in our office covered by insurance, much of our defense effort for Vitek went uncompensated. Some of the defense lawyers with heavy caseloads really took a bath.

Some of the national plaintiffs' lawyers continued claims against Dupont for the Proplast material. Some months later all of those claims were dismissed. Some claims were also made against the doctors who installed the initial implants. These cases also went nowhere, as the surgeons had no reason to doubt the integrity of the Vitek products at the time they were implanted. No doubt many patients with the Vitek implants suffered permanent damage with no compensation. These folks did not have many favorable alternatives. An FDA Safety Alert of December 28, 1990, recommended the following:

If either loss of implant integrity or progressive bone degeneration is found, explantation [implant removal] may be appropriate. If explantation is chosen, patients should be evaluated to determine what alternative procedures might be appropriate, e.g., a non-Proplast coated implant, an autologous bone graft, or no replacement (symptomatic management).

CHAPTER 23

DEFENSE PARANOIA AND SURVEILLANCE

Insurance companies are unduly paranoid. No matter what type of injury is claimed, insurers in this country do not ever believe that an injured person is as seriously injured as he or she contends. Perhaps the only type of liability claim that doesn't immediately arouse paranoia about "fraud" and "exaggeration" is a wrongful death claim. But even that raises questions about whether the claimed losses of the decedent's heirs can be trusted, whether the decedent had the earning potential claimed, and whether he or she was fooling around on the spouse. Even if the claimant is a saintly preacher or preacher's wife, the insurer will automatically assume that the extent of the damage claim is exaggerated. Unfortunately, this attitude pervades defense lawyers' view of injury claims as well. In addition to this built-in paranoia, defense lawyers have a certain amount of self-interest in keeping their defense files open as long as possible. This often forces a legitimate claimant to spend months or even years in emotional and often financial agony to bring a claim to a conclusion. As a defense lawyer for over fifteen years, I must confess that I shared the belief that injury claims were always grossly exaggerated by the claimant and his or her lawyer.

This paranoia is fostered by the ready availability of several favored defense doctors who routinely find nothing wrong with an injured claimant. These doctors conduct so-called independent medical evaluations (IMEs). These exams and the opinions they produce are far from independent. The doctors are paid extremely well by the insurers for their favorable opinions. Of course, the defense doctors do not want to come back with an opinion contrary to the insurer's position, because the gravy train of lucrative business would disappear. When I was doing defense work, we had one old defense doctor who consistently found no basis for any legitimate injury and opined that the claimant had "functional overlay" and "compensation neurosis," polite words for fraud and exaggeration. Another of the regularly used defense doctors, a man named McCain, was still doing IMEs even into his late seventies. He was known throughout the profession as "No Pain McCain." I fought as hard as any of the defense lawyers to prove that the plaintiff was a dirty liar and that the plaintiff's doctor was a quack. With many of the injury claims and trials involving soft-tissue neck and back injuries, with no objective evidence, it was easy to cast doubt on every claim before the jury.

As the years passed, my attitude towards injured persons gradually changed. It may well have been partially due to my own soft-tissue back problems. For many years, I would strain my back about once a year doing something stupid, like trying to singlehandedly move a three-hundred-pound boat. I would suffer for two weeks in a hunched-over position with a low backache. Comparing what I was going through with the claims of the many back-injured workers or automobile crash victims, I did begin to appreciate their struggles. Just maybe the back pain complaints were legitimate, even when there were no objective signs of injury. It was only after I made the voluntary decision to leave the defense practice in 1994 and handle only plaintiffs' cases that I truly started to understand the pain complaints of my clients. I now fully believe that most of the injured claimants I represented were truly injured and deserving of the money damages for their losses.

One of the fascinating elements of the defense paranoia of insurers and their attorneys is their expenditure of significant defense funds on behind-the-scenes surveillance of injured claimants. Surveillance is the preferred defense tool in workers' compensation cases, where no paying insurer believes that a lower-back injury can't heal within a few weeks and that an injured worker has to remain disabled for months and years. Readily available to the defense are lots of super-sleuths with video cameras and long-range telescopic lens cameras, all able to cleverly conceal themselves behind tinted windows in vans parked outside the claimant's residence or place of work. Injured claimants are usually caught unawares by the spy as they go about their normal business, never realizing their movements are filmed.

Usually the surveillance accomplishes little, and sometimes it backfires. One memorable story was that of a defense attorney presenting before a jury his surveillance film of a young boy with a claimed serious leg injury playing baseball and running the bases. The boy and his parents had testified that he no longer could play baseball, which actually was not true. But when the jury saw film of the boy limping as he struggled to run the bases, it was such graphic evidence of the boy's real disability that the jury awarded the boy a huge amount of damages.

As a defense attorney I used surveillance several times. More often than not it proved to be a waste of time and money. But on a couple of occasions the results created fun memories. We had a workers' compensation claimant with a supposedly disabling back injury who was filmed painting his house and garage, in the process climbing ladders, carrying buckets of paint, and repeatedly bending and twisting contrary to his doctor's supposed employment restrictions. A second claim I defended involved a young man who had been working for a landscape company when a high-tension chain struck him below the knee, badly fracturing his leg. His doctors described significant disability and inability to run, climb, and do strenuous labor with the leg injury, as did the young man in his own deposition. During that deposition, when innocently asked about his home address, he volunteered that in a week he was moving to a new home. With that information in hand, I had a surveillance crew stationed outside the old address on moving day. Parked outside the home was a rental moving truck with a ramp from truck bed to ground. On film we repeatedly caught the young man hauling out of the house and up into the van heavy pieces of furniture such as large stuffed chairs and mattresses. For whatever reason, every time he exited the truck he would jump down to the ground and run back into the house, showing no limp or evidence of injury. When the plaintiff's attorney saw that film, the case settled cheap.

Only once as a plaintiff's attorney did surveillance of my client come into play. For several years I had fostered a favorable relationship with several highway patrolmen who did accident reconstruction work. One of these was Dave, who lived in Shakopee. When Dave's wife, whom I will call Denise, sustained an injury, Dave called me for legal help. Denise had stepped out of the shower and while standing with wet feet on a tile floor, picked up her Conair hair dryer to dry her hair. With the base of the handle and end of the electrical cord in the palm of her right hand, she hit the dryer switch and immediately got a severe electrical shock through her hand and arm. This injury persisted and turned into a serious, painful condition called reflex sympathetic dystrophy, or RSD. Denise's neurologist had conducted a thermogram study comparing the temperature on Denise's good hand with that of her injured hand. Thermogram studies are controversial, but for RSD they can be a good diagnostic tool. Denise's thermogram produced beautiful color pictures showing much hotter, and thus injured, areas in the palm of her right hand compared to the left hand. At trial the enlargements of these pictures, along with the testimony of the treating neurologist, were most convincing on the RSD claim.

Proving fault on Conair was also interesting. My two hired engineers examined the hair dryer and rendered opinions that there must have been a break in the electrical cord where it entered the handle. I then took the hair dryer to a testing lab, where an X-ray of the handle and cord showed a clear break in one of the two wires within the plastic insulation. With this beautiful X-ray, the engineers quickly theorized how the shock had passed through Denise's hand down through her wet feet to ground. Our defective design theory easily explained that the place where the cord entered the base of the handle was subject to repeated movement and bending, resulting in the break in the wire. A better design would not have allowed the excessive motion of the cord.

Sounds like a good case and a sure winner, right? Well, Denise may have been one of those clients whom I did not recognize as exaggerating and possibly falsifying her symptoms. The defense attorney obviously suspected this before I did. In Denise's deposition she had described many things she could not do. As she testified she held her injured right arm stiffly across her midsection, as if cradled in a sling. Before the injury, one of her favorite pastimes had been playing on two different ladies' softball teams, which she claimed she could no longer do since the injury. Even though she had returned to her job as a legal secretary, she described limited ability to type and hold a phone with her injured hand. Denise smoked, and she testified that she could not "flick her Bic" with the injured hand.

Not even suspecting that there had been surveillance on Denise, we went to trial in Shakopee. The defense witness list contained a name unknown to me. Upon inquiry I learned that the person was an investigator who had recently done surveillance on Denise. In a big argument I persuaded the judge to order the defense to disclose to me beforehand both the full-length videotape and the edited version they intended to show to the jury. That evening my trial prep was interrupted as I plowed through three and a half hours of the investigator's unedited tape. Most of it was very benign, for instance, following Denise and her daughter around Target while they shopped for clothes. But the defense liked other portions and pieced them together in the edited version. They caught Denise several times flicking her Bic with her injured hand. They also filmed her at her daughter's basketball game, jumping up several times and clapping enthusiastically with her injured hand.

One section of the edited courtroom version was filmed in the waiting area of the law firm where Denise worked. After viewing this segment with amazement I called that firm and relayed that an outsider with a hidden camera had sat for hours, listening to and recording conversations in the office, no doubt including many confidential client communications. I invited the attorney to appear in Shakopee the next morning to discuss the video with the judge and defense attorney. The morning session was quite exciting. Denise's employer was irate and threatened all kinds of retaliation against the investigator and defense lawyer because of the unauthorized infringement on the attorney client relationship. I argued strenuously for total suppression of the surveillance film. After considerable thought, the judge probably made the right decision in allowing the edited version to be shown to the jury. He also advised Denise's aggrieved employer that he could sue or bring accusations of ethical violations against the defense attorney.

So, I started trial with a good liability case but potentially big trouble with my client's credibility. The defective hair dryer evidence and my two experts testified well on the liability issue. The jury clearly liked our X-ray of the broken wire. I tried my best to prepare Denise for the impact of what was coming on the videotape. The defense lawyer appropriately set her up with his cross-examination, asking questions like, "You can't light a cigarette with a Bic lighter, correct?" But surveillance doesn't automatically come before a jury and win a case. It requires "foundation," or testimony from the investigator who took the film to verify what is going to be shown to the jury. This is often where surveillance falls apart. To do the filming in the first place, the investigator must usually lie and deceive people. They become patent liars to do their job.

On my cross of this investigator, which the judge allowed before the showing of the video, I had some fun. His story about getting into the law office to film Denise's work went like this: He came in with a lunch pail in which the video camera was secretly hidden. He told the receptionist he was to meet a client of the law office and asked to wait; he then settled in with his concealed camera sitting on the coffee table, recording everything said by any lawyer or secretary and all phone calls coming into the office for about two hours. Of course, he did get Denise picking up the phone a few times with her injured hand. I had no qualms about really going after this guy to show that he was a deceitful liar who could not be trusted in anything he said. He also had to admit that he had edited out large portions of film showing no evidence contrary to Denise's claim of injury. By the time the video was shown, the jury viewed this guy and the defense attorney as real schmucks and no doubt questioned the validity of what they were seeing.

The defense attorney argued strongly, based on the video,

that Denise was a fraud and not deserving of an award. I stressed the serious defect in the hair dryer and confirmation of the RSD by the doctors and thermograms. The jury was not out too long and came in with a nice plaintiff's verdict finding Conair strictly liable for a defective product and awarding Denise $146,000, a large verdict at that time for Scott County. Obviously, the surveillance in this case backfired and probably inflated the amount of Denise's verdict.

Most of my large verdicts and settlements have made for interesting epilogues from my clients. Some of us old-timers recall the television show called *The Millionaire,* in which average people were given a million dollars and then cameras followed their stories as, in most cases, their lives disintegrated. Most of my clients' stories have happy endings involving favorable uses of their newfound wealth. Denise's was not so. A follow-up call to Dave a few months later disclosed that Denise had quickly spent nearly all of her verdict amount in lavishly decorating their house and buying personal things. Then Dave disclosed to me that Denise had returned to playing softball and had run off with a male softball player not long after. Dave had moved out of the well-decorated house and was pursuing divorce. He said she had been showing few signs of ongoing problems with her RSD. So, in summary, Denise fooled me just as she fooled the jury, but not the video camera. I can honestly say that Denise was the only client for whom I obtained a large award where convincing proof surfaced that the injury claim had been seriously exaggerated by the client.

CHAPTER 24

THE WONDERS OF A FOCUS GROUP

One of my great wins was the direct result of conducting a focus group. A focus group is just a sample gathering of average citizens who are presented a set of facts or issues and asked to give feedback about their views on the subject. Politicians commonly use them to test the water on their appeal to voters or how the public views their positions on issues. Over the last twenty years, use of focus groups has become routine for trial lawyers as well. There is really no better way to gauge the attitudes of jurors than to present an abbreviated version of your case to a sample group of typical prospective jurors and get their verdict and comments on the facts.

There are numerous professional groups that will put together a focus group for one or two thousand dollars. My first use of this technique, however, was a lot cheaper and easy to put together. I sent a memo around to all lawyers and staff in our office, asking them to contact friends and relatives who might be willing to come to our office for a day to assist us in evaluating a case. In return they would get fifty dollars, free parking, and a free lunch. I got a good response and a nice mix of people, young and old, male and female. I believe we selected eight or ten people out of the volunteers. A focus group can give great advice on liability issues, such as which driver is more at fault, as well as demonstrating what a reasonable jury award might be. In the case I will describe next, we were seriously concerned about whether we could win, so our primary interest was in the group's views on the liability issue. We knew that if we won liability, the damage award would be substantial.

The Berg case, as it was known, came into the office from a friend of one of my partners who ran a successful printing business. His thirty-two-year-old son, Michael, who was married and the father of two young children, had been killed in a motor vehicle crash on Interstate 94 northwest of Minneapolis, about halfway to St. Cloud. Here are the facts: Michael, an insurance salesman, was driving a small compact car on a mid-winter interstate highway. Behind him in his lane of travel was an unloaded flatbed semi driven by an experienced over-the-road truck driver for the Clark Equipment Company. Clark Equipment is a big, successful company located in Melrose, North Dakota, and is famous for its Bobcat loaders. Its over-the-road trucks were insured with high liability limits protecting its drivers. Coming southbound on I-94, in the opposite direction from Michael and the Clark semi, was a young lady in a pickup heading to her job in the Twin Cities. Probably due to going too fast for the slippery conditions, she lost control of the pickup, went into and through the center median, and collided with the left front corner of Michael's vehicle. Michael's small car was brought to almost a complete stop in the northbound inside lane, and a second or two later the Clark semi collided with the rear of Michael's car with great force. The semi crunched the rear of the small car and pushed it almost three hundred feet down the highway before coming to a stop. Michael was dead at the scene with multiple fractures and internal injuries. These facts supported two clear conclusions. First, Michael would not be found at fault, as he had no place to go to avoid the collision with the pickup. Second, the pickup driver would be found seriously negligent for excessive speed for the road conditions and losing control of her vehicle. The problem was that she had only $50,000 of liability insurance coverage on her vehicle and had no assets beyond her insurance coverage. Early on, the lady's insurance company offered the policy limit to eliminate her from further exposure. Our goal in representing Michael's wife and children was to attach a very high percentage of the accident fault to the Clark semi driver, who was protected by the generous insurance coverage.

One of the things that appealed to me most about doing plaintiff's work is the opportunity to be creative in developing the theories that support a winning case. This Berg case was an exciting challenge. I have always loved working with expert witnesses. To put together a winning scenario you need to be fully educated on the technicalities surrounding the accident. Accident reconstruction experts supply this input. One such expert was Myron Lofgren, a retired Minnesota highway patrolman who taught accident reconstruction to other highway patrol officers. I had worked with him on prior cases, several involving semis and issues of speed, stopping, skidding, momentum, and other technical factors. With Lofgren's help we developed the argument that the Clark driver was going too fast for the conditions, was following too close to Michael's car, and failed to take any evasive action in the several seconds as the pickup crossed the median.

As would be expected, the competent defense lawyer also hired an accident reconstruction expert who drew totally oppo- site conclusions. His basic opinion was that the semi driver was not speeding and had only a few seconds to react, so there was no way he could have avoided the collision. His final opinion was that the collision was solely the responsibility of the woman in the pickup.

At this stage of the case, with conflicting expert opinions and several months remaining before trial, we decided to do our focus group. Another lawyer in our office had assisted me in the preparation of this case, and he took the role of the plaintiff's lawyer and I played the defense lawyer. We welcomed our mock jurors and suggested that they would find their time with us interesting as they helped us to evaluate this legal case. We did not tell them whether our firm was on the plaintiff or defense side. The widow and two small children were purposely not present, as that sympathy factor could have affected the outcome. We did a short jury questioning, then described the basic facts of the accident and read the main portions of the conflicting expert reports. We did not call any witnesses, but we did provide the test jury with abbreviated closing arguments for each side. We then gave them a couple of hours to do their deliberation and give us a verdict. We purposely saved two hours at the end of the day for informal discussion and feedback.

Was this ever an education! Their verdict was one short of unanimous in finding no fault on the Clark driver. Only one person thought that he was some small percentage at fault. The majority actually felt sorry for the Clark driver, believing the defense expert's analysis that he had no time to avoid the impact. We found that the strongest supporters of the verdict had some truck driving experience in their background. They had advocated strongly and convinced several other jurors of the Clark driver's innocence. They even said they had figured out that our firm was representing the plaintiff in the case. Even with that assumption, plus the fifty dollars and a free lunch, these folks did not want to help us out with a favorable result. By the end of the question-and-answer session I was quite discouraged about our chances on the case.

But lessons can be learned from adversity. One clear conclusion was that we had to eliminate any jurors with truck driving experience. That would also eliminate spouses of truck drivers and people with any part of their business related to trucking. Furthermore, it was apparent that we needed to place much greater emphasis on the failures of the Clark driver and somehow illustrate them in a persuasive manner. We had to continually emphasize that the Clark driver was the target defendant.

To better illustrate Lofgren's opinions, I retained another reconstruction expert from Iowa who created a computer generated video animation of the crucial seconds of the accident sequence. Computer animation was a new technology at the time, and animated reconstructions were just starting to be used in lawsuits. It was controversial, and some judges were not allowing these "cartoons" to be played before a jury. In our case my Iowa guy worked with Lofgren to illustrate the former patrolman's theories in the animation. This enabled Lofgren to testify that he had helped prepare the animation and that it correctly represented his opinions about what had happened. This satisfied our trial judge as adequate foundation to allow the video to be played before the jury.

Lofgren always made a scale drawing of the roadway for a half a mile or so on either side of the impact area. He usually used a scale of about one inch to ten feet, so the overall drawing was some eight to ten feet long. I discovered that his scale was precisely that of some of my son's Matchbox cars. I visited a toy store and purchased a model car like Michael's, a pickup like the woman's, and a flatbed semi like the Clark driver's. We then took Lofgren's large scale drawing, glued it onto foam core backing, and laid it flat in front of the jury. Lofgren could then place the toy vehicles on the diagram and show the movement of the pickup through the median, the semi's proximity to Michael's car, and most dramatically, how far down the highway the semi pushed Michael before coming to a stop.

The third creative tool I utilized was analyzing the different injuries to Michael's body as described in the autopsy. I hired another expert, a biomechanical engineer who could identify which of Michael's many injuries were caused by each of the two different impacts. This expert concluded that the left front impact from the pickup would have caused the two broken bones in Michael's legs, the broken bone in his arm, and some facial lacerations and injuries from striking the steering wheel. His solid opinion was that the cumulative effect of the injuries from the pickup impact would not have been fatal. His analysis of the injuries attributable to the rear-end semi impact began with photos taken by the highway patrol. Those images made it clear that the semi impact had broken Michael's driver's seat and propelled him forward into the dashboard and steering wheel. Several internal injuries, like his torn aorta and lacerated liver, could be directly traced to the crushing impact from the rear. My expert, with his pictures and anatomical diagrams, as well as the autopsy report, gave a firm and convincing opinion that the fatal injuries were caused only by the rear impact from the semi.

Since I started trying plaintiff's cases, I have advocated my personal theory on how best to win them. In client meetings and in the seminars I have taught, I would illustrate this theory with a simple horizontal line on a piece of paper. At the start of a trial, with an unknowing jury, we assume that both sides start out in neutral at the horizontal line. Except for the jury questioning, the plaintiff's attorney always goes first. I believe that everything our side does should push the defendant and his or her lawyer farther and farther below that neutral horizontal line. Even in the jury questioning, if it is done right with subtle—and sometimes not-so-subtle—advocacy for my client's cause, the case should be going downhill for the defendant. Next, I give a lengthy opening statement, coming as close to the objectionable line of argument as possible. If done effectively, this should push the defendant a lot further downhill. The defendant's attorney's opening statement follows and is seldom very effective. This may give the defendant's cause a slight bump upward, but it should never get back to the neutral line. Thereafter, every witness I put on the stand will hopefully push the defendant farther and farther away from the neutral line. If my witnesses perform properly, the defense's cross-examination, which may score a few points and a few bumps upward, will never get the case back up to the neutral line. When I finish with my witnesses and rest my case, I hope the defendant is so far below the line that nothing the defense attorney will do with their witnesses and their part of the case will ever get them back up to or above the neutral line to support a defense verdict. Having the last closing argument should let me bury the defendant so far below the line that the jury will be forced to reach only one conclusion, and that is the one for my client.

In our brief focus group trial of the Berg facts, we had little opportunity to apply these concepts. To the focus group jury, the defense case looked good and would have ended above the neutral line. But with the animation, Lofgren's diagram and model cars, and the biomechanical expert strengthening our case, I was able to give an opening statement of nearly two hours explaining what this powerful evidence would show. As I listened to the defense attorney floundering around in his opening, scoring few points, I felt the case was well on the way downhill. My experts and graphic exhibits were very credible, and the defense attorney could accomplish nothing significant on cross-examination.

Michael's widow and their two small children added a lot of sympathy to our case from a damage standpoint. One interesting item of damage evidence was testimony from Michael's father. Under Minnesota's wrongful death law, you can claim the decedent's "likely future earning capacity and prospects of bettering himself had he lived." At the time of his death, Michael was a struggling life insurance salesman earning only about $16,000 a year. His past earning history did not project any significant number for his family's loss of his future earning capacity. But Michael's father, who owned a successful printing company, was able to testify, over strong objection from the defense, that he had planned to retire in a very few years and bring Michael in to learn the printing business and take it over. He projected that Michael would have earned about $80,000 a year in his first years, with a larger income ahead.

This case concluded in 1992 with the jury awarding what was then the largest wrongful death verdict in Minnesota history. Of most satisfaction to me was their finding of the Clark driver 90 percent at fault, Michael zero, and the pickup driver 10 percent at fault. Judgment was entered for the plaintiff on July 15, 1992, for $2,766,333.43. Without the insight from the focus group we might not have prevailed in this case. Their forthright opinions caused a major restructuring of our case and created a favorable framework for the real jury trial. I owe a lot to that focus group.

CHAPTER 25

THE OUTSIDE LAW FIRM CONSULTANT

Management of a law firm is a difficult task. Historically, law firms have been governed solely by the elder partners, who believe that time and amount of gray hair determine the right to control the destiny of the firm, its lawyers, and staff. More recently, more enlightened firms have selected a rotating management group and given every partner or shareholder an equal vote on issues governing the firm. The former is like the United Nations Security Council; the big nations with lots of power and prestige have the major votes on all significant issues. The rest of the firm and its junior partners are like the UN General Assembly: Powerless figureheads who might believe that they have position and authority, but in reality have little. The more progressive firms try to function like a democracy (one equal vote per member). But even those firms frequently confront the mentality that every lawyer has the correct answer and can rigidly stand by his or her personal opinion. In every form of law firm management, the task is destined to be fraught with internal strife, confrontation, and dissent. Our firm progressed through both of these forms of management. When I became a new shareholder, the elders of the firm—John, Owen, Mark (the other Mark), and Phil—were the governing body. Decades of tradition created this structure of seniors destined to have control of the firm. Each of those gray-haired senior partners had climbed the same ladder from new associate to partner level. If you toiled long enough in the field, earning for the firm (and primarily for the senior partners) several times your take-home salary, then when you became a senior partner you had the same right to coast along, living well off the labors of the young producers in your firm. This system was self-perpetuating. Since our firm was a corporation, the seniors had given themselves, by their own decision in organizing the firm, many more shares of stock in the firm (which only had value to you on your retirement or, upon your death, to your surviving spouse). They thus controlled voting on every issue. The four seniors had eight hundred voting shares among them, and the six junior shareholders had a hundred shares apiece; it doesn't take a rocket scientist to see who ran the show.

It is a constant quandary for the powerful elders in a firm whether and when to add new partners and shareholders. Each year worthy senior associates with major client control, impressive billable hours, or other favorable lawyer attributes are chafing at the bit to join that elite group. From the elders' point of view, adding new voting shareholders regrettably dilutes control and should be tightly controlled or totally discouraged. Our firm encountered this precise problem. Many well-deserving young trial and appellate attorneys were "up for partner" and had to be made shareholders to prevent their departure. To the elders' chagrin, the "youngsters," with their hundred shares of stock each, soon became a voting bloc capable of overruling the senior dynasty. At one lengthy shareholder meeting, the new partners prevailed on a firm resolution that even though shares of stock for buyout or retirement purposes would remain top-heavy, every shareholder would have an equal vote on all issues. Democracy had prevailed.

As in every free democratic society, not everyone can govern. We lawyers duly elected officers—in our case the management committee—by secret ballot. The seven anointed ones ran the day-to-day business of the firm and brought major issues requiring a vote to the monthly shareholders' meeting. The weekly breakfast meetings of the management committee went well until the sudden death of our senior shareholder, John Lommen, and our merger soon thereafter with another law firm. Shortly after the merger it became apparent that the newly constructed management committee was fraught with dissention. The replacement firm president clearly lacked the support of some members. The addition of an opinionated and confrontational managing lawyer from the newly merged firm further fractured the committee.

Caught in the middle of this rapidly developing power struggle was Jack, the office manager. Jack, who was not a lawyer, had held his position for years as the firm grew from ten to thirty lawyers with more than sixty support staff. Jack's responsibilities had expanded with this growth, and he was held responsible by the management committee for most problems in the firm. Jack was becoming an easy target for the strong personalities on the committee. Soon the previously congenial breakfast meetings became so confrontational that oatmeal and eggs were hard to digest. I frequently left the meetings with heartburn. Throughout the firm, the once cheerful atmosphere had changed; Jack was constantly morose, and one partner was often overly loud and demeaning in his criticism of Jack and the staff. Secretaries and legal assistants were looking for greener pastures, and lawyers were dividing into power groups on even minor issues. Nothing was running smoothly. These internal management problems were not unique to our firm. The large firm that solves such systemic problems is the exception. It again is the nature of the beast. Trying to blend into a cohesive working unit a bunch of strong-willed, egotistical sons-of-bitches is destined for problems. It was time for our firm, as many firms have, to hire an outside law firm consultant. Realizing that our management difficulties required help, we unanimously voted to hire Mr. P. and his consulting firm for a fee of several thousand dollars.

At the first management meeting with our consultant, he outlined his plan to interview lawyers and staff at all levels, become familiar with our practice and production, prepare a written report of his recommendations, and provide practical ways for the firm to return to smooth-running operations. For several weeks Mr. P. bounced around the firm, conducting private interviews. The much-awaited "P Report" was finally delivered to the firm president. Mr. P. had minced no words.

Recommendation number one was to fire Jack, as he was way over his head in responsibilities. Recommendation number two was to remove one powerful personality from the management committee. The remaining suggestions, although helpful, were insignificant compared to bombshells one and two. With management approval, our president put into operation Mr. P.'s recommendations. Even with a generous severance package, Jack was not a happy camper as he cleaned out his desk.

One of Mr. P.'s other big recommendations was a need for more togetherness. Mr. P. was a master of setting up firm functions and retreats to create employee cohesiveness and better working relations. His résumé was replete with platitudes from management teams who had followed his seminar and retreat suggestions. So off we went to Grandview Lodge for our next shareholder meeting, with Mr. P. and all partners and associates present, to work on teamwork. At an unused Boy Scout camp we launched into a series of teamwork activities. Lawyers were divided into teams to solve mentally or physically challenging tasks. Like kids playing Twister, we were joined together holding hands and left to undo our tangled mess through cooperation alone. It was, no doubt, the first time most partners ever physically touched each other, but no one complained. Mr. P. then took us to a head-high bench and instructed each of us to close our eyes and fall backwards off the bench to be caught by our colleagues. Although scary for most, the point was easy grasped: Your coworkers were to be trusted to be there for you in times of need. At the end of the session, even those who came with skepticism and ridicule had to acknowledge the good feelings and camaraderie created by the team events. Most of us were still happy to gravitate back to the lodge for a cold beer.

Mr. P.'s other agenda item was an inside session in which the elder partners sat in a circle and the younger partners were given license to speak their minds with no rebuttal from the senior members. With a few pops under their belts, some young partners took great liberty with their freedom of speech. The session became rather tense, with some management members growing more and more agitated without the ability to speak and power to put the rebellious youngsters down. Although much was said and heard, it did not do much for team morale. Though it might not have accomplished much else, every lawyer in attendance recognized the value of Mr. P.'s efforts and the need for a better working relationship in the firm. Unfortunately, the overall atmosphere of the firm did not improve, and over the next few years many valuable young lawyers and partners, including myself, left to seek better opportunities elsewhere.

The law firm consultant story does not end there. Even with his severance package and assistance in finding new employment, our discharged office manager sought out legal assistance to sue the firm for discrimination. Being over age fifty, Jack claimed age discrimination in his firing. Not only the firm, but also individual partners were named as defendants, and even Mr. P.

became a defendant for his "fraudulent" recommendation to fire Jack. The lawsuit complaint, yet to be filed in federal court by Jack's lawyers, was mailed to the firm with a $2 million settlement demand. The language the lawyer used in its allegations was outrageous. Among many claims, it alleged slander and defamation against one partner and quoted many four-letter words used by the partner to browbeat Jack.

I was assigned to handle the firm defense and seek our insurance carrier's involvement to defend the firm. With so much slanderous language in the complaint, I did not want it filed in the federal court to become a public document. Jack's lawyers would no doubt involve the press once the complaint was filed. If these unproven allegations were published it could do great damage to the firm. To stop the filing and force the lawyers to draft a more civilized complaint, I prepared a temporary restraining motion for the federal court. Following their cast-in-stone rules, however, the federal clerk of court would not accept my motion papers, open a court file, and assign a judge to the case. In one of the great Catch-22s I have encountered, the clerk firmly stated that a file could only be opened by the filing of the complaint in the lawsuit. In total frustration I replied, "I can't file the complaint, because that's what I am trying to prevent! If I file the other side's complaint to open a file, there won't be any need for my motion to stop the complaint from being filed." Having some level of standing with the federal judges, I went to Judge David Dody's chambers with my problem. After reading the complaint, he had no problem with setting my motion on for a full oral hearing with a different judge without the necessity of formally opening a file.

A few days later, the motion hearing before Judge McLaughlin turned into a memorable event. Without any argument from me on the motion, Judge McLaughlin tore into Jack's lawyer. Every attempt by the lawyer to justify his complaint allegations was soundly put down by the judge. I had only to sit back with a grin on my face and watch the lawyer take the abuse. The lawyer was directed to redraft the complaint and present it to the judge for approval before filing it. With such a disastrous start to Jack's discrimination lawsuit, the disheartened lawyer chose to start his new and tamed-down lawsuit in state court.

I was successful in persuading the firm's insurance company to defend the firm and individual partners in Jack's lawsuit. Although pending for close to a year and involving several time-consuming depositions of firm partners, the case was eventually totally dismissed on our summary judgment motion. Mr. P. was also dismissed from the case. Unfortunately, he had to use up most of our consulting fee for his own defense attorney. So much for the law firm consultant.

CHAPTER 26

CHALLENGING A JURY VERDICT

Once the evidence and arguments in a trial are completed, the jury departs to a secluded room to begin their deliberations. What goes on in that jury room is to remain secret. A glimpse of what can happen in jury deliberation was portrayed in that great Henry Fonda movie, *Twelve Angry Men*. Unless jurors wish to describe their deliberations after rendering their verdict, lawyers and the public often wonder, and sometimes remain totally befuddled, about how the jury reached it decision.

When I started trying cases I was always looking for feedback on what brought a disputed case to the winning side. As a young lawyer I routinely called one or two jurors after a case, whether I won or lost, to try and find out the what, why, and how-come of their verdict. I would usually also ask a question like, "What did you like or dislike about the trial and my presentation?" Occasionally some outspoken juror would give me an earful. I used this learning experience to become a better trial lawyer for the next time.

The rules of professional conduct do not prohibit contacting jurors after a verdict. For example, Rule 3.5(c) of the Rules of Professional Conduct allows jury contact with some restrictions:

"(c) After discharge of the jury from further consideration of a case with which the lawyer was connected, the lawyer shall not ask questions of or make comments to a member of that jury that are calculated merely to harass or embarrass the juror or to influence the juror's actions in future jury service."

This leaves the door open for lawyers to contact jurors about the case and their deliberations. However, in federal court trials, most of the time the judge will impose a flat rule of no contact with jurors.

Some interesting problems arise when a lawyer (usually on the losing side) finds out that some indiscretion occurred behind the closed jury room door and seeks to impeach or challenge the jury's verdict. Long ago the Supreme Court laid out the procedure for challenging a verdict. It is called a *Schwartz* hearing, after the 1960 case of *Schwartz v. Minneapolis Sub. Bus Co.* 258 Minn. 325, 104 N.W.2d (1960). A challenging lawyer can schedule a *Schwartz* hearing with the judge and present evidence by affidavit or by bringing back the jurors to provide in-person testimony. The casebooks are full of a multitude of different lawyer challenges, the vast majority of which are turned down. Merely presenting evidence that the jurors violated some of the judge's instructions, like restrictions on using a dictionary or a calculator, will not justify overturning the verdict. Similarly, if the deliberations went off on a tangent and the case was decided in a strange way not supported by the evidence, it would not be sufficient for a new trial. If outside influences affected the verdict, that still might not be enough. A 1999 decision of the Minnesota Court of Appeals in *Baker v. Amtrak Nat. R.R.*, 588 N.W.2d 749 (Minn. App. 1999) stated:

"Although trial courts are urged to be fairly lenient in the granting of *Schwartz* hearings, their purpose is to determine juror misconduct, such as outside influence improperly brought to bear on jurors. The purpose of a *Schwartz* hearing does not include the correction of a miscomprehension by a juror or jurors. The assertion that the jury was confused and did not understand the effect of the verdict has been rejected as a basis for a *Schwartz* hearing. Jurors may not impeach their verdict on the basis that they did not understand the legal effect of that verdict."

I remember one challenge where during the deliberations there was an important front-page newspaper article about one of the parties in the lawsuit. The bailiff in charge of the jury had left his newspaper in a place where the jurors could see the headline as they walked in and out of the jury room. At the *Schwartz* hearing each juror testified under oath that even if he or she had seen the headline, it did not influence the verdict. The new trial request was denied.

I may have had one of the most interesting jury verdict challenges in Minnesota litigation history. It all started with a head-on collision on a sharp curve on State Highway 101 in the south metro suburbs. My client was a young tradesman driving his pickup north on 101. Coming south was a woman about sixty years old in a full-size sedan. As they came around the curve one of the two vehicles crossed the center line, causing a fairly high-speed collision. Both drivers were injured. The case came to me as an insurance defense case, but soon I was also representing the young man on his injury claim. On the other side, the woman also had a single lawyer both defending her and prosecuting her injury claim.

Both sides hired accident reconstruction experts to render opinions as to who crossed the center line. The cars were gone, but the sheriff had taken many photos of the badly damaged vehicles. I had hired probably the best and most-respected reconstruction expert in the state. He made paper models of the two vehicles to demonstrate the crush damages to each vehicle at the point of collision. His opinion was that the woman's car was crossing the center line when the impact occurred. As you would expect, the expert on the other side had exactly the opposite opinion.

To illustrate how sharp the curve was at the point of impact, I set my video camera in the windshield of my car and recorded as I drove around the curve several times from both directions. Although not very scientific, it did show that the lady coming around the curve from the north might have had difficulty controlling her vehicle if she was going a bit too fast. My expert liked the video, and the jury was also quite interested in seeing the place of the collision.

The trial was in Scott County district court in Shakopee. The case presentation was quite routine. I remember that my young client made a very appealing witness. We argued to the jury, and the judge gave the usual instructions. The verdict was to decide the comparative negligence of the two drivers. One interesting exception under Minnesota comparative negligence law is that if the jury found equal fault—that is, 50 percent negligence on both drivers—then both sides would win and recover 50 percent of their damage award. In this case that did not happen.

Six jurors were to deliberate. Under the Minnesota rules, if the six jurors come in with a verdict within the first six hours of deliberation, it has to be a unanimous verdict. After six hours of deliberation, if there is one holdout on all of the questions, the jury can return with a five-sixths verdict, which would be valid.

I received a call from the clerk that a five-sixths verdict came back finding my client 60 percent negligent and the other driver 40 percent negligent. Fairly large damage amounts were put down for each side. But because of the percentages, my client would recover nothing on his injury claim, and my insurance client would have to pay 60 percent of the lady's damages. Since

I thought we had put in the better case, I was quite shocked. I found out from the clerk which of the jurors had held out in our favor against the other five. That evening I called the dissenter. I started the conversation with something like, "Since you must have been arguing in my client's favor, could you explain what factors supported the verdict for the lady?" There was a long pause, and then the juror gave an uncertain initial response that I must be mistaken, that he was voting in favor of the lady and not the young man. After further confusing discussion, we together determined that on the written special verdict form, the juror who filled in the blanks had misunderstood the comparative negligence instructions and questions and put the 40 percent and 60 percent numbers in the wrong blanks. No matter what the verdict said on the paper, what was intended by five jurors was that my side was to win, with one dissenter favoring the other side. Ecstatic, I called my young client and then poured myself a stiff one.

To get the verdict right we still had to pursue a *Schwartz* hearing and convince the trial judge to change the verdict. All six jurors were called back, given an oath, and then asked to explain what they had really meant with their verdict. All six definitely agreed that the verdict form was inaccurately completed and that the intent of five was that we would win. The opposing lawyer vehemently argued that the judge could not interfere and overturn the verdict. He cited many past precedents, none of which had such an obvious clerical error on the verdict form. The judge agreed that he had to change the result, and we were declared the winner. Thus, not only did my young client get 60 percent of his damage award, but my insurance client also had to pay nothing on the lady's claim. Oh, what sweet justice!

CHAPTER 27

INTRIGUE WITH INTERPOL IN ITALY

Does a person get wealthy being a lawyer? The public's perception certainly is that attorneys are at the top of the income scale. This belief is fostered by the occasional multimillion-dollar payout broadcast in the local papers or the report of Wall Street lawyers charging their corporate clients a thousand dollars an hour for their time. Some lawyers have undoubtedly struck it rich with big verdicts or high-paying corporate clients. But the vast majority of lawyers are working the daily grind just like rest of the population, toiling to reach a decent middle-class standard of living. I remember reading several years ago a statistic that the median income for lawyers (whether nationwide or just in Minnesota I do not remember), was well below $100,000—something like $50,000 to $60,000 a year. Keep in mind that "median" means that half of the lawyers are making less than this number on an annual basis.

Where did my legal career take me financially? After my second year of law school in 1968, my summer clerkship in New

York City paid me $250 a week, which at the time was very adequate for my lifestyle. Similarly, my first real job with a law firm in 1969 paid an annual salary of $12,000. Under the economic conditions of the time and with my wife working, we lived quite well. It was not until about twelve years later, at age thirty-six, after I became a partner at Lommen, Cole & Stageberg, that I made over $200,000 a year. This provided for a comfortable upper-middle-class lifestyle, including some funds for investing for retirement. Working until 1994 at an insurance defense firm gave me an income at or somewhat above that same level. Starting out on my own after that meant a couple of pretty lean years, with frequent reliance on a line of credit from a friendly banker. Then good things started happening with my contingent fees, and my income reached its peak in 2005 with an eight-million-dollar verdict in Florida in a Coleman heater case. Even after sharing the contingent fee with three Florida lawyers, the payout was spectacular for this small-town boy from northern Minnesota.

I recite the above not to brag, but to reinforce that my legal career has been good to me in many respects. One thing it has provided is the opportunity for a lot of travel. I have probably handled cases or taken depositions in more than half of the fifty states. And as I discussed in an earlier chapter, many of those trips included a few days of vacation. Another Coleman heater case allowed for skiing Utah slopes in the winter and hiking three of the national parks in the summer. From the early years of my practice I was fortunate to be able to take frequent and great vacations, skiing, hunting, golfing, sailing, and exploring in many places throughout the United States, Mexico, Canada, the Caribbean, and Europe. This is not meant to turn into a boring travelogue. But I will recount my rather remarkable encounter with Antonio and the intrigue of the Interpol on a trip to Florence, Italy.

When my son, Jeffrey, was sixteen and my daughter, Mindy, was twelve we took a two-week family trip to Italy. How can I forget the wide-eyed look on my son's face when he encountered his first topless ladies on the beaches of the Mediterranean, or Mindy posing for a picture as if she was holding up the Leaning Tower of Pisa. The travel plan included two days of sightseeing in Florence. At midmorning on the day of our arrival we were standing in a central square, a block or two from the famous Uffizi Gallery, when a strange little man came up to me and spoke in a very agitated manner. He said things like, "Are these your children? It is not safe here. There have been shots fired down by the Uffizi. You should come away from here to be safe; follow me." We hurriedly followed him to a place a couple of blocks away from the square, where he introduced himself as Antonio, a British journalist here in Florence to research a story. He advised that he knew a lot about Florence and its history and that he had the morning free and would show us some sights where we would be safe. Now picture this fellow: He was about five feet tall, fairly well dressed, with dark olive skin, looking somewhat like Dustin Hoffman's Ratso in the movie *Midnight Cowboy*. I was quite concerned and cautious about following him, and I quietly warned Jeffrey to watch for trouble. We followed Antonio to a cathedral off the beaten tourist path, which confirmed at least some of his historical knowledge. In this church were the tombs of some of history's greatest, including Michelangelo, Machiavelli, and Galileo. We were impressed. Heading back to the city center, Antonio suggested we stop for an aperitif, so we sat down at a café for a break.

Antonio's story continued to unfold. He was quite a talker. He claimed to be on assignment from one of the big world news magazines, like *Time* or *Newsweek*, investigating the "white slave trade" of transporting vulnerable young women to Russia for prostitution. As proof of this problem he claimed that he had observed, the evening before, a couple of young female Americans getting intoxicated at a local restaurant owned and managed by a Russian lady. When the two girls asked for a ride to wherever they were staying, Antonio claimed, the Russian lady had called two of her helpers, who placed the girls in a car and disappeared. Antonio was sure that the girls were now drugged and on their way to Russia. He claimed to be involved regularly with the British secret service, the CIA, and Interpol, the international super-sleuth organization. When Antonio found out that I was a lawyer, he started soliciting my help with his undercover work.

Mixed in with this rather bizarre story was an ongoing narrative about the history and important sites of Florence. Our visit to Michelangelo's David included an unforgettable half-hour history lesson. Antonio suggested that if we wanted to buy jewelry or the famous Florentine leather he would take us to the best places. At a fancy leather store, the proprietors seemed to know Antonio and welcomed us into the store. Feeling somewhat obligated to buy, I did purchase a nice leather belt. Antonio led us to a small Italian restaurant, where the owner again happily greeted Antonio as a regular customer. Lunch, with some good local wine, was on me. As the afternoon wore on and the historical narrative continued, Antonio led us to the Uffizi. There was a long line at the entrance, and closing time was about an hour away. Ignoring the line, Antonio marched us up to the ticket booth and told the staff that he was escorting an important American diplomat and we needed immediate entrance. I dug for ticket money, and in we went. Over the next hour we hustled from one famous painting after another. Antonio knew where every great work was and explained the background of each painting like an art history major. The last event of the afternoon was taking our car across the River Arno to the bluffs opposite to watch the spectacular sunset over downtown Florence. Another great tourist stop off the beaten track.

During the busy day we hadn't stopped to find a hotel, but Antonio assured us he could find us a satisfactory place. What became apparent was that Antonio did not have lodging for himself. So, in about a two-star hotel, we obtained two rooms across the hall from each other, one for Antonio (which he did pay for after negotiating with the hotel registrar) and the other for my family. Quite exhausted by the day's activities, we begged off from an evening meal with Antonio. Having learned about our plans for a second day in Florence, he was already laying out the itinerary for the next day's touring, including a drive up into the hills surrounding Florence.

After dinner, Antonio came to our door, requesting that I go with him to do more surveillance on the Russian lady's restaurant. I could not resist this bizarre story, and so away we went. The restaurant was on a famous square with open-air seating on the piazza. Rather than sitting down at the Russian lady's tables, we sat next door, where Antonio could carefully observe the operation of the restaurant. I bought us a bottle of wine and we sat for an hour or so, Antonio still talking nonstop. He claimed he had contacted Interpol, and their operatives were also observing the restaurant. The Russian lady was about fifty, attractive and stylishly dressed. She was the maître d', so she was prominently stationed at the center of activity. When she spoke to a female customer or a male employee, Antonio would say, "Did you see that?" or "See, what did I tell you?" and "Watch her now and see that customer disappear." Even though I was sitting right beside him, I saw nothing happening out of the ordinary. He claimed Interpol was getting pictures of these events. Because it was so secret, he could not tell me where the Interpol photographer was located. If there was such a person, he was certainly well concealed. Maybe I wasn't as astute at finding the bad guys as Antonio, but hardly did I see any worldwide conspiracy and kidnapping happening in this peaceful Florentine square.

With no encouragement from me, and in fact ignoring my strong exhortation, "Don't do it," Antonio got up and charged toward the Russian lady to confront her on his suspicions. I decided to follow as Antonio's trusted witness (and now probably his trusted lawyer). Standing some ten or fifteen feet away I watched Antonio aggressively come face to face with the Russian lady and accuse her of kidnapping the two drunk girls the night before and engaging in the white slave trade. She appeared totally astounded at the accusations from this strange little man, and she soon called her bouncers to remove him. Before they arrived, I intervened and grabbed Antonio to usher him away. I looked at the Russian lady and said something like, "Sorry about that, I will take care of him." We beat the security people out of the restaurant, but all the way back to the hotel Antonio babbled on that he had proven the conspiracy and the Interpol people had it all recorded. Back at the hotel, I found my family awake and wondering whether I was alive or unconscious and on my way to Russia. They were most interested in my evening adventure.

The next morning we packed up and left early to avoid waking Antonio and spending another day with him as our tourist guide. We talked and laughed a lot about Antonio and speculated at what he was really about. Sometime during the prior day he had pulled out a small, tattered notebook to record our names, address, and telephone number. I noticed that we were certainly not the first entries in the notebook. It appeared that he had been doing the same type of guiding for some time, cornering unassuming tourists and later recording for some strange reason the names of his victims, conquests, new friends, or whatever. What I find puzzling is that his motivation in his pursuit of the white slave traders seemed pure, and some of his story, even our surveillance of the Russian lady's restaurant, had some credibility. Of course, his embellishments about the involvement of Interpol had no fact or substantiation. Still, Antonio was one of the most unforgettable people in my life. If there was some realistic way of searching him out for further talk and enlightenment, I would certainly pursue it. One thing I know is that my kids, too, would follow me without hesitation to a reunion with Antonio, anytime and anywhere.

CHAPTER 28

DEALING WITH A MASTER SWINDLER

In this narrative I have been careful to use pseudonyms for clients and others featured in my stories to assure that challenges to my recollection of facts, which may be somewhat flawed, will not lead me to some disaster, or maybe a slander and libel suit. However, one case rises to the top of the list of individuals whom I could not slander or libel due to a not just damaged, but in fact destroyed reputation. But still, out of caution and the desire to avoid encountering this fellow again, I will call him Paul. I will now tell the almost unbelievable tale of Paul, the biggest and most successful swindler I ever encountered.

I was referred by one of our insurance companies to provide the defense of a prominent individual in the community and his lovely wife, who were being sued in a civil suit by this fellow named Paul. At that stage in my career I never turned down an insurance defense case, especially one that sounded as interesting as this one. With the defense appointment in hand, I met with my new clients and their personal lawyer to ascertain the facts of the case.

I will call these clients Bill and Mary. The tale that they unfolded could probably be the first three chapters of an X-rated novel. Bill and Mary were high school sweethearts, and Mary had stuck with Bill through college. They eventually married and lived in the suburbs with children and a high lifestyle. Not only was Bill very successful and highly paid, but Mary came into the relationship with some family money. Bill had been working very hard at his business while Mary, like many wealthy suburban wives, did volunteer work on various projects. At one of Mary's volunteer board meetings, she met another board member named Paul. It seems that Paul had other aspirations in addition to helping the needy with his extra time. At our first attorney client meeting, Mary revealed that Paul had swept her off her feet, claiming that he was satisfying needs left unfulfilled by her hard-working husband. This led to a long-term clandestine affair.

Paul had convinced Mary not only of his serious romantic intentions, but also that he was trustworthy and that Mary should be loaning him money. With her own family money and investments, Mary had fallen for Paul's poor-me stories and gave him three different loans of many thousands of dollars. The exact amount now escapes me, but the total was something like $180,000. His promises to repay these sums repeatedly resulted in missed payment deadlines, but his sweet talk and apparent bedroom prowess had dissuaded Mary from pursuing any collection remedies. To avoid explaining the depleted monthly investment reports to Bill, Mary would rush out to pick up the daily mail before he had a chance to peruse it.

How does a routine extramarital affair result in this couple needing a defense attorney for a lawsuit? After some period of time, Bill became suspicious of his wife's frequent departures and followed Mary to one of her secret meetings with her lover. Bill confronted them in a parking lot. Lots of shouting ensued, but no blows were struck. Mary then confessed everything to Bill, but with a twist in the story. Claiming that Paul had coerced her with threats of revealing the affair to her husband, Mary declared herself an unwilling participant in the loans. This brought Bill to a boiling point, and he disclosed the whole swindle to the county attorney, vowing to get the money back and prosecute Paul.

Local community newspapers routinely print recent criminal charges, so Paul's name, his arrest, and the charges against him appeared in the local suburban paper. Obviously having planned for the day when the roof might cave in on his escapades, Paul had kept numerous letters he had received from Mary as well as audio recordings of bedroom activity and a quite revealing video tape. (I never did see the video.) When Paul and his attorney disclosed these items to the county attorney, Mary's coercion story really fell apart. The county attorney told Bill and Mary that proving coercion would be very difficult and there was insufficient evidence to prosecute any further. As I learned later, even if the prosecution had proceeded to trial, it is very unlikely that Bill and Mary would ever have agreed to testify about the whole mess in a public trial. With the prosecution dropped and Bill and Mary giving up efforts to recover the loans, they felt that Paul would be satisfied and go away. They hoped never to see or hear from him again.

Alas, the best laid plans often go awry. A libel, slander, and abuse of prosecution lawsuit arrived from Paul suing Bill and Mary for damage to his reputation by this unwarranted and defamatory prosecution. This is where I came in, as the insurance company's defense lawyer, to defend Bill and Mary against this multimillion-dollar suit, amazingly and brazenly brought by the man who had swindled my clients out of nearly two hundred thousand dollars. Talk about balls! Well, at the time this case got started, I did not know just how big my opponent's balls were. As Mary had unfortunately learned (as had many others, as I will soon relate), Paul had a remarkable facade of believability and an unabashed confidence in his ability to weave a tale out of false-hoods to gain some personal advantage. He had gone to a prominent law firm in Milwaukee and convinced an experienced senior partner of the justification for his lawsuit against Bill and Mary. This prominent attorney had agreed to represent Paul on a contingency fee with no money advanced for expenses. It is quite clear that Paul never leveled with his own lawyer and did not disclose much about his background. Had he done so, no good lawyer ever would have taken a contingency gamble with this guy. The Milwaukee lawyer turned out to be a formidable oppo-nent. The lawsuit discovery process commenced in earnest. As part of the lawsuit we filed a counter-claim to try to get Mary's money back, even though we knew there was no realistic chance of ever recovering a dime from Paul.

In every lawsuit you try to do some investigation on your adversary. Digging into Paul's past, we found it to be a gold mine. We hired an investigator, and with the insurance company's blessing turned him loose to track Paul's past. Paul was president of several corporations, none of which were more than shells with no assets or moneymaking capability. He had created phony financial statements and had borrowed money from some of the largest banks in Minnesota. Our investigator located several of the phony loan documents. Some of Paul's many unpaid credi-tors had forced him and his corporations into an involuntary bankruptcy in Minnesota. This didn't slow down Paul's behavior. During the pending bankruptcy he had again convinced a Minneapolis banker, using a phony financial statement, to make him a six-figure loan. As his past record showed, he had no inten-tion of repaying any of the borrowed money. Court documents disclosed a multitude of creditors seeking enforcement of judg-ments against him both in and out of the bankruptcy. Since the abolition of debtors' prisons centuries ago, the only way to recover bad loans is through a lawsuit obtaining a judgment against the debtor. This still does not ensure any type of recovery unless the debtor has some assets to levy against. As Paul had hid from his creditors any significant assets, he could walk away untouched with the borrowed money in his pocket.

Our investigator tracked Paul's trail back to Boulder, Colorado. There he had used a fake credit card to buy a girlfriend a diamond ring worth $10,000. The jeweler had determined that the credit card was invalid and had the authorities apprehend Paul just before he boarded an airplane out of Denver. After being booked and charged, Paul had spent a couple of days in jail, entered some kind of nominal guilty plea with an explanation, paid a minimum fine, and returned to Minneapolis. When we later questioned him as to whether he had ever been arrested and charged with a crime, he denied any such past history. The Colorado documents were going to be powerful, particularly the ugly mug shot.

One of Paul's more intriguing transactions was his ownership and sale of a condo and boat slip at the Port Superior Marina in Bayfield, Wisconsin. For years I had chartered sailboats out of Port Superior and knew the charter master, Dave Nixon, very well. As our investigator found out, and as Dave verified, Paul did own a condo and boat slip at Port Superior, but he seldom made his mortgage payments or paid the fees for his ownership. Dave had been after him as a slippery owner for some time. Again, right in the middle of his bankruptcy, Paul somehow doctored up the ownership documents and sold the condo and boat slip to an innocent buyer for cash. Even though these properties had been listed as assets in the bankruptcy court, this sale was never reported to the bankruptcy court or his creditors. It was reported to me that Paul drove away with some $40,000 plus in cash in his car trunk.

For some period of time, Paul had been driving and living out of a Winnebago RV. Our investigator traced him through small towns in Wisconsin, finding numerous small businesses, such as grocery stores and gas stations, that had accepted checks and credit cards from this handsome, fast-talking swindler, none of which were any good. The amount involved was usually so small that the swindled recipient wouldn't involve the authorities and chase after the crook and his Winnebago.

Paul also owned an airplane, another area of interest for me, and it turned out that he had been flying around the country without a valid pilot's license. When Mary got involved with him he owned a fast V-tail Bonanza airplane. Somehow he had learned to fly and communicate with flight controllers at airports, and without a current pilot's license, he flew in and out of airports without incident. Mary had apparently been along on several flights. The airplane provided the basis for most of Paul's money swindles from her. Claiming that an insurance or maintenance payment was due on the airplane and that he was temporarily short of cash, he had convinced Mary to make loans with promises of immediate repayment. After Mary complied, he would start a series of excuses for why the money could not be repaid. Even if the money actually went towards the airplane, he never repaid any of it.

Back to the lawsuit. Paul's high-powered lawyer was taking the case seriously, having obviously been deceived on the true facts of his client's past. Lengthy depositions of Bill and Mary were scheduled. I spent several hours preparing them for the anticipated questioning. As much as they tried to recount the facts of the affair and Paul's taking of money from Mary, they faced aggressive questioning on why they initiated the prosecution, the publicity, and why the case had been dropped. No matter what kind of bastard Paul may have been, my clients were vulnerable in this civil suit for their actions in pursuing Paul through the authorities and the press. This deposition experience was very emotionally trying for these clients.

We scheduled the deposition of Paul for a full day, intending to confront him on all of his misadventures while under oath. This, our first face-to-face meeting with Paul, was a most interesting deposition. This swindler's appearance and demeanor were truly remarkable. He was handsome, with blond wavy hair like former Green Bay Packer great Paul Hornung. He had beautiful baby-blue Paul Newman eyes. Upon meeting him you would immediately like the man. As I said many times after this deposition, I would not want my wife to be alone with this fellow for two hours, as she probably would be seduced by his good looks and smooth presentation. His confidence overflowed as he answered the questions. When asked directly, even with our documentary proof of some of his swindles, he denied the transactions, claiming the documents were mistaken. He even denied that it was his signature on some of the phony documents. Never had I then, or even since, encountered such a confident liar. He clearly felt that he could talk his way around whatever solid evidence was presented to him. I have seen many a tough witness over the years, but this fellow was the best. At the conclusion of the deposition, with the record replete with his denials under oath, I was confident that before a jury the contradictory documents bearing his signature, together with the witnesses I would call, would overcome this showman's claims of innocence.

My recommendation to Bill and Mary as well as to their insurance company was to defend this case through trial and put this guy out of business. But, as often is the case, other considerations intervened. Bill and Mary's personal attorney argued with the insurance company about the trauma of going through a probable two-week trial, even when the prospects of winning were very good. Against my recommendation, the insurance company agreed to pay Paul and his attorney some dollar settlement with a stipulation that the two sides would have no contact whatsoever in the future. Of course, this settlement included Bill and Mary giving up their counter claim for return of the thousands loaned to Paul. As a defense lawyer, I find that settlements like this, in cases that should have been tried, really hurt.

This was not the end of my contact with Paul. Sometime after the lawsuit ended, we were alerted that Paul was being prosecuted in federal court in Michigan. Through our investigation we knew that he had been building a fancy home on an island in Lake Michigan and flying back and forth in his airplane. In typical Paul fashion, he had not been paying his suppliers and laborers. He had again used a phony financial statement to persuade a Michigan bank to loan him something like $50,000 to complete the construction of the home. This time, however, his luck ran out and he was charged with federal bank fraud. The Michigan prosecutor had contacted us for our background on Paul, which we were more than happy to relate in detail to him. We offered our investigator's services in full cooperation, and I recall that our investigator was present in the Michigan courtroom for Paul's sentencing. Apparently, when Paul stood up to bullshit the federal judge as he had done to dozens of his victims, the judge cut him off and immediately sentenced him to the federal penitentiary for something like two or three years. I wish I could say that jail time would change the stripes on this rogue's back, but I know better. He is a committed con man, and only a bullet in the head from a swindled businessman or the husband of a future lover would put this guy out of business.

I must add at this time that Bill and Mary were great clients and weathered the whole civil lawsuit mess well. They eventually resolved their marital problems and have remained together ever since.

CHAPTER 29

A BAD EXPERIENCE IN CALIFORNIA

Early on in my career the thought of venturing outside Minnesota to handle a lawsuit in another state was a very foreboding one. Since I was struggling to handle the law and litigation procedures of my home state's different courts, trying to master the law and procedures of a foreign jurisdiction seemed an impossible task. Then I had occasion to watch a polished trial lawyer from California handle a trial to a successful conclusion in a complex aviation case in a Minnesota state court. That convinced me that trying cases out of state could be done without too much sweat and strain. As my trial experience deepened, I was soon handling cases in Wisconsin, Iowa, and North and South Dakota, all of which were similar to Minnesota in court rules and procedure. Unfortunately, one of the really low points in my career was venturing into California on an injury case. Not only was the case unsuccessful, but it may have contributed to the demise of one of my law partners.

My partner, Glenn Kessel, had a pleasant blonde girlfriend

named Lori. On several occasions I had socialized with Lori and got to know her fairly well. After a while, though, Lori made the decision to leave Glenn and her family and move to Los Angeles. After being there a short time she sought employment at a temporary employment agency. They placed her as a receptionist with a small company that had just moved into a new office building. One of Lori's duties was making coffee in the new lunchroom. On perhaps her first effort at coffee making she reached up to open an upper cabinet door, and as she swung the door open it separated from its hinges and struck her on the forehead. It was a heavy fiberboard door, and it knocked Lori to the ground, leaving her semiconscious. Coworkers found her, observed the evidence of the head injury, and escorted her to an emergency room.

Lori ended up with some fairly serious residuals from this incident. She experienced headaches, neck problems, and most significantly some level of a traumatic brain injury, commonly called a TBI. She was not able to work and flew home to Minnesota to be with her family while she underwent medical treatment. She saw respectable doctors who confirmed that she was experiencing residuals from the TBI along with ongoing headaches. Through Glenn I became Lori's personal injury lawyer. Having been involved in several TBI cases, I knew that proving a TBI claim was difficult because there is usually no objective evidence of brain injury on X-ray, EEG, CT, or MRI scan. The claim would be proven by intelligence and memory testing by a neuropsychologist. Our chosen neuropsychology expert in Minneapolis conducted his testing and rendered an opinion, though a somewhat equivocal one, that Lori did have a TBI with resulting memory loss caused by the impact of the heavy cabinet door.

The case obviously had to be brought in California. All of the liability facts, defendants, and witnesses were in California, while most of Lori's medical witnesses were in Minnesota. It looked a bit complicated, but worth the time and expense to pursue if

Lori's claim had some significant damage potential. With the brain injury, which looked like it was going to be permanent, and with a probable significant loss of earning capacity for a woman now in her mid-thirties, plus the prospect of trying the case in big-verdict California, it looked like a potentially high-damage case for settlement or trial. I agreed to handle the case on the usual one-third contingent fee.

A Minnesota lawyer cannot just waltz into another state and handle a case in its court system. Special arrangements can be made on a case-by-case basis, on what is called *pro hac vice* counsel, if you associate with a lawyer practicing within the state. Perhaps it was Glenn or someone else in the firm who gave me the name of a Los Angles lawyer to associate with to commence the case in Burbank state court. Taking on this lawyer, who was not an experienced personal injury lawyer, and agreeing to split the contingent fee with him were the big mistakes in the case. The California court system and its procedures are different from anything I had experienced. My new co-counsel was unfortunately not up to speed on the rules and deadlines either.

Our investigator had determined that several companies were potential defendants, one or all of whom were responsible for not securing the hinges on the cabinet door. So the lawsuit was started against the general contractor, architect, cabinetmaker, and installing carpenter. We were soon facing four seasoned defense attorneys fully comfortable with the local court procedures. It was shocking to find out that our case would not reach trial for up to five years after its commencement. This delay proved disastrous to our case in several respects.

Proving the liability case was easy. We quickly zeroed in on the installing carpenter who had the responsibility to attach all of the hinges on the cabinet doors. This fellow had only limited liability insurance, so in order to have enough insurance for our anticipated huge verdict for Lori we needed to keep the other defendants around. Thus, on every aspect of the case, my marginally competent local lawyer and I were facing the four experienced defense lawyers. Being paid on an hourly basis, they were content to work the case with lots of depositions, motions, and makework. This necessitated several trips to Burbank.

The biggest problem we encountered was the judge's scheduling order, which set out deadlines for completing different parts of the case. Even though the trial would not be called for five years, the discovery deadline to complete depositions and do all pretrial work was at the end of three years, still two years short of an anticipated trial. My local counsel had no clue how seriously this discovery deadline was regarded by the Burbank judge. From my experience in trial procedure in several states, there is a well-recognized distinction between discovery depositions and trial depositions. Usually there is no need to complete depositions of treating doctors to be used at trial until shortly before the scheduled trial. This makes logical sense for several reasons. Doctors' depositions are quite expensive and should be delayed until settlement appears impossible and the case will proceed to trial. Also, a doctor's deposition taken two years before trial may be outdated and stale if there is continued post-deposition treatment of the injured plaintiff. With this routine procedure in mind, I delayed the depositions of the Minneapolis neuropsychologist and treating doctor until a few weeks before the scheduled trial. When the defense lawyers flew into Minneapolis for these trial depositions, no one raised an objection that they were untimely. With the one California treating doctor agreeing to come to testify live at trial, I felt that the medical end of the case was in good shape.

As I have often stated, a case never gets any better than the day you take it on. It can only go downhill from there. This case was no exception, and over the five years from start to trial, a lot did happen. Many changes in Lori's life made her TBI look temporary or even nonexistent. She obviously had to support herself, so she found employment and was doing just fine at her job. Sometime in this five-year period she moved in with a fairly wealthy guy, did some major traveling, and acquired a pricey automobile. The defense's chosen adverse examining doctor rendered a report contending that Lori was a real phony with no residuals of a head injury. As the months went by, the value of this case was sliding downhill and the defense lawyers knew it. They blew off my high settlement demands and, to my recollection, only offered something like $25,000 before trial. But the worst was yet to come.

As we approached the five-year mark, the Burbank judge scheduled a calendar call of several cases on his docket to set trial dates. This was my first time in the Burbank courthouse. The building was old and decayed. The hallways were filled with traffic and criminal defendants talking with their lawyers and public defenders. There were no private rooms for attorney-client discussions. Our courtroom looked like the inside of an office warehouse, with file cabinets and boxes piled around the perimeter. The no-nonsense trial judge rattled off case after case, asking lawyers only if their case was ready for trial, then assigning a definite trial date. Our trial date was set about six weeks in the future. As I already had a firm Minneapolis federal court trial date set on that date in a major class action lawsuit expected to last two to three weeks, I politely advised the judge of this trial conflict and asked for an alternate trial date for Lori's case. With no explanation, he quickly denied my request, reaffirmed our start date, dismissed us, and moved on to the next case. I remember seeing the defense lawyers smiling at my distress. I had clearly been "hometowned" by my adversaries.

I cannot remember any judge rejecting out of hand a scheduling conflict as I had just experienced. I was the lead counsel in the class action suit, and no way was the federal court going to alter its trial schedule on this major case which had been set for trial for several months. It was clear to me that my California local counsel was incompetent to try Lori's case. With the help of my firm's appellate department, we made a pretrial appeal to the California appellate court to overturn the judge's trial setting. This was quickly rejected. My only option was to pass Lori's case off to another trial lawyer in my office. The one available lawyer was Mike Shroyer, a thirty-five-year-old partner with good trial experience, almost all of which was on defense cases. Mike agreed to handle Lori's case, and I spent many hours bringing him up to speed. With assistance from my fine legal assistant, Mark Lloyd, we felt that Mike could still win the case. When I advised Lori of this change, she was less than happy but agreed that we had no choice.

The trial proved to be a disaster. As I was also in trial, Mike reported to me each evening. He was getting no help from the trial judge. The defense lawyers made a motion to exclude the trial depositions I had taken of the Minneapolis witnesses, claiming that they were late and not in compliance with the discovery deadline that passed two years previously. The judge quickly agreed, throwing out the best medical support for the claim. This left Mike with only the one California doctor who really could not support the TBI claim. The next evening Mike reported on Lori's courtroom testimony. He described that she came across as exaggerating and not at all credible. She claimed to have no memory on things that were obvious and inconsistent with her upper-middle-class lifestyle. Mike believed that the blue-collar Burbank jury just hated her after the defense lawyers finished with their cross-examination. He was actually laughing about how badly the case was going. We decided to take what he could get in settlement and get him out of Burbank. At the end of that day the defense lawyers had improved their offer to $50,000. Lori, of course, felt that her testimony went well and blamed us for the failure to use the Minnesota medical testimony. Mike and I decided that he should tell Lori that she must take the $50,000 offer, and to resolve her complaints against us we agreed to totally waive our contingent fee so she could keep the whole $50,000. She agreed, and the case was closed.

I don't remember how much lawyer time and out-of-pocket expense went into handling this case, but it was a lot. The worst consequence of this fiasco was that my partner and good friend, Mike, within a few weeks of his California experience, was diagnosed with terminal cancer. I was aware that while in California he was not feeling well. In retrospect it is clear that he was already suffering from the cancer. It was Mike's last trial; what a crazy way to end a trial lawyer career. He was dead within about six months. I volunteered to prepare the bar association eulogy, and I praised Mike's friendship and skills as a trial lawyer. I never mentioned the circumstances of his last trial. It took me quite a while to get past the guilt of sending a friend and a fine trial lawyer into the bizarre world of California trial work.

CHAPTER 30

MY ONE ADVENTURE IN BANKRUPTCY COURT

Nowhere in our profession is there a group of legal specialists that exists so far outside the mainstream as the bankruptcy lawyers. It's easy to go through law school without learning anything about how individuals and failed businesses go through bankruptcy. The commonly accepted understanding of bankruptcy is that, if your expenditures have somehow outstripped your ability to pay, you can easily and cheaply go through bankruptcy, wipe the slate clean, and start over from scratch. In hard economic times thousands have chosen this escape route rather than trying to resolve their indebtedness. Lawyers feast on these poor souls, lead them into the bankruptcy courts and take out most if not all of their paltry assets in attorney fees in exchange for that clean slate. The bankrupt parties, who are relieved of their past debts and transgressions, are also usually left with no credit and unable to borrow a dime for years into the future. Furthermore, what society does not recognize, much less rebel against, is that the multitude of legitimate creditors that graciously extended services to these folks and their businesses get nothing out of the bankruptcy but write-offs for tax purposes.

I learned early on to stay out of bankruptcy court, as it is a specialty governed by about a thousand federal statutes and regulations that I could hardly understand and integrate into my civil law practice. But over the years I counseled many destitute clients in disastrous financial situations to go down to the federal court and file for bankruptcy.

My one venture into bankruptcy court was interesting. One of my clients, whom I had in the past bailed out in a complex sexual harassment case, called me about a problem his company was having with a Florida company that it had merged with about a year before. This small but very profitable collections company in St. Paul, operated by two fellows whom I liked, had involved in their management a slick-talking insurance broker and made him the chief operating officer in the company. This guy had connections with a bigger collections outfit in Florida, and he convinced the two Minnesota principals that they should sell out to the Florida company. A loosely drafted sales contract was prepared (without any of my input, thank goodness) transferring ownership of the St. Paul company to the Florida company with promises of stock ownership and future profit-sharing.

My involvement began when one of the owners called me at home at 6:00 a.m. He reported that police officers were at his St. Paul office, refusing to let him or his employees in to go to work. It seemed that the Florida company had gone to court and obtained a court order to assume control of its new subsidiary. This was their move to take over the physical property and complete operation of the business. I drove over to the company and confronted not only the police, who had a valid signed court order, but also the slick takeover specialist from Florida. This fellow looked and talked like a muscleman for the Mafia. After looking at their documents, which appeared legitimate, I ushered my frustrated client away to analyze further what had just happened. I quickly found out that the slick insurance broker to whom the St. Paul partners had given primary management control had helped orchestrate this takeover by the Florida company. Amazingly, my principal client was a lawyer who had been involved in the legal collections business for twenty years, and yet he had no idea what control he had given up in this merger.

To try to resolve the immediate issues that morning, I negotiated with Florida attorneys and the local police to let the employees into the office to continue work as usual, even though management now appeared to be with the new company. I then started to unravel the whole matter of how the trusted local insurance broker had convinced the two naïve businessmen to give up the control of their company for future promises from the company in Florida. I found out that one of the broker's close personal friends was a principal in the Florida company. This obviously created a serious conflict of interest. In analyzing the contract documents, I found that the local guys could rescind the deal if the Florida company did not make a public stock offering during the first twelve months of the merger. The Florida company had not held up its end of the deal and had not completed a public offering. As it was still within the one-year window, the St. Paul clients could demand the rescission. I helped the clients draft the rescission letter demanding the return of the stock and control of their company.

Within days of mailing the rescission letter, we received word that the Florida company had been forced into involuntary bankruptcy by several of its large creditors. It had not been making money and had stopped paying bills long before the Minnesota takeover. Here then was the legal dilemma: A valid contract for the transfer of a business had been executed prior to the declaration of bankruptcy, with the attempted rescission by my clients occurring just days after the filing of the bankruptcy. Since all business transactions with the Florida company had technically stopped as of the filing of the bankruptcy, was the late-filed rescission valid to void the sale of the business?

In an attempt to prove the failure of the contingency and the validity of the rescission that would allow my clients to reassume ownership of their company, I filed all of the necessary bankruptcy papers, creating an issue for trial in the Florida bankruptcy court. Sometime in June my clients and I went to a Tampa, Florida, bankruptcy court for a two-day hearing on the challenge by my Minnesota clients. I was very pleased with the smart and astute bankruptcy judge. This evidentiary trial was something else!

The lawyer for the Florida company not only looked, but also acted just like a Mafia attorney, a greasy Sicilian counselor. I was able to expose a multitude of lies and false documents he and his clients had created. The Minnesota insurance broker, supposedly a trusted confidant who had been brought in to help expand my client's business, was just as dishonest as the Florida people. Some of my best aggressive cross-examination of these witnesses disclosed the fraud and dishonesty of these people and their attorney. At one point I proved that they had prepared an important document during the trial and then back-dated it several months prior.

If you have crooks by the balls, it can be fun. The broker's good buddy was a physician named Dr. Nuckols. This fellow maintained that he had been given the rescission letter by his Minnesota buddy but had never presented it to the board of the Florida company to get formal approval. A short excerpt from the trial transcript shows my distaste for Dr. Nuckols:

"And so you claim you didn't get board approval, and it was your decision not to do that?"

"Correct."

"So you were trying to screw these guys, weren't you, sir?"

"No, I was not, and I resent that."

"Well, you're sitting here fighting from them getting their company back because you did not fulfill your obligations to take that agreement to the board, isn't that right, sir?"

"No, sir. I'm not accustomed to being called a liar."

I could tell the judge was enjoying this questioning. At the conclusion of the testimony, the judge said he would take an hour to digest the evidence and then come out and report his decision. When he returned he ruled against us, finding that under the bankruptcy law the filing negated the attempted rescission of the merger agreement. His order not only complimented my efforts, but also concluded that much of the evidence presented by the Florida company was unreliable. However, he felt compelled by the bankruptcy rules to rule against us. Great words from a good judge, but a bad result. Before we left the Tampa courthouse one of the new investors in the Florida company cornered me to discuss how we might keep the St. Paul operation in business under his new management. After everything was resolved, we were able to essentially keep the St. Paul collections operation going as a new entity working with the new Florida investors.

A most fitting epilogue to this story was information that I received about two years later out of Florida. The totally unscrupulous Mafioso lawyer, that I battled head to head with for a two days, was being prosecuted in Florida criminal court for sexual abuse of a minor. With an Internet follow-up I found that he had been convicted, sentenced to jail, and lost his license to practice law. Oh, what sweet revenge!

CHAPTER 31

DEPOSITIONS IN LONDON

As defense lawyers on an hourly payroll with insurance companies, we were always looking for opportunities for out-of-state depositions requiring airplane travel at the expense of the insurance company. Usually it required convincing some claims adjuster that the trip was truly necessary. The adjuster would almost always inquire if we could contract with a lawyer in the deposition city who could attend the deposition and represent our client at less than the cost of an airline ticket. I would then offer, in my most convincing manner, my usual self-serving response that the case was so complicated, or of such magnitude, that my personal presence was definitely needed.

I do not remember all of the cities I visited over the years, but there were many. Back in my early defense years, Western Airlines (long gone out of existence) flew between Minneapolis and California and allowed for a stopover at any place in between without any additional charge. This created great opportunities during ski season. Several times, on the way to California for a Friday or

Monday deposition, I would pack my skis and stop in Salt Lake City for two days on the great Utah ski hills. On trips to warm-weather places I would always take my running shoes and find interesting places for a run, such as around the college campuses at Stanford, UCLA, and Harvard.

Two such deposition trips were especially memorable. In the first, a serious northern Minnesota sawmill case required a deposition in Alaska. Having grown up working on my father's sawmill, I knew everything about the operation. My client was a typical, small-time owner of a junky little sawmill operating out in the woods north of Duluth. This sawmill, just like my dad's, had moving belts and pulleys and unprotected saw blades, all within easy reach of the workers on the mill. On my dad's sawmill, to get into my edgerman's work area, I had to step over an unprotected, whirling belt. It tore my pants several times when I did not step high enough. Even if the federal government's OSHA standards had been in effect then, no Minnesota sawmill was ever inspected for work-safety compliance. By today's standards, this kind of sawmill would be shut down on an inspector's first visit.

Among my client's sawmill crew was a young man, probably eighteen years old. He had little work experience and was assigned to catch and pile the lumber at the back end of the sawmill. He had a question, and he walked up toward the boss man (my future client), who was the sawer, or the main man on the sawmill. With the loud diesel engine running next to him, the young man leaned forward over a spinning pulley to talk to the sawer. This particular pulley had some studs extending out of it, and they caught the fellow's jacket, whipping him over and around the spinning pulley. He somehow survived, but with devastating injuries, including several internal injuries and the amputation of both of his arms above the elbow.

The resulting lawsuit was against the out-of-state sawmill

manufacturer, the owner of the land on which the accident occurred, and my client, who owned the sawmill. By the time the lawsuit got going my client had packed up his sawmill and moved his operation to Seward, Alaska. The lawyers involved, including the plaintiff's lawyer, were all good guys. Early on we all concurred that we would have to go up to Seward to take my client's deposition. It obviously would have been far more economical to fly my client back to Minnesota than for four lawyers to fly to Alaska and spend several days of billable time. But a trip to Alaska—with the potential for big-time fishing—was a must on this case. Considering the severity of the plaintiff's injuries, it was no problem to convince the insurance company of the need for me to take this trip.

Several months of planning went into this Seward deposition. Most of that planning was related to finding the best time for halibut, salmon, and trout fishing. The deposition in Seward was clearly important for all parties, but it took no more than two hours to complete. The next morning we left on our chartered halibut-fishing trip out on the ocean. We caught our limit of halibut, the largest being eighty-five pounds. We then drove back to Anchorage to start our five-day fly-in salmon and rainbow trout trip. Being a good, honest defense lawyer, I only billed the insurance company for transportation and real time spent on work, with the rest on my own nickel. The case eventually settled, with an appropriate lifetime annuity for the injured plaintiff.

Some lawyers have the good fortune of taking depositions in foreign countries. My most memorable trip was to London. I don't remember the specifics of the case, but it involved claims of several million dollars in fraud against insurance agents in Minnesota. I was representing one of the main defendants. After several months of investigation and depositions with two other defense attorneys, we concluded that insurance brokers at the home office of Lloyd's of London had sufficient knowledge about the fraud, without appropriate intervention, that Lloyd's should be brought into the lawsuit as an additional defendant. Again, because of the multimillion-dollar claims, it was a no-brainer that we had to go to London to complete depositions of several Lloyd's brokers.

When there is more than one defendant in a case, the attorneys for the defendants usually submit cross-claims against each other, frequently relying on the paltry claim that if my client is at fault, so is yours, and you should pay part of the damages. Even though these defense combatants are fighting against each other, the combined common goal is still to shut out the plaintiff. In this case there were three of us in that boat, each representing a possible defendant liable for some or all of the plaintiffs' damages, but also united in our attempt to pass the liability off to these Lloyd's brokers. One of the defense attorneys, who has remained a good friend since this trip, was a good lawyer named Boyd Ratchye. Boyd was a Harvard Law graduate who belonged to the Harvard Club in New York. Through that connection he made arrangements for hotel space for all of us Minnesotans at a London establishment called the East India, Devonshire, Sports and Public Schools' Club. This place was most memorable. It was a private club on St. James Square, located about one block from the Queen Mother's private dwelling and within easy walking distance of Buckingham Palace. We arrived to turmoil and armed guards stationed across the square from the club. We found out that the building across the square was the Iranian embassy, where someone had been assassinated the prior week in a racial attack. That was a bit unnerving. But the doorman at the East India Club was most cordial in ushering us through check-in and assuring us of our security.

The East India Club was old English all the way. Men were required to wear jackets and ladies to wear skirts at breakfast. The heavy, wood-paneled bar required jackets and was off-limits to the ladies. One afternoon after depositions I went down to the bar, then occupied by several meticulously dressed, elderly businessmen. I was appropriately dressed in suit and tie. Stuffy but lively conversation ensued. I grossly exaggerated the merits of my lawsuit and my need for cocktails with these gentlemen. Their credentials were impressive. The one I remember was the CEO of Phillips Petroleum for Europe. With the assistance of several scotches and my unflagging bravado, I fit in, just like one of the boys.

Boyd had arranged for the depositions to be held in a conference room in the basement of the East India Club. It was a small, windowless room with a steady supply of coffee and water. The only problem was that during that era in England everyone smoked, and smoked heavily. Each of the Lloyd's witnesses smoked constantly, which from my standpoint kept the depositions as short as possible. One of our defense lawyers sat through the first deposition, as Boyd and I did the bulk of the questioning. The next day this chap took off for the rest of the week to visit his relatives in Ireland. No doubt he billed his client for five days of depositions and made sure they never saw a transcript that showed his lack of appearance as counsel of record.

Depositions seldom go all day and almost never go into the evening. Thus, we spent many hours sightseeing and touring London. After work, our first stop was always a pub for a pint or two. We saw all of the main sites of London while doing a decent job completing the depositions.

Given the opportunity of a free trip to London, taking an extra week for vacation travel seemed in order. We had taken our own court reporters with us for the depositions. The husband of one of the lucky court reporters was a good friend of mine. So my wife and I planned with the two of them to rent a car and travel throughout England for the next week. In our week we traveled to Oxford University, to Stratford-upon-Avon to see a great

Shakespeare play, and to Bath to see the Roman ruins. With a bit of careful concentration, driving on the wrong side of the road and navigating the round-abouts, returned the rental car unscathed.

Vacation aside, this trip was very worthwhile from a business standpoint. The depositions of the Lloyd's brokers were beneficial, and the case eventually settled with an appropriate contribution to settlement from the Lloyd's brokers. I could feel absolutely no guilt about the pleasure of those hours of work in London.

CHAPTER 32

RENT-A-CENTER

We have all heard about loan sharks who extract exorbitant rates of interest from borrowers in times of their distress. *Godfather*-type tactics still exist to enforce late or missed loan payments. What is most distressing is that the guy doing the borrowing is usually in dire financial straits, badly in need of cash or credit and with no power to negotiate on payback interest rates. Historically, the legislatures and courts of our country have tried to protect consumers who must borrow money for personal or business reasons. Unfortunately the neediest folks suffer the most. Excessive rates of interest are called usury, and usury laws exist to put a cap on the interest rates lenders can charge to their borrowers.

One needs little background in math to understand the meaning of an annual percentage rate of 15 percent. If you borrow $1,000, you will be required to pay back $1,150. Most troublesome are the lenders who sell borrowed money in obscure and complex transactions where the eventual interest rate is vastly greater than anticipated. The legal world of consumer protection simply does not have enough lawyer power to challenge these usurious tactics. Most often it is the little guy who is the victim without a remedy.

This gets us to Rent-A-Center, a national company that is for the most part set up to extract hidden and extremely usurious interest from the low-income customers their business attracts. The concept behind the Rent-A-Center business is what is commonly called rent-to-own. For example, say a hardworking family needs a new television. The family members' credit ratings are too low to open credit cards or to buy the television from Sears or Ward's on a payment plan. Rent-A-Center gives these folks the chance to take home the television immediately for what appears to be a modest monthly payment. Little or no favorable credit history is required. They sign a contract whereby after making thirty-six monthly payments they will automatically become the owner of that television, free and clear of any further obligation. The contract has all kinds of penalties for late payments and gives Rent-A-Center the right to literally come into the home and repossess the items for nonpayment. What is not disclosed to the customer, who thinks the modest monthly payment is wonderful, is that over the full thirty-six month term the interest rate is huge. The customer will have paid something like $800 for a television sold at Sears for $400; interest rates of 100 percent or more are not uncommon.

Our firm got involved with Rent-A-Center in an effort to assist Legal Aid lawyers in their claims of usury against the company. Another law firm and ours agreed to share work and any eventual legal fees on an equal three-way arrangement with Legal Aid. I ended up being lead counsel in the battle that ensued. The lawsuit was going to be a class action on behalf of several years' worth of Rent-A-Center customers. Our class plaintiffs were two black ladies who had each had been burned in several transactions with Rent-A-Center. The lawsuit alleged several consumer protection claims, including usury, but also a RICO claim. RICO, or the Racketeer Influenced and Corrupt Organization Act, is a federal statute enacted originally, as the name suggests, to attack Mafia-type racketeering. But because of some broad statutory drafting, lawyers across the country began applying RICO in civil litigation where two or more parties were acting in collusion against another party's interest. RICO claims were creeping into all kinds of lawsuits. I remember at one point reading an article entitled "RICO, RICO, Everywhere." What was perhaps most appealing about a RICO claim was that it allowed for the recovery of treble damages, or three times the amount of damages that could be proven at trial. With our class action claiming millions in excess interest charges, the prospect of tripling that amount was a big incentive to go full-bore in the lawsuit.

Rent-A-Center's defense team was from the largest law firm in Kansas City. They were formidable opponents, but we clearly held our own. A lot of expense went into expert witnesses to calculate the amounts of the high interest rates. I did have a nice weekend in Palm Beach, Florida, while taking the deposition of one of their experts. I recall an interesting jury response when the defense's expert economist from Palm Beach was on the stand. In reply to one of my cross-examination questions about what he was being paid for his work, he sheepishly admitted to $700 per hour. There were audible gasps from several persons on the jury.

Federal Judge Magnuson was our trial judge. There was one memorable pretrial motion hearing where my co-counsel got royally reamed out by the judge. In federal court they have a page limit, a maximum of around thirty-five pages, on legal briefs submitted on motions. My colleague's first draft on some pretrial motion issues was something like fifty pages in length. The substance was pretty good, but it was obviously in need of some severe editing to get within the page limit. I reminded him to keep the brief under thirty-five pages. Feeling very proud of all fifty pages, instead of editing out fifteen pages he had reduced the type size and added the same material in footnotes on almost every page. On some pages, more than half a page was in a footnote. I distinctly remember telling him that the court might not like it. He went ahead and filed it. And when my colleague stood up to present his substantive oral argument before Judge Magnuson, the judge laid into him for the excess footnotes in the brief. His law clerk had found some circuit court case on point criticizing excess footnotes, and the judge quoted at length from the authority. The tongue-lashing went on for several minutes. Towards the end my colleague was literally shaking at the podium. The judge calmed down finally and politely said, "All right, let's hear your argument." How's that for a lead-in to a very important legal argument?

The trial was big-time and took two weeks. Every day the courtroom was full of interested Rent-A-Center customers. I handled almost all of the questioning, cross-examination, and arguments. Towards the end of the second week we felt quite good about our chances. We put a lot of time into the preparation of the jury instructions and the written verdict form, in particular because of the complexity of submitting the RICO issues to the jury. The final verdict form to be presented to the jury had a total of sixty-eight questions. We didn't need favorable answers to all of the questions, as we could win on any of several different theories, including different options on the RICO claims. The problem was this: The jury was told that if they answered the first two questions "No," they did not need to answer the other sixty-six questions.

The timing could not have been worse. Closing arguments started on Friday morning of the second week of trial. I followed the defense attorney and argued for over an hour and a half without using any notes. Afterwards I received more accolades than I had ever received following a closing argument. By the time the judge finished his complicated and lengthy instructions, it was about three o'clock in the afternoon. The death knell for our case came when the judge told the jury they could deliberate until four-thirty, and if they hadn't reached a verdict then they would have to return the following Monday to start a third week of their jury service. As we sat around the courtroom for that last hour and a half, I knew we were sunk. As anticipated, the jury came back at 4:25 and handed in their verdict with questions one and two both answered "No." No matter how sympathetic our poor clients were, and how great a case I tried, there was no way that jury was coming back on Monday to answer sixty-eight tough questions. Sometimes things other than the merits of your case dictate the results.

Even though this jury trial eliminated part of the Rent-A-Center claims, several additional issues worth several million dollars were yet to be decided. Before reaching those issues I had made the decision to leave the Lommen, Nelson firm to go out on my own. The Rent-A-Center case stayed at the law firm. Some two years later, after favorable rulings from Federal Judge Michael Davis, a victory was declared for the plaintiffs. The class members received some reimbursement of their overcharged interest, and the lawyers divided up a substantial fee. For all of my hard work on the case, I did not share in the rewards.

CHAPTER 33

MARY—THE ELECTROCUTION CASE

In any lawyer's career there is a client who can never be forgotten. Mary is mine. In 1987, two lawyer friends from Mankato, Minnesota, called and explained their involvement in a double wrongful death case arising out of an electrocution of two high school teachers. They explained their potential conflict in representing the families of both of the decedents when there might be claims of negligence brought against one decedent by the family of the other decedent. I hesitantly agreed to look at the case. The facts disclosed that the two young schoolteachers, each in their mid-twenties, had been painting farm buildings during their summer break from teaching. The two teachers were working on a three-story farmhouse outside of Chaska, painting the building while using a long, aluminum extension ladder. While both young men were maneuvering the ladder, a gust of wind blew it into a 7,200-volt power line, resulting in their immediate electrocution. The lawyers' theory was that the power line, installed years before by the local cooperative power company, was too close to the three-story farm building. Before accepting the case for one of the families, I told my Mankato friends I wanted to look carefully at the farmhouse and the location of the power line.

I will never forget this trip to the death scene. On a nice spring day I drove west of Chaska and found the gravel road leading to the farmhouse. The farmstead was located alone on the south side of the gravel road with a few farm buildings further south, bordering the cornfields. The farmhouse dominated the farmstead. As I drove closer I saw the bare power line traveling south from the gravel road, close to and past the west side of the house toward the other farm buildings. As I gazed on this scene my overriding impression was, "Why did they run the power line so close to the house? There were many safer alternative routes!" My second thought was, "I can win this case; that power line is way too close!"

After I agreed to get involved, my Mankato friends gave me Mary's case. This was the bigger potential damage case but the one with more complications. Since the other widow had been first to come to them, they felt obligated to handle that death case. With some trepidation they explained the problems with Mary's case. On the surface it looked great. Mary's husband was a bright, good-looking, prominent teacher. He and Mary, also a teacher, had two young children, J. and A., then ages four and two. Mary had suffered psychologically since this horrible tragedy. The Mankato lawyers recommended that I meet my new client in her psychiatrist's office, where she would have immediate support in adjusting to the change of attorneys. I arranged a meeting at the office; when I met her there she was curled in the fetal position in a beanbag chair. Hardly able to make eye contact or respond to a greeting, Mary laid there as her loyal psychiatrist tried to explain my involvement in her legal case. Whatever we lawyers may hope for in client relations, this was at the far deep end. It took months before Mary was comfortable with me and willing to trust me in representing her and her children's issues.

Because Mary's case had a greater magnitude than the case being handled by the Mankato lawyers, I soon took over as lead counsel. After numerous depositions and the involvement of expert witness, the case went to trial in Shakopee, Minnesota, before Judge Eugene Adkins (the same Adkins who was the plaintiff's lawyer in the Chinese murder case). Our trial judge, recently appointed to the bench, felt the only way to try a lawsuit was to start at 8:00 a.m. and work until 6:00 p.m. or later. This trial schedule is fine if you are working at an hourly rate, but really grueling for a plaintiff's lawyer. This three-week trial was about as tough as anything I have done as a trial lawyer. The case, however, gave me some wonderful memories.

The co-op's lawyer was a very bright, methodical guy who never missed an opportunity to establish and preserve his record for a future appeal. During the trial, Mary sat behind the rail, away from us trial lawyers at my insistence. From that position, without my soothing and quieting hand, Mary loudly voiced her objections to any adverse argument or testimony presented by the defense. Even with admonitions from me and Judge Adkins, Mary did not slow her running commentary on the trial. Because of Mary's erratic conduct and verbal outbursts, the defense attorney asked Judge Adkins for a mistrial sixteen times, by my count. With appropriate restraint, the judge repeatedly denied the new trial motions.

Because of my first and very favorable impression of the power line being too close to the house, I requested that we take the jury out to the farm site for a viewing of the accident scene. A short digression is warranted here. Early on as a defense lawyer I learned the great advantage of a jury viewing of an accident scene. I was defending the City of Bloomington for an injury occurring during an adult education course at Lincoln High School. A woman attending a golf class in the recreation room at the high school had fallen and seriously fractured her wrist. She and her lawyer claimed that the floor was slippery. In the preparation for the defense of the case I visited the recreation room and found the floor to be a rubberized surface and anything but slippery. During the trial I requested, and the judge agreed, to take the jury to the school to view the scene of the accident.

I hired a bus to transport the jury, judge, clerk, court reporter, and lawyers out to the scene. Appropriately, the judge instructed the jurors to view only the premises and not discuss their viewing or ask questions of the judge or lawyers. As we departed the bus and entered the school, we found hallways filled with smoke and firefighters dragging fire hoses about. It seems some wise-acre student had started a paper fire in another student's locker, causing the fire alarm and evacuation. Well, after parting the waves of smoke and convincing the school administration of our legitimate purpose in being there, our group found the recreation room. Much to my pleasure and the chagrin of the plaintiff's lawyer, the jurors entered the recreation room and immediately began scuffing their feet on the rubberized floor. To a person, they all found the floor to be not slippery at all. As much as the plaintiff's lawyer would later argue and protest, this viewing of the scene was the best possible evidence for the jury. Needless to say, I won this defense case.

Back to the power line viewing. After the judge granted my request to view the scene, the defense lawyer acknowledged, for the first time, that his cooperative power company, since the deaths, had been out to the farm and had raised the power line so it now was in a higher location than on the day of the deaths. Even with this late disclosure, I convinced the judge that the scene viewing was still important to show how close the line ran to the house and that the raised line was evidence of the safe height at which it should have been maintained by the power company in the first place. Just as at Lincoln High School, this viewing by the jury was critical. With the wide-open spaces around the farmstead the jurors saw the many safer alternatives for the placement of the line. Also, after being advised of the post-accident change of the line's height, the jury could easily visualize how much more dangerous a lower line would have been when the teachers were painting the farmhouse.

In a case of this type, expert testimony is critical. We had three excellent experts testifying that the co-op was negligent in the location and maintenance of its power line. As is usual, these experts cost us plaintiff's lawyers many thousands of dollars on a questionable case. The more interesting part was the defense's hired-gun experts. Both had been brought in from Chicago by the defendant power company. One defense expert, one Dr. Armington, a PhD in electrical engineering, had testified in many prior electrocution cases, often as an expert against power companies. With a little background checking I obtained several transcripts of past deposition and trial testimony from this electrical expect. One of our contentions was that the power company had failed to put safety inserts in their monthly electric bills, thus failing to repeatedly advise consumers about the danger of high-voltage power lines. Dr. Armington testified at trial that this was not negligence on the part of the power company and that it had no duty to provide such inserts. In two of his prior testimonies, however, when working on the other side in plaintiff electrocution cases, this high-powered expert had given exactly the opposite opinion, that it was negligence for a power company not to include these safety inserts. As a trial lawyer, I felt like a kid in a candy store. But one does not want to jump in too quickly for the kill. Drag it out and give the witness a lot of extra rope to hang himself. And indeed he did!

He was not the defense's only memorable expert. Triodyne, Inc., a very large, reputable engineering firm from Chicago, supplies many kinds of engineering experts, principally to defendants who can afford their outrageous fees. When it came to trial, none of the low-level engineers would appear as a testifying expert, but Dr. Ralph Barnett, the president and founder of Triodyne, agreed to be the company representative at trial. No matter which of the Triodyne engineers might have done the workup on a case, it always somehow gravitated to Dr. Barnett to appear at trial, and he would testify as though fully conversant with all the issues in the case. Of course, in his direct defense testimony this smooth-talking engineer discounted and rejected all of our theories.

Again, having done my homework on Barnett's background, I found a paper he had written for an engineering seminar entitled something like "How to be a good expert witness." Believing himself to be quite a humorous writer and speaker, Barnett ridiculed lawyers throughout the article and playfully suggested to his readers things like "How not to answer a question with a straight answer" and "How to be evasive and frustrate the opposing lawyer." With Barnett's article in hand, once again my cross-examination was a real delight. After reading a phrase from his article to him and the jury, I would ask, "Is this how you have been answering questions here before this jury?" Glancing at our trial judge, I could tell he was really enjoying these putdowns of the mighty Mr. Barnett. The judge let me go for ten minutes or so and then called us to the bench. With a smile on his face he said something like "Stageberg, you've done enough damage, so let's move on."

The damage case for Mary and her two children was challenging. How could we best present this very troubled woman and her losses to the jury? A wrongful death case in Minnesota is carefully controlled by state law and rules. We do not try to put a value on the deceased person. The damage standard is to show what has been taken away from the survivors in economic losses and noneconomic losses relating to the love, guidance, care, comfort, and so forth that would have been provided to the surviving family had the death not occurred. Mary, with her severe psychological problems, would be a sympathetic witness but emotionally unable to testify to many of the losses suffered by her and her children. Another restriction on wrongful death damages is that no amount can be awarded for the grief and sorrow suffered by the survivors. To get around this, I convinced Mary's psychiatrist to be our key damage witness. Records indicated that Mary had lots of psychological problems before she was widowed. The death of her husband added greatly to her dysfunction and inability to cope with reality. With the psychiatrist's help we shifted the emphasis from Mary's grief to describing how her decline after her husband's death showed how important he had been to maintaining her stability. The catchphrase we coined was, "Michael was the glue that held Mary together." Presenting the psychiatrist's testimony this way fell within the acceptable rules of showing the importance of the deceased to the surviving spouse. (When the power company later appealed, this type of damage testimony was approved by the appellate court and established a good precedent for future wrongful death cases.)

After three weeks of trial the case went to the jury. The surprises were not over yet. I had strongly urged that Mary and her two children remain with me and the other widow and her lawyers at the courthouse until the jury returned with the verdict. It is an old lawyer's trick to keep your damaged client around the courthouse so that when jurors come and go for lunch or breaks they will see the worried client eagerly awaiting their verdict. I like to tell my clients that if the jury is going to shut you out, make them look you in the eye when they reject your claim. When our jury did not reach its verdict the first afternoon, they were sent home and scheduled to resume deliberations the following morning. I similarly sent Mary and her kids home with clear instructions to be back in the morning, before the jury returned, so they would see us again, waiting in the courthouse for the verdict. The next morning arrived, but no Mary and kids. My phone calls could not locate her.

Sometime during that next day the jury brought in its verdict. The power company was found 58.4 percent negligent and each schoolteacher 20.8 percent negligent. Damages of $850,000 were awarded to the other spouse and family and $1,112,650 to Mary and her children. A clear victory! But where was Mary, and how could I share this joy and excitement with her? Several days later, Mary and the kids surfaced and the story she told is almost unbelievable. This verdict was very large and so noteworthy at the time that it was written up the next day in a big article on the front page of the Minneapolis paper. Mary's name and the amount of the verdict were discussed in the article. Because of the unbearable stress of waiting for the verdict, Mary had taken her kids and had driven a hundred miles north and stayed in a Holiday Inn in Brainerd, Minnesota. At breakfast the next day, Mary paid the cashier with a personal check. The cashier looked at the name on the check and said, "Congratulations." Mary asked what she was talking about. The cashier said she just read about her in the paper and that she was now a millionaire.

Mary's sad saga was far from over. Mary was never really happy about the verdict, as she repeatedly said it could never replace Michael. We carefully set up annuity programs for Mary and the children with their portions of the damage award. With careful planning, Mary and her children were made financially secure for life. Unfortunately, Mary still had major psychological problems requiring repeated hospitalizations, psychiatric care, and medication. I kept in touch with Mary and her children for many years, giving legal advice and encouragement when needed. It became an annual ritual for me to deliver Christmas presents for Mary and the kids. Mary tried different teaching jobs but always seemed to find ways of misbehaving so as to not have a contract renewed for a second teaching year. She also got into as many car accidents as jobs. My contact with the family decreased as the kids reached adulthood. Last I heard from Mary, however, she remarried and is happily getting along. Her son J. finished college and went on to law school.

An interesting postscript is needed. With the negligence percentages of 58.4, 20.8 and 20.8, the trial judge ruled that each plaintiff's recovery would be reduced by the 41.6 percent negligence of the both decedents, i.e., each plaintiff would receive 58.4 percent of the damages awarded them by the jury. When the power company appealed to the Court of Appeals, raising all kinds of issues and demanding a new trial, we cross-appealed, contending that the trial judge miscalculated and that each death case award should be reduced only by the individual decedent's 20.8 percent negligence. We won the appeal, not only winning on all of the power company issues but also convincing the appellate court on our cross-appeal. Thus, the end result was a happy recovery of 79.2 percent of the verdict damages in each death case. The appellate decision is found at 392 N.W.2d 709 (Minn. App. 1986). I wish Mary could have really understood what a great job we did for her.

CHAPTER 34

DYING WITH YOUR BOOTS ON

In chapters of this memoir I have expounded on my very favorable relationship with my senior partner of many years, John Lommen. Although eighteen years my senior, he conversed frequently with me, and we laughed often about business and nonbusiness issues. He was the one and only mentor in my legal career. I admired him as a superb trial lawyer, a patient and understanding law firm leader, and a personal friend. Every good thing must come to an end, however, and our relationship ended dramatically in a courtroom in April of 1987.

For some three years John and I had been working on the biggest single defense case in our law firm. We were defending the Japanese conglomerate Mitsubishi in a product liability airplane crash case. In addition to cars and television sets, Mitsubishi manufactured airplanes. One of their main models was called the MU-2. This high-performance twin-engine turbo-prop plane was certified by the FAA for single-pilot operation. That is, it did not need a copilot. It was a very fast aircraft and a favorite of busy corporate executives who liked the freedom of flying their own planes and getting places in a hurry. Being an "executive hot-rod," as the type was sometimes called, the MU-2 required skillful piloting to stay in the air.

Every airplane has an envelope of safe operation. This is a combination of several elements including speed, altitude, air pressure, and carrying weight, all of which are calculated into the safe operating range of the aircraft. If a pilot operates outside of the envelope, bad things can happen very quickly, like losing control and heading for the ground. As the MU-2 was a high-speed, high-performance aircraft, it had a quite narrow envelope of safe operation. As could be expected, high-powered corporate executives who liked the MU-2 often lacked the training and experience of professional pilots. As a result, the MU-2 had a bad track record of accidents, especially with corporate execs in the pilot seat.

The MU-2 involved in our case was owned and operated by a wealthy Minneapolis corporate executive named Held. He ran beef processing plants that sold meat products to supermarkets and restaurants. He had huge cattle ranches in several states. Someone said that between land he owned and the land he leased, he controlled one tenth of Nevada's real estate. One winter's day Mr. Held was flying his MU-2 from Fargo, North Dakota, back to a suburban Twin Cities airport at Crystal. Several miles short of the runway assigned for Held's landing, the MU-2 crashed, killing all aboard. Accompanying Mr. Held on this fateful flight were his two sons, the fiancée of one son, and the company book-keeper. The primary plaintiff in the following lawsuits was Mrs. Held, who had tragically lost her husband and two sons. Several lawsuits were commenced alleging that product liability defects in the MU-2 and not pilot error had caused the crash. Mitsubishi's primary attorneys were from New York City. They had contacted John Lommen because of his past aviation trial work and retained our firm as local counsel. As the case developed, I ended up doing most of the trial preparation with consultation and help from John and the New York lawyers.

The plaintiffs' product liability theory was interesting. Weather conditions near the Crystal airport on the day of the crash had been conducive to icing on airborne craft. Ice accumulating on the wings, fuselage, and tail sections of an aircraft destroys the aerodynamics of the aircraft, as air can no longer pass smoothly over the important parts that keep the plane aloft. When there is added weight (*drag* is the technical term) on the aircraft from the ice and the airflow over the wings and tail is disrupted by uneven iced surfaces, the plane's envelope of safe operating conditions narrows. With a load of ice and a narrowed operating envelope, it becomes very difficult for the pilot to keep the plane aloft, especially in a high-performance craft like the MU-2. For obvious reasons, pilots try to avoid weather conditions where ice may develop.

It was the plaintiffs' claim that Mr. Held had piloted his MU-2 into unexpected icing conditions, and when ice covered the rear horizontal stabilizer (the tail), its poor design reduced the plane's envelope to such an extent that the plane could not be kept aloft by any pilot, inexperienced or experienced. The plaintiffs' chief design expert was an aeronautical engineer from Stanford. He had prepared a mockup of the horizontal stabilizer and conducted wind-tunnel tests to demonstrate the faulty design. With many complex calculations he concluded that only a quarter inch of ice on the horizontal stabilizer destined the MU-2 to crash. This was going to be tough testimony from a well-qualified academic. Of course, our team of experts challenged the design theory as well as the claim of significant icing conditions in the area.

One interesting bit of investigation that I pursued related to the weather and claimed icing conditions. I gathered the transcripts of the air-traffic controllers at several Twin Cities airports for the hours surrounding the time of the Held crash. Air-traffic controllers identify aircraft by their SN, or serial number, when talking to pilots. With the SN numbers I was able to request from the FAA the names and addresses of the owners of five or six private planes flying in the vicinity of Crystal airport around the time of Held's crash. With a series of phone calls I located and interviewed the pilots of those planes and gathered statements of their recollection of the amount of ice on their planes. Two of the pilots I contacted turned out to be flight instructors who had flown that afternoon with the express purpose of finding icing conditions as training for their student pilots. The planes involved were all smaller and much slower planes than the MU-2 and thus much more likely to gather quantities of ice. All of my witnesses described little or no ice on their planes and certainly not a quarter inch or more. On a wall-sized blowup of an aviation chart of the Crystal airport and surroundings I plotted the location of each of these pilot witnesses at the time of the crash. Coming from totally disinterested witnesses, this seemed to be a very powerful contradiction to plaintiffs' icing theory.

With an unlimited defense budget from Mitsubishi and good companion attorneys from New York, the case preparation was a lot of fun. We made several trips to the Mitsubishi aircraft plant in San Angelo, Texas, in part to learn how the MU-2 was assembled and tested. We also found absolutely the best Texas-size grilled steaks at San Angelo restaurants. As we approached trial, New York counsel decided that we attorneys and all of our experts needed a retreat to review the issues and our trial preparation. The chosen location was a swank resort in Scottsdale, Arizona. The meetings were very useful, but we also ate and drank well and even played a couple rounds of golf.

The case was scheduled to be tried before Federal Judge Harry McLaughlin in Minneapolis. Several weeks before trial I was nominated to give the opening statement for the defense. For me this was an exciting opportunity in a major-league case. I began my preparation early. Unfortunately, events intervened. I ended up having to try two Minnesota state court cases back-to-back, ending only a day or two before the Held case commenced. With those complications, I had insufficient time to do the final prep for the Held opening statement. In consultation with New York counsel, it was agreed that John would do the opening. He willingly concurred, and I spent several hours prepping him.

With his experience, John Lommen was totally capable of doing the opening and becoming lead counsel at trial. John had tried lawsuits for over thirty-five years. He was one of the old-time lawyers who tried cases every week, often with only a few hours of preparation. His reputation among Minnesota lawyers was outstanding. He was often called The Barracuda because of his aggressive courtroom cross-examinations. Yet outside of the courtroom he was always congenial and fun-loving, even with opposing counsel. He told great stories of the early days, when lawyers from both sides and often the trial judge would meet in a saloon after a day's trial. My only hesitation in turning the opening statement over to John was that he had been recently devoting more time to office management and had not tried a full jury trial for over four years. But at age sixty he still appeared up to the challenge and ready to go.

The Held jury trial was projected to take up to two months to try to a conclusion. The morning the trial began, our trial team walked the six blocks in the skyway to the federal courthouse. John was quiet that morning, and he asked the young New York associate to carry his briefcase. John lagged a few paces behind us all the way through the skyways. In the courtroom, the federal judge quickly picked the jury and the five plaintiff attorneys began their opening statements. At the noon break, John again was somewhat subdued and quiet, but not enough to cause anyone concern. The last plaintiff's opening statement ended a little before 3:00 p.m. Then John got up and began his opening. In classic Barracuda style his delivery was polished and forceful. Adding to John's impressive delivery were the half-reading glasses propped on the end of his nose. About half an hour into his presentation, John was using a pointer to trace the path of the MU-2 on my wall-sized aviation chart. He unexpectedly paused, laid the pointer down, politely said to the jury, "Excuse me," and fell to the floor.

I was seated six feet from John and was the first to reach him. He was on his back, his eyes rolled upward. As I knelt beside him on the floor, my first thought, which I will never forget, was "My best friend is dead."

To digress a moment: John's sudden collapse at age sixty was not totally unexpected to me. John smoked and drank heavily through many of his early years. He was so social that rounds of cocktails till quitting time were routine. Recognizing his drinking problem, John had quit cold turkey before age fifty. He first had tried drinking only wine, but he soon gave that up and switched to Perrier. For at least ten years John had neither smoked nor touched a drop of liquor, but he was overweight and exercised little. I knew he had an exercise bike at home but seldom used it. A few months before that fateful day he had an angiogram that showed some cardiac blockages, but none serious enough for surgery. I knew John was concerned about this heart condition, but he wasn't doing much about it. Knowing all that, I was always concerned that my friend John did not have a long life expectancy.

Back to the turmoil in the federal courtroom. Reaching John's side, I began yelling, "Does anyone know CPR?" and "Someone call an ambulance!" The young New York associate was a former lifeguard trained in CPR. He rushed forward, and he and I began CPR. Right in front of twelve jurors, the judge, and a full courtroom we tore open John's coat, shirt, and tie and began compressing his chest. In his dying moments John had lost control of his bladder and bowels, so we had quite a mess as we continued our efforts. Judge McLaughlin appeared dumbfounded by these events. I finally got up and went to the judge and requested that he dismiss the shocked and gaping jury. He responded, "Oh yeah, I will do that." The paramedics arrived, and before carting John to an ambulance they applied electroshock to John's chest. Nothing happened. From the moment John hit the ground, not a glimmer of life showed through all of the lifesaving efforts.

I rode in the ambulance for the short trip to Hennepin County Medical Center. All efforts at resuscitation by the attendants appeared futile. At the hospital, John disappeared for more lifesaving efforts. I then had the unpleasant task of delivering the bad news in a call to the law firm and also to John's lovely wife, Betty. I couldn't tell Betty what I thought, only that something serious had happened to John in court and that she should come immediately to the hospital. Betty, other family members, and my law partners arrived. About six o'clock or so, a doctor came out with the news that John had not made it. No surprise to me, as I had known that three hours earlier, within seconds of when John hit the floor.

I stumbled back to the office to find many lawyers and staff still present, some openly crying. Several lawyers with more practical and less emotional responses questioned what would happen to our law firm with its leader and major business producer suddenly gone. As we sat around the conference table, not really knowing what to do next, I went and retrieved a bottle of scotch that John had kept for a dozen or more years in one of his office cabinets. I proposed to lawyers and staff alike that it would be appropriate for all to toast our fallen leader with a shot from his personal bottle. With tears in our eyes we raised a goodbye toast to John Lommen.

The day after this devastating event, we received a call from Judge McLaughlin that he wanted us back in his courtroom at nine o'clock the next morning. Not knowing what to expect, my New York counsel and I appeared before Judge McLaughlin. This turned out to be one of the most distasteful and traumatic events in my legal career, and I will hate this judge literally till I die, hopefully long after he does. We arrived and the judge took us back into his chambers. Without a moment of sorrow or compassion for our personal loss, he launched into a brusque speech on how he wanted this case settled or we would proceed to finish the trial, starting again the next morning. He was obviously irritated with me for taking over his courtroom as he had sat speechless and stunned behind his desk. His exact words were, "We will start this trial tomorrow morning and you [dramatically pointing at me] will try this case." Remarkably, he said that we would use the same jury (the members of which were obviously traumatized and in no way able to provide a fair trial to either side). He said he had assigned his magistrate to spend all day talking settlement with both sides. He perfunctorily dismissed us to a private conference room and said he was next going to talk to the plaintiffs' attorneys.

We retired to the conference room, and before the judge's settlement magistrate arrived I broke down in tears in front of my New York friends. I told them that I did not believe I could start trial the next morning under these conditions. Conservative settlement offers had always been under the control of New York counsel, but these circumstances seemed to greatly change the equation. New York counsel relayed to Mitsubishi that the case was going to go to trial the next morning with their lead trial counsel an emotional wreck.

I must now relate what else happened that morning with Judge McLaughlin, an event later disclosed to me by the plaintiffs' lawyers. As background, the two lead plaintiffs' lawyers had always had a friendly and respectful relationship with John and me. They were deeply saddened by John's death. After calling us in and saying, in no uncertain terms, that trial would proceed the next morning with the same jury, the judge had given the plaintiffs' attorneys a completely different scenario. He told them that we could not use the same jury because of the traumatic events and that the trial of this case would be delayed three months or more for a new trial setting. He strongly urged these attorneys and their clients to settle the case with the magistrate that day. Obviously this judge had seen an opportunity to dispose of a big case and was not above lying to experienced lawyers and their clients. The judge's magistrate had also been enlisted in his mission to force a settlement that day.

The leading plaintiff, Mrs. Held, was a beautiful, sophisticated lady. John and Mrs. Held had created a friendly relationship, or at least a mutual respect for each other, due in part to John's personal charm and real compassion. When John went down in the courtroom, Mrs. Held, who had already lost three family members, went into hysterics. I vividly recall her screaming in horror at the events happening some thirty feet before her.

Mediation by a federal magistrate often is successful in settling cases. Before the magistrate began his efforts that day, the two sides were many millions of dollars apart. But because of the divergent scenarios the judge had given to each side, both sides' settlement positions changed dramatically. The plaintiffs' lawyers later confided in me that Mrs. Held had said she could not go through this again. Their settlement demands came down by several million. Similarly, after my New York attorneys discussed the situation with the Mitsubishi officials who controlled the purse strings, the previously low settlement offers increased significantly. By five-thirty that afternoon all issues in the case had been settled. The esteemed Judge Harry McLaughlin had seized upon a tragedy for clients and lawyers alike, and with misrepresentations on the trial's status he had manipulated both sides into a settlement to avoid a several-week trial. I will never forget or forgive this judicial impropriety.

A few days later John had a royal send-off in a large memorial service attended by a multitude of judges and respectful attorneys. In no way could I have given any kind of eulogy. My partner, Phil Cole, with a tougher skin than I, said magnificent words about our beloved John. As related in other chapters, the unexpected death of the senior partner in our firm was to greatly change the dynamics of the firm. Had John not suddenly died, I likely would have ended my legal career with Lommen, Nelson, Cole & Stageberg. Ah, how unexpected events out of our control can change our lives.

CHAPTER 35

THE DECISION TO LEAVE

At the end of 1993, I was less than a year away from turning a half-century. I was restless and in need of a change. May could be called a midlife crisis, but that doesn't really fit. D chanted with the status quo would be more appropriate. I now senior partner number four in a forty-two-person law with beautiful offices on the eighteenth and nineteenth floor the IDS tower, the most prominent office building in downto Minneapolis. For several years I had been on the firm's mana ment committee. For several years I had either been the larg annual income producer or close to it, and as a result I enjoye nice salary and annual bonuses. Nice contributions went ann ally to my 401(k) retirement plan. My brother, Roger, with who I had a good relationship, had joined the firm and was headir up a successful corporate-law department.

Doesn't sound like a bad situation for a lawyer to be in, right I recall thinking that I could end my career in fifteen or twent years, having fought exactly the same battles every day to sav

insurance companies some money, and retire with my nice collection of investments. I thought a lot about a seminar I had attended many years before, where the great Wyoming trial lawyer Gerry Spence described facing the same quandary of having a secure career as a defense trial lawyer, but finding something missing. I remember his story as follows: Spence had defended an injury case, successfully convincing a jury to award minimal damages to a lady with a damaged leg. Sometime thereafter he was in a supermarket and watched the same lady limp out with her groceries. They exchanged words, and the lady said something like, "I don't hold it against you, because you were just doing your job." Thereafter Spence gave up the insurance defense practice and began his tremendous career as a plaintiff's injury lawyer. Forgive me, Gerry Spence, if I am somewhat misstating the facts, but this version, which I so strongly remember, helped to drive me out of a stagnant career as an insurance defense lawyer.

The downsides of a decision to leave the firm and its security were significant. My good friend and mentor and the leader of the firm, John Lommen, had died suddenly in April of 1987. John's good-natured attitude towards people and the law practice had created and maintained a most pleasant atmosphere in the firm. After John's death, things changed. Strong personalities clashed as partners asserted management authority. No longer were management and partner meetings fun and lighthearted. The younger lawyers and even the staff showed discontent. My very nice office was on the end of the oval-shaped IDS Center, with the offices of six of the newer partners surrounding it. These were all good trial lawyers with whom I socialized and shared good experiences. Within about three years of John's death, all six were gone. Five left to set up their own firms, and Mike Shroyer died of cancer. The group of people who were fun to practice with was reduced to my secretary, Ruth, my legal assistant, Mark, and my brother. Also, at the urging of partner Phil Cole we had

merged with a six-person firm. From a social standpoint, these new lawyers were not much interested in collegiality, and none of them made any attempts to build a personal friendship with me or, as far as I knew, anyone else. The new lawyers felt that the partner retreats were a waste of firm money, so that much-anticipated social event vanished. Practicing law with this group was no longer much fun.

Since 1983 I had gotten a good taste of representing clients on the other side of litigation. My first million-dollar-plus verdict for the plaintiff's side was in the *Dalhbeck v. Dico* case in 1983. Several large injured plaintiff or wrongful death verdicts followed. Getting these favorable results for clients was a pleasure I had never before experienced. It is a real high to share champagne with clients and law partners after a successful jury verdict. Several of these plaintiff verdicts were so large and of such interest to the community that they were reported in the print and television media. This success gradually had a downside. My insurance company clients showed their lack of true loyalty. After publicity on the plaintiffs' verdicts, I found that defense referrals from the insurance clients were drying up. At one point I discussed this with a good friend who was a senior claims handler at one of our good clients, the St. Paul Companies. I had never lost a trial for this insurance company, and it was one of my best clients. Over lunch I inquired of the claims guy why I was not getting new referrals. He said quite openly that at a meeting the claims manager had directed that no more files go to Stageberg because he was doing plaintiff's work.

Thus, as 1993 came to a close, there were many good reasons to leave the Lommen, Nelson firm. But the agonizing question remained: Could I sustain myself and continue to make a living on my own until retirement? I first interviewed at two prestigious Minneapolis firms. Each would have taken me on as a partner doing their major litigation. But being part of another big firm, with all of its personalities and problems, no longer looked exciting to me. More and more I thought about taking the gamble and going out on my own, trusting that my experience and reputation as a trial lawyer would somehow produce business.

All of the above culminated at Christmas time in 1993. I was on a ski trip in Aspen, Colorado, over the holidays, and the prospect of leaving the firm had been a constant topic of discussion with my wife. We would ride up the chairlift together, discussing on one trip the reasons for leaving and on the next trip up the benefits of staying with the firm. A big issue was the giving up the security of a high salary, a good working staff, health coverage, and the firm-funded 401(k). Departing looked like a major gamble. Sometime in the middle of the week, my wife and I went to a movie at the theater in downtown Aspen. It was the now-classic *Grumpy Old Men*, starring Jack Lemmon, Walter Matthau, and Ann-Margret, about ice fishing in Minnesota. Midway through the movie, Jack Lemmon was debating whether to hustle Ann-Margret, and she said, "I know that the only things in life that you regret are the risks you don't take." About five minutes later in the movie, Jack Lemmon repeats, "The only thing in this life that you regret are the risks that you didn't take." (I have again watched the movie and the quotes are exact.) At that very moment I looked at my wife and said, probably too loud for the rest of the movie audience, "That's it. I am going to make the move."

It may sound kind of corny, but it is the absolute truth that a phrase in that movie was the factor that tipped the scales in my decision to venture out on my own. Somehow that phrase was so significant to me that it changed my whole legal career. I, and probably a multitude of people over the centuries, would have forever regretted not taking the risk of starting out on a new, unproven adventure. From the moment we left the movie I was totally committed to the decision to leave, and on the next Monday morning I had no qualms about typing a resignation letter and delivering it to the firm president, advising that by the next Friday I would be leaving the firm. Looking back on how successful and enjoyable the results of taking the risk and leaving has been, somehow I feel I should have long ago thanked Jack and Ann and the movie makers for deciding the issue for me.

My last week as a senior partner in a major law firm was forgettable. My brother was not too surprised by my decision, as he had known of my discontent. Most of the lawyers and staff were quite surprised. Many of the staff came in to wish me well. Few of the firm's lawyers stopped into my office as I was packing to leave. By the end of the week, no partner was offering a good-bye lunch or dinner, and only Roger was there to buy me a drink after work on Friday. It was obvious that the others felt anger that I had "abandoned ship," especially as my departure meant a loss of revenue for most of the partners. I remember feeling quite lost as I departed the firm's offices for the last time, not really knowing if I could make it on my own.

After a few years of being my own boss, making more money than ever before, and thoroughly enjoying the plaintiff's solo practice, I concluded that I should have made the move five years earlier.

PART III

IN NEED OF A CHANGE, IN 1994
I LEFT THE BIG FIRM AND MOVED FROM DOWN-
TOWN TO THE SUBURBS, WHERE I SET UP A SOLE
PRACTITIONER LAW FIRM ABOUT FIVE MINUTES
FROM HOME. AFTER A SLOW START THIS NEW
VENTURE PROVED PLEASANT AND PROSPEROUS.
ALTHOUGH STILL WORKING AS THIS GOES
TO PRINT IN 2011, I WILL RETIRE SOMEDAY
AS A HAPPY SOLE PRACTITIONER.

CHAPTER 36

SETTING UP A NEW PRACTICE

As I described, I made my decision to leave the firm over the Christmas holidays in 1993. I had done almost no real planning for the practical aspects of setting up a law firm. By contrast, three of the young partners who had already left had just come in one day, passed around a departure note, and immediately left, with paralegals and staff in tow, for a new, fully set-up office several floors above us in the IDS Center. They had planned ahead carefully to secure clients and to be a fully functioning law firm and producing income within days.

My home had a large walkout basement overlooking Christmas Lake. That was going to be my first office. That first weekend I bought a computer, a copier, and office supplies. At the old firm I had refused to have a computer on my desk, ignoring new law firm reality, assuming that I could finish my legal career without ever knowing how to use one. I did have one of the secretaries train me on the new machine, so I could at least produce some basic correspondence. Having struck out on my own, I realized that I would need to hire an experienced secretary with some office management skills. I had always had office managers and bookkeepers to handle the business end of the law practice, so I didn't have a clue how to do those things.

About two weeks into January of 1994, I went to another law office for a deposition on one of my few files. It was a very snowy day, and the witness was a no-show. While waiting in the office I asked a secretary if she knew of some secretary who might need a job. She gave me the name of a person who was to become my good friend Marilyn and my secretary for fourteen years. Marilyn, who was three years older than me, had partially retired from a legal secretary position. My call to her obviously piqued her interest. She enthusiastically joined my little operation and appeared quite excited about helping this fledgling business get off the ground. Over the years Marilyn proved to be multi-talented, working as a receptionist, a good typist, a computer whiz, and a bookkeeper with the skills to keep me out of a tax audit. A lot of my initial success I owe to Marilyn.

Looking ahead to months with only a few files soon to close, and with the ongoing expenses of my new office, I was fortunate to obtain a $100,000 line of credit with a banker who had a good understanding of the cash-flow ups and downs of a plaintiff's contingent-fee practice. Over the years I developed a great relationship with different bankers at U.S. Bank, and they kept me afloat in times of slow cash flow.

A few other interesting events transpired in the first year of my sole practice. I felt I needed a paralegal to assist on my cases. I interviewed and hired an experienced gal who was quite talk-ative and attractive. At that time, my office, shared with Marilyn and the paralegal, was still in a downstairs room in my home. Within days of their first introduction, my paranoid wife was sure that this paralegal and I were having an affair while she was at work. She insisted that the young lady be fired. I had to provide an awkward excuse in discharging the young lady that the paralegal job just wasn't working out.

About six months into working from home, all hell broke loose. As an experienced trial lawyer, I did get some defense referrals. One was from the owner and operator of the Wagon Wheel Stables in the south suburbs of Minneapolis. In my younger days I had gone horseback riding there. Lots of young boys worked at the stables. It seems that the owner, my defense client, had decided that these young men needed exposure to the sexual side of life, and he had sexually abused several of them in the bunkhouse. In the early 1990s, sexual abuse lawsuits were all the rage, with many plaintiffs recalling (legitimately or not) sexual abuse that had been inflicted upon them many years before. Several lawsuits had therefore been brought by the ranch hands, now adults, against the abusive owner of the stables. As the many acres of the land comprising Wagon Wheel Stables had since been replaced with Burnsville housing developments, the now-wealthy owner looked like a pot of gold to the plaintiffs' lawyers. The conclusion of these sexual abuse cases, however, is not the focus of my story. All of these cases were dismissed because they were brought beyond the six-year statute of limitations. My client paid nothing in any settlements.

The true impact of this client was in the opening of my first office. My wife, Jane, was a psychologist specializing in sexual abuse issues in children. She had such a bias in favor of the victims that she never doubted their stories of abuse. She frankly despised the abusers of children. Well, she knew about my representation of the stable owner. Everyone deserves a defense, no matter how guilty, right? That's fine in principle, but I found that my wife had limits. When I met with clients in the home office, I would often sit with them at the dining room table. When Jane saw me meeting there with this abuser (who actually looked the part), she blew up and demanded that I move my office out of the house.

Thus, after six months of paying no rent, I was out looking for office space.

Within five miles of my home I found a two-story office building with several lawyers sharing space. Another office, an ugly space formerly occupied by the building owner, had been vacant for several years after the owner went to federal prison on a bank fraud charge. The office was spacious, with a gas fireplace, but it was decorated in dark colors and lime-green shag carpeting. I cut a deal with the building's new owner to totally remodel and redecorate the office, at their expense, and to set up an adjoining office for Marilyn. The office turned out great, with a winter-warming fireplace and a great commute. It was to serve my purposes quite comfortably until retirement.

CHAPTER 37

TRYING TO DRUM UP LEGAL BUSINESS

When I left the security of the Lommen, Nelson law firm, I purposely did not take any of the firm's defense files so as to avoid a dispute with my old employer. I did take the ten plaintiffs' injury and death files I had worked on during my practice there. With not a lot of business and the expense of setting up a new law office, I had a lot of shaky moments in the start of my new business. A constant worry of sole practitioners is when the next case will come through the door. Until realizing that ups and downs are the norm in the plaintiff practice, I had lots of sleepless nights and second-guessing my decision.

About ten years earlier the U.S. Supreme Court had determined that bar association and lawyer ethics rules prohibiting advertising by lawyers were a violation of free speech. This opened the floodgates for all types of lawyer advertising. Many lawyer ads were obnoxious and drew widespread criticism. But statistics started showing that ads on television and in newspapers, mailings to the public, and in the yellow pages were successful in bringing new clients into a law office. The most used (and most often abused) advertising was done by the personal injury lawyers. A no-name lawyer or law firm, with no experience, could produce a full-page yellow pages ad or a half-minute television commercial and sound to an uninformed public like a most experienced and competent lawyer. Starting out on my own without a lot of clients compelled me to get on the advertising bandwagon. With no fees coming in and working with the line of credit from my friendly banker, my advertising budget was quite limited. I had missed the deadline for an ad in the current year's Minneapolis yellow pages. But I could still get an ad in the St. Paul book. A full-page ad, of which there already were twenty to thirty in the first pages of the yellow book, would cost me $13,000 a year. A quarter-page ad was about $6,500. I chose that route. I consulted with a friend in advertising who recommended using some kind of catchphrase that would separate me from all of the other lawyer ads. We came up with a lead line of "Proven Success" and followed it with comments about my several million-dollar verdicts and experience in major litigation. This one-year advertising experiment was very disappointing. Several calls came in but provided only a single case worthy of pursuing.

As the one-year ad was running out, a case came in that I liked. It involved a woman whose son had been riding his bike on a path in a Coon Rapids park.

He rode out onto a residential street and was hit by a car. It looked like the boy had some minor degree of brain damage. I found that the Coon Rapids Parks Division did not have a stop sign where the bike path intersected the street, which looked like a decent negligence claim against the city. I started the lawsuit and began putting the case together.

I must shorten this story because of its bad ending. The boy's mother had in the past worked in a law firm and thought she could control the case. My relationship with her went steadily downhill. We got to the settlement negotiation stage and she, on the advice of a lawyer relative in Missouri, demanded that we seek a million dollars in settlement. When I advised that the maximum municipal liability limit in Minnesota was only $300,000, she demanded that I challenge that statutory limitation. She became impossible for me to deal with, and I decided that enough was enough. I made a motion in court to withdraw from the case while making sure that the boy's interests were protected if another lawyer would get involved. The judge granted my discharge from the case. Considering that I was out $3,500 in out-of-pocket expenses, I still felt lucky and relieved to be away from this demanding woman. Well, not so fast. Several weeks after my discharge, I received in the mail a multi-page ethics complaint that this woman had filed with the Lawyers Professional Responsibility Board. It was my one and only ethics problem. The response required several hours of work to prepare my defense against many allegations and to supply supporting documents. The board actually called a hearing of about three hours in which I had to defend my representation before a hearing officer that cross-examined my tactics. My former client's goofy allegations were easy to refute, but listening to this lady badmouthing me was still a most unpleasant experience. The case was totally dismissed with no findings against me. And thus did my first advertising effort cost me over $10,000 and a lot of time and grief without producing so much as a dime of business. So much for the yellow pages!

Two times I tried group advertising. There are well-published groups that solicit lawyers to produce, for a fee, television ads with the promise to direct call-in clients to the subscribing lawyers. My first effort cost $3,000 and produced not a single client worth pursuing. My second try had a better-sounding gimmick: Gathering clients and passing them on to member lawyers. Again, my investment of $2,000 or $2,500 was a total waste of money.

In setting up my own practice I had hoped to get case referrals from other lawyers with whom I had developed favorable relations in my past trial work. Throughout my years of defense practice, one of my principles in dealing with other lawyers, even those I battled in the courtroom, was to never be dishonest or to attempt to screw them over. As a result I had good rapport with many different lawyers, and I was optimistic that when my name got out as a solo that some cases would come from other lawyers. Although starting slow, this proved to be the most profitable part of my new adventure.

To promote this area of business I placed an ad in the *Minnesota Lawyer* magazine that went out monthly to all of the members of the Minnesota Bar Association. I again used the "Proven Success" headline and advertised myself as experienced and ready to help other lawyers with their complex cases. I identified my five past million-dollar verdicts for clients. This ad proved to be my one great advertising venture. After two years on my own I recorded my sixth million-dollar verdict for a client. That year I changed my ad, crossing out the 5 with a slash and putting a 6 next to it. A few years later, after my seventh million-dollar verdict, I put a slash through the 6 and added a 7 next to it. This ad produced amazing results. At almost every professional meeting I attended, lawyers, many of whom I did not even know, would come up and ask me when I was going to change the number again. I was very pleased with how that simple ad kept my name before lawyers throughout the state. I received several referral calls from lawyers I had never met who asked me to review their cases to see if I would get involved.

The early nineties also saw the creation of a new kind of advertising. A few weeks after setting up my home office I received an unsolicited call from a fellow with an accent. He asked, "Do you have a website?" This was early in 1994. I had no idea what a website was, and I told him so. After he explained it to me, we reached a deal in which, for $600, he would help create the website and get it up and running. Believe it or not, that turned out to be the third lawyer website in Minnesota. It still exists, although updated, at www.stageberglaw.com.

The website produced some fascinating contacts. Two calls and possible cases came from Canada. A fellow in Saudi Arabia sent an e-mail because he wanted to sue the Mayo Clinic in Rochester for a failed eye surgery. The one good case I pursued was for a Swedish fellow, Bengt Strid, who wanted to sue Polaris Industries for a product defect that caused him injury. Mr. Strid, a contractor, had suffered fractures to both legs when he could not extricate himself from his snowmobile when it tipped over. He claimed that in the Polaris design the foot space was too small and had trapped his boots and legs when he tried to exit the machine. After I measured and photographed a similar Polaris snowmobile and most of the competitors' models, I agreed that the Polaris boot opening was inadequate in size, compared to competing machines. Bengt became my client, and on two occasions he and his wife came to Minnesota for parts of the lawsuit against Polaris. The case settled for a nice figure without going to trial. Bengt and I have remained in contact, and on one vacation I visited him in his hometown in Sweden.

CHAPTER 38

HELPING OUT LAWYERS

As I started out on my own, I was counting on my past experience of trying 150 or more civil cases, many in complex areas of litigation, the kind of expertise that I could sell to lawyers needing assistance on their cases. My hope was to find inexperienced trial lawyers who had good cases but felt that they were in over their heads. Pointing out five verdicts of over a million dollars for my clients, I subtly encouraged other lawyers to ask for my assistance in developing and if necessary trying their lawsuits, in return for a share of the attorney's fee.

One young lawyer named John, who had worked for me a couple of months as a law clerk, called one day with loads of questions. John had passed the bar and set up an office just off Lake Street in Minneapolis in an area inhabited by many Spanish-speaking immigrants. John's little South Minneapolis office was like a sponge soaking up personal injury clients with minimal English, most of them seeking help with auto collision injuries. John had this naïve idea that all of these cases he'd signed up meant a stream of regular settlements, providing money to his clients and a nice one-third contingent fee for his legal efforts.

After a year or two of this successful representation his of clients, John realized that the insurance carriers were really tough, especially on injury claims from non-English-speaking claimants. John called me and asked, "What do I do on all of these cases that I can't settle?" My short and simple answer was, "You go to trial and try them to a conclusion." John replied, "But I thought they would all settle, and I have never tried a jury case." He relayed to me that he had six jury trials scheduled during the next two months. I reviewed a number of John's cases and convinced him to accept nominal settlement offers on some and try the others. I agreed to associate with him on a few others. When my name was added as co-counsel, the insurance companies realized that I would try the cases, and they quickly settled. Fortunately, I never had to try one of John's cases to a conclusion. My best advice to him was that you never take on a case at the beginning unless you plan to try it to a conclusion. Then, if it settles sometime before trial, you consider yourself lucky and walk away with your fee.

One interesting referral case came from a young lawyer in Detroit Lakes, Minnesota. His client, a local deputy sheriff, had been badly injured when a rear wheel separated from the axle of his pickup. Investigation showed that earlier on the day of the accident he had had four new tires installed at Tires Plus in Moorhead. Apparently the mechanic had failed to tighten the lug nuts on the left rear wheel. The deputy had paid the bill and headed home in his truck. About twenty miles away from Moorhead, the wheel fell off, sending the client and his pickup into the ditch. To the young local lawyer this seemed like a tough case. To me it was a piece of cake. I hired a metallurgist to examine the wheel and confirm that the lugs had not been tightened. Putting together the medical end was also easy; a vocational expert predicted that the client could not return to his good paying job as a sheriff's deputy. Mediation produced a nice settlement and a contingent fee that I shared with the local lawyer.

Before I relay my most interesting case referral, I must diverge on a pet peeve of mine relating to big-firm litigators. These litigators, with an unlimited budget drawn on the client's defense money, just feast on the little-guy plaintiff's lawyer. A multitude of times I have witnessed the big-firm litigation departments attempting to bury sole practitioners with a mountain of paperwork, legal motions, unnecessary depositions, and out-of-state trips. The tactic is clearly to so overburden the little guy that he will give up or stumble somewhere along the way, providing the big guy with an easy out. As described in later chapters, I have personally experienced this intentional avalanche of paper in my Coleman cases. The fascinating thing is that the big-firm litigators really do not know how to try a jury trial, and they do not want to go to court. So, if a little guy with a good plaintiff's case recognizes this and gets past the bullshit preliminary paperwork, the trial may well go in his favor.

At some seminar early on in my career, I heard a speaker differentiating between a "trial lawyer" and a "litigator." His analogy stuck with me. He said, "If there are a field of stones out there with evidence underneath them that will help the case, the trial lawyer will selectively choose a few stones to turn over to reveal the necessary evidence to try the case. Whereas the litigator will take the time and expense to turn over every stone in the field." The speaker was clearly advocating for attendees to try jury cases and hone our skills as trial lawyers, not just litigators. After hearing that story, I never again referred to myself as a litigator.

About five years out of law school I ran into a former classmate who had graduated ahead of me in our class and had gone to work for Minneapolis's largest law firm. I inquired about what he had been doing at the big firm. He replied that he was a litigator in the litigation department. I asked if he had been trying cases. He proudly replied that he had handled several very important pretrial motions and settlement conferences. As far as I could tell, he had never tried a jury trial to a conclusion. At that stage in my career I had tried at least thirty jury trials to a conclusion. I remember thinking that it would be a lot of fun to get this fellow against me in a full-scale jury trial. The downside, however, was that he was making about twice as much as me at the big firm.

This leads to my most entertaining referral, a case sent to me by my friend Jim. He was working as a sole practitioner in suburban Chaska and had a general practice heavy on divorce and criminal work. Jim was a really nice fellow, capable in his limited specialties and ready to admit his inexperience in handling injury cases. Jim had asked my assistance on a couple of personal injury cases where he felt that he was in over his head. One was a complex insurance case of the type that I found routine. Such referrals were great for both of us, as Jim and I both made money with good results for the clients.

Over several months, Jim had been calling to talk about a big rape case he had, thinking that he would probably need my help to try it. I said, "Sure," but I stressed that he had to get me involved sometime soon. Nothing happened for over a year. Then Jim came to me and said, "I need help now." The facts of the case were fascinating. He represented a couple, let's call them Jerry and Lisa, who were suing a big up-and-coming national corporation headquartered in Minneapolis. Jerry was a project manager for the company and had been assigned to Scottsdale, Arizona, to manage the construction of a new plant. Jerry and Lisa had moved down to Scottsdale, and a vice president of the company had taken them out for dinner and lots of drinks. The VP gave them a ride back to their motel. Jerry passed out or went to sleep in their room, and the VP started putting moves on Lisa. They ended up in the motel pool where, Lisa claimed, the VP forced her to perform oral sex on him.

Lisa didn't tell Jerry until some months had passed. By that time the management claimed to be unhappy with Jerry's work on the Scottsdale project and was considering firing him. Jerry could not understand why he was on the way out, so Lisa disclosed to him that she had been raped by the company VP. Obviously, fuming, Jerry went to the company president in Minneapolis and told Lisa's whole story. The long and short of it was that the VP denied the rape and the company fired Jerry. The company claimed that Jerry's firing was because of poor performance and had no relation to the rape allegation. In representing Jerry and Lisa, my friend Jim had started two lawsuits, a rape and battery case for Lisa against the VP and a whistleblower firing case against the company, its president, and the vice president. The several defendants were represented by four of the big law firms in Minneapolis.

Jim had done a lot of good work, taking many depositions of the key players and establishing the existence of a really messy attempted cover-up of the rape and the real reason for the firing. The defense efforts had then begun in earnest, and Jim was besieged with motions, demands, and expensive discovery trips down to Arizona, all of which really taxed his time and finances. In addition, the opposition made repeated accusations, most of them totally false, that Jim was hiding things and doing under-handed legal work. Jim simply did not know how to handle this constant barrage of big-firm litigation. After getting way behind on responding to motions and demands, a flustered Jim came to me for help. His case now filled four banker's boxes, most of the paper coming from the four defense firms.

After listening to the whole story I agreed with Jim that both lawsuits had real merit and good settlement or jury-verdict poten-tial. The whole case, however, was so bogged down in paperwork, unnecessary legal work, and peripheral battles that the trial preparation had been seriously neglected. Trial was only four or five months away, and the case was nowhere near ready to go to trial. Jim had missed several deadlines and was already on the bad side of the assigned trial judge. He needed several expert witnesses. My first task was to line up three experts, get them key material, and get Lisa and Jerry back from Arizona for interviews. With Jim I tried to prioritize his multitude of issues and get the case back on track for trial. I decided there was no merit in my taking several days to read the several thousand pages of depositions and documents filed in the case. I told Jim to serve a notice to the defense lawyers that I was now associate counsel for the plaintiffs, which let me appear at all further proceedings. I knew I was not going to be fully prepped on the details of the case.

By this time in my career I believed that I had established a fairly well-known reputation as an aggressive trial lawyer. I did not know any of the defense lawyers from the big firms, as I had never seen them in court or anywhere close to a jury trial. I don't mean to sound too pretentious, but I made the assumption that they would research my background and realize that I meant business as a trial lawyer. At our first few meetings of counsel and with the trial judge, I was treated with unusual respect by the lawyers and the trial judge (even though I knew very little about the facts or issues at hand). On several critical motions, at which I was present only for support, Jim did a decent job arguing before the trial judge, succeeding and requiring that the first of the two cases move ahead for trial. The judge ordered a pretrial settlement conference to be attended by all lawyers and clients.

The background for the settlement status of this litigation was interesting. Early on, Jim had demanded for his clients five million dollars in settlement. Sensing Jim's inexperience, the defense lawyers offered a pittance of around $50,000 or $75,000. That was the situation as we went into the judge's settlement conference. Our client Jerry arrived, and I met him for the first time. Jim had described Jerry as being smart but somewhat volatile. He was confident that Jerry could be portrayed before a jury as a victim of an improper firing whose wife had been raped by a company vice president. As they say, first impressions are most lasting. When I met Jerry, my impression was that a jury would absolutely hate this guy. He was strong-willed, arrogant, and had a snide look about him. After five minutes with him I was convinced that there was no way we could turn this fellow into a victim in front of a jury. I pulled Jim aside and told him, "My friend, there is no way we can try this case with this guy as our primary client. We have to settle this case."

Some really fun hardball negotiations then took place. The judge went back and forth between the two sides with a high offer of $200,000 forthcoming. Jim and the client wanted a million, but as a last effort to settle I said to the judge, "Have them pay $800,000 or we go to trial next Monday." After relaying that final position to the four defense lawyers and their clients, the judge reported that no settlement was possible. I then told the judge and the attorneys, "We will be ready for trial next Monday." There was little response from the four defense lawyers.

Jim and I went out into the hall to talk about our trial presentation, and I then asked Jim to go into the courtroom and advise the defense attorneys that I wanted the company vice president available on the first morning of trial for my cross-examination. Under the court rules a plaintiff can call a defendant, or a corporate officer, as part of the plaintiff's evidence and cross-examine the defense witness before questioning by the defense lawyer. This is usually a good plaintiff's tactic. Jim went into the courtroom and relayed my message to defense attorneys, then came out and said to me, "They won't produce the vice president as a witness." That was total nonsense as far as I was concerned, and I stormed into the courtroom and went up chin-to-chin with the lead company defense lawyer, saying, "You don't think you have to produce that guy for cross?" He stammered a reply, "The VP is not a corporate officer and does not have to appear." Putting on my toughest trial-lawyer façade, I poked my right index finger into the front of this lawyer's three-piece pinstriped suit and said, "That is total bullshit. Of course he is an officer, and you will have that guy in court on Monday morning for cross-examination." There was no response other than a shrinking retreat to his colleagues and clients.

A bluff? Or did I really want to go to trial? Hardly, with our unappealing client. But, what the hell, I am a trial lawyer and these defense "litigators" were not. Jim and I and our client left the courthouse with no real idea what would happen. I had assured Jim that over the next few days I would spend whatever time was required to get fully up to speed and try the case as lead counsel. Midafternoon that day I got a call from Jim. The lead defense litigator, the one I had terrorized in the courtroom, had called Jim with an agreement to pay the full $800,000. The only condition was that it be confidential to prevent publicity damage to the image of the corporation. Quite to my surprise, both Jim and our client were somewhat disappointed, claiming that we should have stuck to our demand at a million. I reassured them that our decision was most prudent.

What was the end result? Four big-firm litigators successfully avoided trying a real jury trial. They had cumulatively billed their clients far more than the one-third contingent fee that Jim and I received from the $800,000 settlement. These so-called litigators will continue to foist onto their clients their false credentials as trial lawyers, extracting huge hourly fees and convincing them that when the chips are down they must settle rather than go to trial. It is nothing more than a big fraud on the public consumers of legal services.

CHAPTER 39

MY FIRST BIG ONE AS A SOLE PRACTITIONER

I started my sole practice with only a few pending cases and no real line of anticipated business. Hardly did I think that clients would start walking into my basement office, but I did expect (perhaps too optimistically) a stream of decent referrals. In about my third week of not being very busy, the first of the lawyer referrals came in, and it was a good one! I will call the client Simon. During the Christmas holidays Simon, his wife, and their best friend, Andrew, flew from Orlando, Florida, to Des Moines, Iowa, to do some cross-country skiing. One day they drove their rented Ford Tempo up toward Mankato to go downhill skiing. As they proceeded north, a garbage truck pulled out from a stop sign in front of them, resulting in a T-bone collision. Simon's wife had been sitting in the right front seat; she flew forward and under the shoulder safety belt, and the seat belt, from the heavy impact, crushed her windpipe, killing her. Andrew, who was driving the Tempo, and Simon, riding in the backseat, both survived with relatively minor injuries.

After the referring lawyer described the case, I immediately contacted Simon in Florida, sold him on my services, and made arrangements to fly to Orlando the next day. My involvement with Simon was favorable from the start. He was a low-key solo-practicing dentist, and his late wife had been a successful commercial real estate agent. Simon described her as a talented and special person with whom he had had a wonderful relationship, although they were not able to have children. During the visit I conducted a thorough interview with Andrew, a successful building contractor and dear friend of Simon and his wife. I flew back home with a signed attorney fee agreement and a big grin about my first big case. This one had all three requirements for a great lawsuit: Good liability (the garbage company at fault), heavy damages (wrongful death of a strong wage earner), and a deep pocket (the garbage company had $1 million in liability coverage). In addition, there was a potential defective seat belt case against Ford Motor Company.

A lot of claims, parties, and lawyers got involved. My wrongful death claim for the death of Simon's wife was against the garbage company, Andrew (as driver of the car), and Ford Motor Company for a defective seat belt. In addition, Simon and Andrew both sued the garbage company for their injuries. The case proceeded at the normal litigation pace until all the lawyers agreed to make a trip to Orlando to complete Simon and Andrew's depositions. That trip proved to be probably the biggest single shocker of my career.

Simon and I had planned to meet at an Orlando restaurant the evening before his deposition for preparation. When I met him that night, he was not the same Simon; he looked horrible and was obviously very distraught about something. He went on to tell me that Andrew had come to him that day to confess that he had had a long-term secret affair with Simon's beloved wife. It seemed that Andrew's defense lawyer, a good friend of mine from Minneapolis, had that afternoon prepared Andrew for his deposition, stressing that Andrew must tell the truth. To Andrew, that meant fessing up to the affair if asked in the deposition. Why Andrew felt obligated to run to Simon and confess to him beforehand is beyond me. But think a minute about how the value of my great wrongful death case would plummet if the defense lawyers found out that Simon's supposedly wonderful wife had been far from faithful. Later that evening Andrew's lawyer and I had a great laugh about these crazy events and decided what Simon and Andrew would have to do in their depositions. We advised both of them that they did not have to volunteer anything about the affair unless specifically asked. But if asked they would have to tell the truth.

So there I sat the next day through two lengthy depositions, holding my breath whenever one of the defense lawyers seemed poised to ask the wrong question. Some questions were close, but not right on, and Simon and Andrew followed our advice. The affair never came up. The defense lawyers believed throughout the case that Simon and his wife had a great relationship and Andrew was nothing more than a nice guy and family friend. All of the claims except the defective seat belt claim were settled by December of 1994. If I recall correctly, Simon's wrongful death claim was settled for $950,000 of the $1 million garbage company policy, plus the complete $50,000 policy from Andrew's insurance company.

What happened next with Simon's settlement money is again a classic tale. In any wrongful death claim there may be several blood relatives of the decedent other than the surviving spouse with a potential claim to some of the proceeds. One relative is appointed as trustee to bring the case on behalf of all potential settlement participants. Simon was clearly the appropriate trustee for his wife's death. At the end of the case there must be distribution of the recovery among the claimants. Usually the trustee's lawyer makes a proposal for a percentage distribution among the potential claimants, and in most cases this is accepted by everyone. Then, after the attorney's fees are paid, the distribution is made out of the attorney's trust account. If someone objects to the distribution it can go into court for a judicial division of the proceeds. Although over my career I handled probably twenty wrongful death cases, only Simon's required a full-blown court hearing.

Simon's wife had come from a Jewish family residing somewhere in the New York City metropolitan area. She was survived by her father, mother, and brother. They claimed to have had a great, close relationship with their deceased daughter and sister, but they had never liked Simon and thought their daughter had married down. Simon's view was that his wife seldom spent any lengthy time with her family, and she thought her brother was an idiot. My proposed distribution of the settlement money strongly favored Simon as the surviving spouse, but it did provide some percentage to the family—perhaps 20 percent, as I remember. This incensed the family, and they hired an attorney in Mankato and demanded a court hearing for a judicial division of the settlement.

Simon and the family appeared before the Mankato judge. The hearing was bizarre! The brother was sworn in and described that his father and mother were survivors of the Auschwitz concentration camp and that their daughter was the center of their lives. As the brother testified to several bizarre family situations, I could see why Simon thought this fellow was goofy. While other witnesses were testifying, the mother continually moaned loudly and cried about the loss of her beloved daughter. To my relief, the judge divided up the proceeds exactly as I had proposed. As could be imagined, Simon wanted nothing to do with his former in-laws thereafter. I kept in touch with him for a few years and found out that he remarried within a year and was very happy with his new wife and the settlement money; he had no regrets about losing wife number one or his "good friend" Andrew.

A bit of follow-up on the seat belt claim against Ford: Lawyers around the country were having success claiming defective design for an automatic shoulder belt that had caused injuries and deaths from strangulation, just as in my case. With the shoulder belt automatically closing when the car started, passengers did not feel it necessary to connect the lap belt as well. Without the lap belt, a person's lower body would slide forward at impact, allowing the shoulder belt to strike the neck area, resulting in serious neck injury or death.

I had lined up national experts to pursue the claim against Ford. Minnesota sunk this claim in a crazy way. For many years the legislature had enforced a "seat belt gag rule" that said no evidence of the lack of use of a seat belt could be admitted in a personal injury lawsuit. Thus, an injured plaintiff could not be found negligent for not wearing a seat belt. This statute should have had no connection to a product liability claim for the defective design of a safety belt system. But on Ford's motion to dismiss my claim the trial judge ruled that the language of the gag rule was broad enough to prohibit all evidence relating to seat belts, even in a design defect case. My appeal of the dismissal resulted in full agreement by the appellate court. This result shocked not only plaintiff's lawyers but also legislators, who openly said the gag rule was being misinterpreted. It took two more years before the legislature amended the statute to clarify that it did not prohibit seat belt design problems. All too late for my claim.

My first year on my own thus ended with great results, even though I had collected no significant fees until Simon's settlement. After paying a percentage of the fee to the referring lawyer, I was left with sufficient income to pay off all my loans with quite a bit left over. Being on my own was looking okay.

CHAPTER 40

THE NASTY WORLD OF SEXUAL ABUSE

Being the parent of two great children, I can hardly fathom the damage they would have suffered if some adult sexually abused them. Unfortunately, sexual abuse of children is rampant and arises in many surprising arenas. The most publicized sexual abuse allegations have arisen against the Catholic Church. Since about 1970 people have come out of the woodwork to claim that they were sexually abused while youngsters, often by their ministers or priests, their own parents, or other relatives. I became involved in sexual abuse cases both by choice and by chance.

My initial involvement relates to my marriage to Dr. Jane McNaught, a psychologist specializing in treating children and parents affected by child sexual abuse. I was assigned as counsel for one of many defendants sued in a much-publicized sexual abuse case coming out of the small south central Minnesota community of Jordan. As the media daily expounded on the multipart investigation, it appeared that for two or more generations in the Jordan community parents and even grandparents had been sexually abusing children. For days on end this breaking story was on the front page of the newspapers as the aggressive Scott County prosecutor Kathleen Morris muckraked through the town, dredging up more dirt against more citizens. Every time she brought charges against a citizen she would call a press conference to brag about her expanding investigation and the atrocities that had occurred in Jordan.

Obviously, the accused citizens rebelled against the accusations and hired good defense attorneys to defend against the abuse charges. If I recall correctly, one or two people did plead guilty to the charges and were sentenced to lengthy prison terms. The first case to come to trial was to be the big test case against all of the other residents charged with abuse of their children. The publicity-grabbing county attorney chose to be the lead attorney to prosecute this case. As it later was revealed, Ms. Morris, for all of her grandstanding, had little courtroom experience. The competent defense attorneys chose to focus their defense on challenging her aggressive tactics in pursuing these abuse cases without adequate supporting evidence. Daily trial reports documented the blunders in her pursuit and development of these prosecutions. In the end, each of the named defendants in this first big criminal case was acquitted of all charges.

Where then do Mark and his future wife, Jane, come into this sordid picture? When those parents were exonerated by the jury, they immediately commenced civil lawsuits against everyone even slightly involved in the unsuccessful prosecutions. Dr. Jane McNaught had been for several years one of the PhD psychologists in the area specializing in the aftermath of child sexual abuse. In that capacity she had been hired by Ms. Morris, along with other psychologists, to evaluate the children and provide professional opinions as to whether or not their stories were credible. At Morris's request, Jane had evaluated three of the child victims of abuse in Jordan. In each case Jane had provided the opinion that the children had indeed been abused.

To jump forward a bit: During our marriage Jane never agreed with my opinions, supported by a lot of scholarly literature, that abuse reports of this type by children are many times either false or grossly exaggerated. The questions posed by investigating police officers while interviewing alleged abuse victims frequently lead the child to the one answer anticipated by the questioner. Psychologists can fall prey to the same unconscious guiding. For instance, in the well-known use of anatomic dolls to help children identify abusive behavior, the interviewer might ask, "Did Daddy touch you on the pee-pee?" while pointing to the doll's crotch, giving the child cues that would not have been suggested by an open-ended question like "Where did Daddy touch you?"

Now, back to the Jordan cases. Jane had malpractice insurance with the St. Paul Companies. When she was sued by the Jordan plaintiffs, I was chosen as her defense attorney. On the surface the case seemed far-fetched. The victims' lawyers had sued everyone in sight, including Morris, the county, all of the psychologists, and the accusing parents, alleging among other things a conspiracy among the defendants. When one of my associates, Paul Peterson, gathered the evidence, the case looked very defensible for our psychologist client. All she had really done was perform a normal type of sexual abuse evaluation of a child and rendered a report with her opinions. How could this have been part of a conspiracy? With this insight into the case I spent little further time preparing the defense case, and left Paul to handle the details. When the attorneys scheduled Jane's deposition, however, I got actively involved in preparing her for the questioning.

My first introduction to Jane was quite interesting. I had just returned from a weekend duck hunting trip up north, where I had tripped and fallen in the brush, either badly spraining or breaking my wrist. I introduced myself to Jane as her lawyer with my bandaged wrist outside of my coat sleeve. As we laughed later, it was less than a powerful introduction to the lawyer who was supposed to protect her professional career. One of the more humorous parts of this deposition stuck with me. One of the several plaintiffs' lawyers (none of whom were the shining stars of plaintiff's trial work) was a fellow named Albright. During the deposition I turned this fellow inside and out with appropriate objections. After the deposition he was known in our office as "Half-bright."

When we and other defendants made summary judgment motions to dismiss the civil cases against our clients, all of them were granted by the trial judge. A good friend who was defending Morris in these civil cases later told me that it was his conviction, after being much closer to the facts than I was, that Morris was dead-on in her accusations against the alleged abusers. After the case closed, my relationship with Jane turned into a romance and eventual marriage. A couple of years later Morris appeared at our firm, looking for an associate attorney job as a trial lawyer. I interviewed her but never took her name to the hiring committee.

Just like other injury cases brought in Minnesota, civil sexual abuse cases for damages must be commenced within six years after the abuse occurred. One exception is if the victim has somehow seriously repressed the abuse in his or her memory and then recalled it years later, usually through extensive counseling. This claim is difficult to prove and is often found to be a false attempt to bypass the limitation.

I also took part in cases brought against Catholic priests and their supporting superiors. Beneath the cloak of the Almighty, priests could convince young victims that their submission to abuse was required by God. Far too often, the supervising bishop would become aware of allegations of abuse or at least the tendencies of the priests toward pedophilia. When abuse allegations surfaced, most often the offending priests were shuffled off to a new parish and allowed to continue their uninhibited abuse of young victims. Catholic Church abuse problems have most recently arisen in Ireland and Germany. After initially denying the events, the Vatican and even the Pope himself have been forced to apologize for abusive priest behavior. This still may be the tip of the iceberg, given the global reach of the Catholic Church.

In my plaintiff's career I represented three members of a family who all claimed abuse by a priest associated with St. John's Abbey in Collegeville, Minnesota, near St. Cloud. The father claimed that his two daughters had been repeatedly abused by the local parish priest. Our investigation showed that this priest took groups of youngsters, both boys and girls, up to a cabin in northern Minnesota on supposed retreats. He would then have them disrobe for games and would even give them wine to drink. In the cabin's separate sauna building, the priest joined the young, nude girls and massaged their bodies, including their genitals. Fortunately for our investigation, this wayward priest had kept a diary about the kids he took to the cabin, including the two girls that we represented. This priest, like many others, was known to abbey officials as having aberrant tendencies, and yet he was allowed to continue on in his position as a parish priest.

Our lawsuits against St. John's Abbey met the usual insurance company defense based on the statute of limitations. Our two clients were in serious psychological distress, much of which could be traced to the abuse. Unfortunately they were now in their thirties and well beyond the statute of limitations. We found that the new abbot had paid some abuse settlements even when the statute of limitations defense was present. He was an honorable man with some real compassion for the abuse victims. We racked our brains for some plausible argument on how to get past the time limitation. We had found that our two clients had visited the abbot directly before our involvement and had extracted some promises from him that he would settle with them under certain conditions. We therefore alleged a breach of the contract the abbot made with his promises of settlement for the clients.

One of tragic sidelights of this case was comments we received from a real Deep Throat–type investigator who had been pursuing St. John's Abbey for years on these abuse issues. He presented to us very credible arguments that our offending priest had actually murdered two young girls in northern Minnesota. Two sisters who appeared in the priest's diary as guests at the cabin were found dead in a gravel pit not far from the cabin. There never was enough solid proof to prosecute the priest, but our Deep Throat was sure he did it. Furthermore, he was convinced that this same priest, possibly together with other offending priests, had abducted a young St. Cloud boy, Jacob Wetterling, whose unsolved disappearance had incensed the whole state. His case has never been resolved.

I wish I could say we did a great job for those two young ladies. Cases against the priests were required to move forward in the legal system, resulting in some resolution or trial. With our quasi-bogus attempt to avoid the statute of limitations, we did work out a settlement for our clients with the abbey's insurance company. The amounts our clients received were minor compared to what they had survived. I still hear from these clients in e-mails about continuing repercussions from the priest's abuse. This is a nasty business!

One fascinating case was referred to me by another lawyer who did not want to get involved in sexual abuse issues. The client, whom I will call Donna, was a psychologist who was struggling to make a living in a small Wisconsin town. Like most in that profession, she went to regular counseling with other psychologists. Scratch my back and I will scratch yours. For depression and related issues Donna had been seeing an experienced psychologist at one of the hospitals in Minnesota. This counselor was a married woman and well established in her profession. After a few sessions, the esteemed counselor started hitting on Donna to develop a lesbian relationship. Donna was not receptive and tried to ward off the advances. She eventually came to me for legal help.

One option was to go gangbusters and sue the counselor and the hospital and seek publicity and large sums of compensatory and punitive damages. Donna favored a much less aggressive approach. My first letter to the counselor brought a quick response from her attorney challenging the merits of the claim. When I presented to him several quite suggestive letters Donna had received, his posture quickly changed. Because the counselor's reputation, job, professional license, and even her marriage were at risk of total destruction, generous settlement offers were forthcoming to keep the whole mess quiet. By this point Donna was really suffering emotionally and was probably never going to re-engage in her own counseling business. The settlement we reached was to supply Donna with regular payments for the remaining years of her working life expectancy. A complex document was drafted to prevent disclosure of any facts and to keep the counselor away from Donna. For over thirteen years regular checks came to my trust account, and after deducting my fee I forwarded the balance to Donna's bank account. As my planned retirement was about the same as Donna's, it proved to be a nice thirteen-year annuity.

CHAPTER 41

A BIG MEDICAL MALPRACTICE CASE

After defending medical malpractice cases at the Lommen, Nelson firm for many years, I was almost guaranteed some malpractice cases against doctors and hospitals when I moved to sole practice. To expand my connections with the plaintiffs' lawyers, I joined the Minnesota Trial Lawyers Association and planned to attend their summer convention in Alexandria, Minnesota, hoping to drum up some plaintiff's referrals.

At that first MTLA convention, a lawyer named Sue came up to me and said that she had seen my ad and wanted me to look at a medical malpractice case she was handling. Questioning her about the case, I learned that two of the prominent medical malpractice law firms in Minneapolis had already rejected it. That is never a good sign, particularly for a sole practitioner with few funds in the bank. I agreed, however, to review the case with Sue and give her my opinion.

When I evaluated the serious injury case for Sue's client, Tom, it seemed to me that there was serious medical negligence involved. Perhaps because I had few heavy cases to fill my cabinet at that time, I agreed to associate with Sue in the representation of Tom against the mighty Fairview Hospital system in Minneapolis.

On Halloween night in 2002, Tom, then thirty-two years old, and his roommate dressed up and went down to one of the then-swinging bars on the east bank of the Mississippi River for a costume party. Upon departing at closing, having consumed their share of libations, Tom and his roommate joined the crowds leaving the municipal parking lot. As traffic backed up in the ramp, Tom's roommate honked on the horn, which apparently aggravated someone ahead of him. The passenger in the car ahead got out, walked up to Tom's open passenger window, and punched Tom in the face. Neither of them retaliated, and Tom and his roommate went home to bed. At about 5:00 a.m. Tom woke up, went into the bathroom, looked at his facial lacerations, and woke his roommate to take him to the emergency room for medical treatment. Tom arrived at the Fairview Riverside ER sometime before 6:00 a.m. As Tom went in alone, his roommate fell asleep in his vehicle.

In the ER reception room no one took great interest in this drunk kid with blood on his face. An intake nurse recorded that he had been drinking and had been struck in the face. He was placed in a room and waited for over half an hour for an ER doctor to evaluate him. The nurse's notes told the doctor that this young man was "intoxicated" and "had been in a fight." The ER doctor correctly stitched up the laceration on Tom's nose and ordered X-rays to determine if there was a facial fracture. Then Tom's real problems began. The X-ray department was over a hundred yards from the ER. (As part of the lawsuit I measured the exact distance.) Even knowing that Tom was intoxicated, the doctor did not offer Tom a wheelchair, though an orderly accompanied him on the walk down the twisted hallways. He arrived just before a shift change for the X-ray techs; the tech who did Tom's pictures was anxious to finish her work in ten minutes and head home.

The direction from the ER doctor was to get different types of facial X-rays. (I am sorry that I cannot remember the technical terms.) For the prescribed shots, the tech required that Tom stand upright next to the X-ray plates for front and side views. After two views standing with his neck and chin outstretched towards the vertical X-ray plate, Tom either passed out or fainted and fell backward onto the hard tile floor.

Tom's lack of response was immediately recognized and a neurosurgeon was consulted. Within a few hours brain surgery revealed a massive hemorrhage from striking his head in the X-ray department. After extensive rehab, Tom left the hospital with major mental and physical deficits from his traumatic brain injury.

How does one analyze this from a win-lose standpoint? It was apparent to me that the deterrent to the other lawyers who had reviewed the case was Tom's intoxication. That is, how could a plaintiff win a malpractice case if he was intoxicated at the time of the claimed negligent act? With some help from trusted experts, I concluded that the intoxication was an asset rather than a liability in this case. Follow me for a moment: If a patient comes into an ER in an obviously intoxicated condition that is known to ER personnel, does that not impose some special care obligations not required for a stone-cold-sober patient? Sure, drinking to the excess is not favored, but at the Fairview ER treating intoxicated patients was certainly not unusual. As ER staff, you must treat the patient with all of his infirmities or imperfections. I saw that angle as the way to win this case.

The defense pooh-poohed our claim and offered no settlement money. But as I did more investigation into what happened in the ER and X-ray room I became more optimistic. I found a leading radiology textbook that described the recommended positioning of patients for that type of facial X-rays. The patient was to lie down, not stand up, for the films. Furthermore, radiology texts stated that for X-rays taken in a standing position the patient should be strapped in with a seat belt–type device to secure the patient against the upright X-ray plates. My inspection and photographing of the X-ray room revealed several of the seat-belt devices that could have been used to prevent Tom's fall.

To succeed with any malpractice case you need competent and believable expert witnesses. With Tom's facts and a plan to present them, I found both a local ER doctor and a competent out-of-state radiologist as my experts. They both supported my view that Tom, as an intoxicated patient in the ER, did not receive the type of care that complied with the appropriate standards of medical practice. With the defense also having several competent expert witnesses, the case was destined for trial.

This two-week trial was as tough as any I had tried before a jury. I was representing a youngish, intoxicated, party guy against one of the finer hospitals in the area and its trained ER doctors and technicians. One must always look to a favorable theme in the case. Mine was this: At an emergency room you take patients with whatever issues they have, physical or mental, intoxicated or sober, and your duty is to treat and heal those patients, giving special consideration to their infirmities, whether self-induced or not. Somehow this approach rang true with the jury. They found the ER doctor negligent for not placing Tom in a wheelchair for the long walk to the X-ray room and also found the X-ray tech negligent for her positioning of Tom during the procedure. They rejected any claim that Tom was negligent for his intoxication. The damage award in favor of Tom was for $1.6 million.

Tom's story and my involvement with him did not end with the trial. When such a big verdict as this came in it was reported on the evening TV news. I was interviewed with a big smile on my face. It was a pleasure to call the lawyers in the two big law firms that had turned down Tom's case and tell them about my result. We took Tom's portion of the verdict and set up a lifetime annuity for him, with sufficient funds to provide for all his living expenses, residential assistance, and therapy. He was set up for life.

During the case I had learned was that Tom was an avid basketball fan, having played high school basketball in Colcraine, Minnesota, about sixty miles from my hometown. He had been a loyal Minnesota Gopher basketball fan for years. Every year since the verdict I have called Tom to see if he is capable of coming with me to a Gopher Big Ten basketball game. A few years after our verdict he developed serious spinal meningitis, related to his prior injuries, that left him more severely disabled. At that time he indicated he could not go to a game. I insisted that he meet me at the game and I would find a way to get him to our seats. With the assistance of ushers, we carried Tom up the stairs to our seats. In retrospect, had I known during trial of Tom's future meningitis and presented that to the jury, his case could have been worth even a larger damage award. Tom still remains my friend, and since he obtained season Gopher basketball tickets in the handicapped seating section, I regularly see him at games.

CHAPTER 42

THE SLAM DUNKS OF TRIAL WORK

The vast majority of the litigation clients who walk into your office do not have cases with all three of necessary elements for a good lawsuit: Good liability, extensive damages, and enough insurance coverage. Every personal injury lawyer has sat across the desk from a seriously injured victim of a motor vehicle accident. But after reviewing the police accident report, the lawyer declines representation because all indications are that the potential client was more at fault in causing the accident than the other driver. Similarly, many seriously injured clients with good liability facts, such as being rear-ended while at a complete stop, are faced with minimal liability insurance on the other driver. This latter type of case, with good liability and big damages, can often be easily resolved with a policy-limit settlement without litigation. For many years I have believed that it is inappropriate for a contingent fee lawyer to take a full one-third fee from such an easy settlement, especially when the injured client clearly deserves a maximum recovery. Unfortunately, most of my colleagues in the plaintiffs' bar do not share this generosity and will often extract a full contingent fee for doing little legal work that truly benefited the client or was instrumental in producing the settlement.

This type of overreaching has contributed to the widely held negative view of personal injury trial lawyers. Perhaps the most egregious example was the tobacco litigation case out of Florida. In the 1990s, individuals as well as attorneys general across the nation sued the tobacco companies, alleging fraud and deception in failing to advise the public, particularly minors, of the addictive nature of cigarettes. The claims brought by the state attorneys general dealt with the millions of dollars that state health programs spent on providing health care to smokers with lung cancer. Most states entered into contracts with private law firms to pursue their claims with some type of contingent fee agreement based on the recovery received by the state. Minnesota's attorney general, Skip Humphrey, a former law school classmate of mine, entered into such an agreement with the Robins, Kaplan, Miller and Ciresi law firm in Minneapolis. Robins, Kaplan did a fantastic job of discovery and trial preparation, far superior to the work done by any other firm. They sent a team of lawyers and legal assistants to England for months to review millions of tobacco company documents that had been stored in a warehouse there. This huge expenditure produced several smoking-gun documents proving that tobacco companies had had knowledge for several decades of the addictive nature of cigarettes.

With their superb preparation, Robins, Kaplan went to trial against the tobacco companies in St. Paul. After several grueling weeks of trial combat, and before the case went to the jury, a settlement of several billion dollars was reached with the tobacco companies. The settlement was quite favorable to Minnesota. The Robins firm negotiated from the tobacco companies its attorney fee on top of what the state received. Although broadcast in the papers as an excessive fee, the attorney fee of millions paid by the defendants was well deserved for the firm's risk and investment of time and expense in the preparation of the case.

What followed is what was most offensive. The Robins firm had laid the groundwork for similar cases to be pursued by the other state attorneys general. Thereafter, one by one the tobacco companies reached settlements with the other states, with recoveries usually in billions of dollars. Florida's tobacco company settlement was for $12 billion. The Florida contingent fee lawyers, riding on the coattails of the great work of the Robins firm, refused to reduce their attorney's fee which, when calculated at the contractual rate of 20 percent, amounted to fees of over $2 billion. Despite vehement public criticism and even a lawsuit by Florida to require a reduction in the fees, the lawyers held firm, refusing to concede anything. They argued that basic contract law required enforcement of the written fee contract, state and public opinion be damned. Although also offended by the amount of the fees, the Florida appellate courts upheld the contractual fee and awarded it to the attorneys. No wonder we personal injury attorneys have a bad name in the opinion of the public.

Contray to this often perceived image of greedy lawyers, personal injury attorneys usually are the little guy's best advocate. They often take questionable cases and expend their personal sums to finance the case. Seldom does the slam-dunk case walk into an attorney's office. I can only recall two different cases that had all three of the required elements for a relatively easy case resolution. The first was a number of years ago, involving the claim of a very charming Filipino lady who worked as a housekeeper in a retirement home. Her husband had died in a local hospital following surgery to replace an artificial heart valve that had been implanted a couple of years before. Investigations revealed that artificial heart valves of that type had been failing across the country and had been determined to be defective and in need of replacement. Dozens of lawsuits were pending across the country. I was able to tap into the network of lawsuits, obtain all of the indicting documents against the valve manufacturer, and begin the negotiation process with the manufacturer's insurer. A written opinion obtained from the deceased's surgeon, stating that the death was directly a result of the need to replace the defective heart valve, put all the pieces of the case together. After some tough negotiation, I reached a high six-figure settlement. As the case involved little legal time, I charged the lady a much-reduced percentage of the attorney's fee.

My second and most interesting slam-dunk case resulted from an eye-out injury to a forty-seven-year-old client who had installed a lawn sprinkling system around his home. After three years of successful operation of the system, he was winterizing it by using an air compressor to blow water out of the lines and sprinkler heads. As he worked, the plastic cap on a nearby pressure relief valve, about two and a half inches in diameter, blew off and struck him in the eye. He lost almost total vision in the eye. In my product liability lawsuit against the sprinkler manufacturer, my discovery requests produced some very interesting results. The defense attorney had been delaying his responses to my probing investigation inquiries. Suddenly, out of the blue, I received a phone call from a claims adjuster from the manufacturer's product liability insurance company. He wanted to talk settlement of my client's case and asked me for a demand. Quite taken aback, I stuttered and said I would call him back. After doing some research on the possible value of eye-out cases in Minnesota, I called the claims adjuster back and suggested that the value of this injury was between $500,000 and $750,000. When pressed I suggested that settlement would have to be for $600,000. Without hardly a moment's pause the adjuster offered $300,000 in settlement. I hung up and said, "Wow." After giving it some thought, I realized that the sudden settlement overture and the delay in producing the manufacturer's discovery responses had to be related. I told the adjuster that no response to the offer would be forthcoming until I received all of my discovery from the manufacturer.

Over six inches of the manufacturer's documents finally arrived in my office. It was great fun to read. Engineering blueprints and memos showed a long history of failures in the pressure-relief caps. To avoid continuing cap problems, the engineers had redesigned the caps by requiring eight rather than four sonic welds to secure them. One of the most astounding smoking-gun admissions in the documents was one engineer's memo analyzing the problem in this way: "When the sonic welds fail, the caps go into orbit." In addition, the manufacturer disclosed a prior injury incident in Denver without disclosing any details. A follow-up inquiry produced the name of the Denver attorney who represented the injured party. When contacted, the attorney described an almost identical eye-out incident to his client from a failed plastic cap. He would not disclose the amount of his confidential settlement with the manufacturer.

With this most interesting material in hand, my follow-up settlement discussions with the claims adjuster were really fun. He was obviously aware of his insured's disclosures. When I advised that this material would support punitive damages against the manufacturer, I strongly suggested that my $600,000 demand was reasonable under the circumstances. In a second phone call the adjuster pleaded with me to settle for something less than my one and only demand. Seeing where this was going, I held my position. Two days later the adjuster agreed to pay the full $600,000. My client was shocked by the large settlement. In this instance I had no qualms about taking my full one-third contingent fee, because my probing investigation of the manufacturer produced the damning evidence and my hard-nosed tactical negotiation resulted in the high dollar settlement for the client.

CHAPTER 43

LUCA THE WONDER DOG

A dog is a man's best friend. Trite? Maybe. But here is my testimonial. Growing up in northern Minnesota, working hard on a sawmill and in a lumberyard since age ten, and being interested in hunting and fishing with my father, I truly wonder why our family never had a dog for a pet. For some reason my mother liked cats, and from the earliest time I can remember we had one or two cats at home as our pets. One old tabby cat named Chester was the family cat throughout my childhood and even into high school. He was quite a cat. He slept outside at night under the crawl space in our house. Even in winter, with temps of twenty to thirty degrees below zero or lower, Chester slept every night in the crawlspace. Fortunately for him, the floor furnace had its burners below the floor level, keeping Chester warm enough at night to survive.

And Chester was a survivor. If you rubbed his flanks you could feel a couple of BBs under his skin where someone had taken a shot or two at him in his past. One of the unforgettable

Chester tricks was when Mother put out the Christmas bowl filled with peanuts and other mixed nuts. Everyone in the 1950s had the same kind of hardwood nut bowl, with the nutcracker and nut picks set vertically in the middle. Well, Chester would jump up onto the living room sideboard, dig around in the nut bowl with his paw, and pull the peanuts in the shell out of all of the other mixed nuts. He would then crack the peanuts in his mouth, discard the shells, and eat the peanuts. Chester lived a long life until age twenty-one. Then my dad, as he said a man had to do, took the 20-gauge and a very crippled-up old Chester into the sawmill yard and put Chester down.

Somehow an anti-dog atmosphere prevailed during my upbringing, an attitude shared by my brother. So as we both married and raised our children, we never even discussed having a dog. Neither family ever even owned cats as our parents had. My family did venture out and get a bird, a cockatiel named Sydney. Since we didn't know when we bought the bird from a breeder whether it would be a male or female, our kids helped pick a name that worked for either a male or female bird. This little bird was great for my kids growing up. We taught Sydney to whistle and say several words and phrases. He was always cheerful when people walked into the room. Whenever anyone was around, Sydney was outside of his cage, sitting on fingers or shoulders, just a part of the family. His regular poops on your shoulder or a curtain while sitting on a curtain rod were just part of the package. Breakfast with Sydney and the kids was memorable. He would sit on the edge of a cereal bowl and bob down to pick out and eat Cheerios along with the kids. On one out-of-town trip, we left Sydney with my brother. He did not believe that Sydney could talk. When we returned Sydney was saying, "Sydney is a fake," just as my brother had been saying to him for a week.

I was raised as hunter in northern Minnesota, and hunting

has always been one of my favorite pastimes. Fall regularly involved duck hunting in our hometown and pheasant hunting in Iowa or South Dakota. For a multitude of years Roger and I and some friends hunted in Iowa with a farmer friend named Jon Horton. Without a hunting dog we had to work incredibly hard chasing pheasants, usually harvesting a fair number but always ending the day dead tired at a motel somewhere. But no matter how tired we were, we had an annual ritual of going out bowling after supper and floundering through two games, trying to break a hundred.

On one hunting trip we invited an accountant named Dave and his Brittany spaniel along for the hunting trip, thinking that a hunting dog of good breeding would be a great addition to our trip. After few hours of our aggressive typical hunting day, Dave and his dog were panting and ready to go home. Dave's dog also had picked up so many sharp burrs in his abdomen and around his legs that he was walking bowlegged, totally useless for retrieving. This hardly created any more enthusiasm for owning a hunting dog.

One fall we went to Iowa and found that our friend Jon had started breeding and raising golden retrievers. His male dog, Freckles, was a great pheasant dog. The next fall we arrived at Jon's to find that he had eight little six-inch-long golden pups from his female, Muffy, who had been bred with a prominent golden stud up in Glenwood, Minnesota. The puppies were so incredibly cute that, after talking with my wife at home, I committed to take one of the pups from Jon's next litter. Sure enough, the next fall Muffy had a litter of seven cute pups. Jon said he would save me one, and I could return to get the dog when he was ten weeks old. Since we had never had a dog, I asked Jon to select a very mild-mannered, easy-to-care-for dog from among the seven pups.

Coming up with a name for a dog is as hard as naming a

child. In our case it arose from a funny naming story that has been frequently repeated. Several years before my golden retriever arrived, my wife and I and my stepdaughter were vacationing in Italy and went to tour the historic town of Lucca. After seeing the sights for several hours, we ended up at a small neighborhood restaurant and pizza joint. As we sat waiting for our food, a local customer came in with a cute little dog that ran around without a leash, making friends with all the customers. Then it stopped in the middle of the floor, squatted, and peed a little puddle, much to the delight of most of the customers. The three of us agreed at that time that if we ever got a dog it would be named Lucca.

When Jon advised that our pup was ready to be picked up, I bought a kennel, dog dishes, and toys and excitedly went down to Iowa to get Luca (for simplicity we dropped one c from the name). At Jon's we found two of the seven pups left, our Luca and a female named Ruby. Jon indicated that Luca was the most mild-mannered pup of the litter. While we sat and had coffee with Jon and his wife, we watched as the rambunctious Ruby ran around the house, knocking over three flowerpots. To our relief, Luca just sat and watched. After coffee we loaded Luca into his new kennel in the Jeep and started out of the driveway. Before we got to the end of the driveway Luca had given us his first major-league dump in his new kennel. A fresh one even from a small pup is quite pungent. Back we went to the house to hose out the kennel and clean up the pup. We set out again, and over the four-hour drive home Luca threw up four times in his kennel. What a way to start a new dog–owner relationship! It had to be all uphill from that point.

Luca had papers, and his breeding as a hunting dog was superb. Muffy had no bloodline, but she had been bred with the son of a dog named Super Trooper, who at the time was the only golden retriever who had ever won the national field trials. Luca was thus the grandson of a national field champion. With about eight weeks of hunter training Luca became a wonderful hunting dog, and over the years I had a fabulous time hunting ducks and pheasant with him. He was not only as a great bird retriever, but also a sweet family pet. I soon openly admitted my regret at not having had a family dog as a pet while my kids were growing up.

When I left the downtown law office and set up my suburban office in Minnetonka, there was already one cocker spaniel that frequently accompanied a lawyer to my building. Luca soon followed me daily to the office. My faithful secretary and legal assistant, Marilyn, was a dog owner, and she soon fell in love with Luca. Luca never barked. (I honestly recall only twelve times that he barked in his whole life.) At the office he always went up to tenants and clients with a big grin, waiting to be petted. Dogs, like people, need regular trips to the bathroom, and with Marilyn's help we soon got into a habit of twice-a-day trips out onto the lawn. Earlier, when Luca was about one year old, I was in the office on a Saturday and didn't notice that he had run downstairs to the building entryway and dropped a big smelly pile. It stunk up the whole lobby and stairway. As I got paper towels and water from the bathroom to do the cleanup, I was so thankful that no other tenants were working on the weekend. Unfortunately, as I emerged from the bathroom with my cleanup tools, another tenant and two clients were coming through the front door into this putrid mess. What can you say? Luca, of course, went up to lick the hands of his new friends. Fortunately, that was the last accident during Luca's career as a legal assistant.

Luca's presence in the office was delightful. Most tenants who walked by the open office door would greet Luca or stop and pet him. The regular mailman, Nate, would always stop and play with Luca and tease him with the dog toys in the office. Luca would wait by the window for Nate and the mail truck. He could hear Nate's footsteps in the stairway and was always alert and ready for playtime. We had several depressing weeks when Nate was transferred and the replacement mailman was a guy without personality who couldn't have cared less about a dog on his route. Some clients or visiting lawyers were taken aback to find a large gold dog in a law office. But, almost uniformly, within minutes of receiving Luca's friendly greeting and my assurances that he was a legal assistant and had never bitten anyone, guests' consternation vanished. Doggy treats were always in good supply at the office. Marilyn regularly brought in cookies, bars, jelly beans, and gummy bears, and Luca happily shared in those as well. He especially liked the gummy bears.

Luca lived to one month short of sixteen years old. At seven times each dog year, he made it to 112 years old. When Luca was getting very gray in the face I knew the end was approaching. He still regularly came to the office, but he was having more and more trouble climbing up the stairs to the second floor. Being divorced by this time and alone at home, I found Luca's companionship a remarkable comfort. He had a daily routine: When the alarm went off in the morning, he was right by my bed. With one pat from me on the bed he would vault up and lie across me for scratches and rubs for as long as I could continue. One day, though, Luca could not jump up onto the bed and needed help to jump up into the back of the station wagon. I knew it was the end. On August 31, 2011, I put him down. It was one of the saddest days of my life. Life goes on, just as it does when you lose any dear friend. But I will always appreciate the smiling, never grumpy companionship of a good dog.

CHAPTER 44

A MONTICELLO SCHOOL BUS

One town in central Minnesota bears the name of Thomas Jefferson's Virginia home, but with few French speakers here in Minnesota, it took on an American pronunciation in which "chello" was replaced with "sello." Monticello is a nice place with a very good school system, and it is the location of the single most tragic accident I dealt with during my career.

A lawyer friend called me the day after this crash, which happened on April 10, 1997, and said he had a call from North Memorial Hospital from a parent of one of the children injured in the crash. I was already aware of the incident from the evening news and the morning paper. With little hesitation I put on a suit and tie and my friend and I went immediately to the hospital to see the parents. We found the parents of two youngsters in the ICU, fretting over whether their boys would survive. Both boys had multiple injuries, including head injuries with bleeding into the brain.

The four parents had no idea what to expect from a legal

standpoint. One of my strengths over the years has been in presenting myself to clients as competent, knowledgeable, and trustworthy (sounds like the Boy Scout oath, right?), while discussing legal issues with them in ways that instill confidence in my abilities. My colleague knew little about injury law, so I carried the ball with both sets of parents. Without a lot of questions I became the lawyer for both families.

What happened on April 10, 1997? A school bus leased to Monticello was heading west to deliver home thirteen grade school kids. A few miles west of town, traffic on an intersecting north–south county road was required to stop at a stop sign and yield to traffic on the road the bus was traveling. Proceeding north was a gravel truck driven by an experienced truck driver, John Doyle. For some reason never determined, Doyle did not slow down for the stop sign and collided at high speed with the school bus in the middle of the intersection. The truck left heavy skid marks at the point where Doyle apparently started to pay attention and tried to swerve left, away from the bus. The right front corner of his truck collided with the left front corner of the bus. An interesting and very significant phenomenon then occurred. Physical forces caused the rear of the bus to swing at high speed in a clockwise direction and the rear of the truck to swing at high speed in a counter-clockwise direction. The sides of the vehicles collided again. This secondary collision was determined by the experts to have been the primary contributor to the deaths and injuries. Students in the rear of the bus were propelled sideways by the secondary impact, flying without restraint across the interior of the bus. Both vehicles ended up in the northwest corner of the intersection.

Of the thirteen students on the bus, three died and ten were injured. The truck driver, Doyle, also died in the collision. The most seriously injured kids were the two boys who became my clients. I don't remember how the three death cases were resolved, but there must have been major settlements from the insurer for the trucking company, Liberty Mutual.

Somewhat to my surprise, the federal National Transportation Safety Board (NTSB), which I had dealt with in several of my aviation cases, had jurisdiction over school bus accidents as well as airplanes and trains. They did a thorough investigation. The NTSB's conclusions were not surprising: A truck blew a stop sign and caused the collision. The investigation also included an interesting exploration of whether seat belts in the bus would have saved the children. This issue had been around for years before this crash, but it had been inflamed recently by several similar school-bus crashes. (I remember that one was an incident where a school bus was hit by a freight train in Indiana, resulting in serious injuries and deaths.) An NTSB investigator duly arrived in Monticello to gather evidence to support the requirement for seat belts in school buses. I supplied documents to this investigator and appeared at his hearing in Monticello. Seat-belt advocates believed that children should be strapped into their seats to endure whatever should happen. With such precautions, some children in the Monticello crash might have survived the secondary impact that propelled them out of their seats. Opponents argued that more serious injuries or deaths would occur if students were confined to their seats and were unable to escape fires or other catastrophes. Our case did not resolve the dispute, and school buses continue with no seat belts and harried bus drivers trying to keep kids in their seats.

My two clients, whom I will call D (age twelve) and G (age eight), both suffered multiple physical injuries as well as, most seriously, closed-head brain injuries (TBIs). MRI scans of both D and G showed bleeding into the brain. Neither were candidates for brain surgery. Thus, lengthy hospitalizations were projected to allow the TBIs to heal on their own. Significant post-hospital time would determine what permanent residual deficits may remain. Both boys left the hospital with various effects of the physical injuries and ongoing cognitive deficits from the TBIs.

I must say I am proud of my legal efforts for these two boys. Liberty Mutual at first raised a defense that Doyle must have had a heart attack or other medical problem that caused an experienced truck driver to blow right by a stop sign. Medical records, the autopsy, and the testimony of another truck driver, who had witnessed the accident while driving behind Doyle, eliminated this defense. The only conclusion was that Doyle just blew the stop sign and was the total cause of the collision.

To put together the injury case for D and G I did the following:

Obtained all of their school records documenting past intellect and mental function and their ongoing struggles in school with the TBI deficits. Recorded interviews with teachers verified the ongoing problems not only with schoolwork, but also with appropriate behavior.

Retained a child neuropsychologist at Children's Hospital in Minneapolis to conduct an initial assessment of the residuals of the TBIs and then a follow-up two years post-collision for comparison purposes. This expert predicted lifetime problems for both boys due to residual effects from the TBIs.

Retained a respected vocational counselor to review the records and offer probable vocational limitations for D and G in completing their education and pursing competitive employment. This expert concluded both boys would never complete college-level education and would have reduced earning capacity of $7,200 or more each year in the future. With the boys having forty-two and forty-seven remaining years of work life, this lost income deficit over a lifetime calculated out to very large numbers.

Prepared comprehensive settlement booklets with reports, school records, photographs, and extensive arguments to justify large settlements for the boys.

Negotiated hard with Liberty Mutual and its attorney for a million-dollar-plus settlement for each boy.

Early in my career, structured settlements had come into vogue. By investing settlement dollars into a structured annuity program with an insurance company, the recipient of the annuity would avoid paying any income taxes on the future benefits received. With the assistance of annuity experts we put together a program for each boy to provide periodic payments of the settlement sums over their lifetime, making them financially secure even if they could never sustain gainful employment. For years I followed the boys with their parents and found that they had mostly recovered from their physical injuries, and most of the deficits of the TBIs had resolved. Maybe it is the wonders of youth and a developing brain that allows for regeneration of cognitive, motor, and verbal skills after a serious TBI. The last I heard, both D and G were doing well, having both finished high school.

CHAPTER 45

CHIROPRACTORS

I do not know what the statistics would show, but there are probably several times more practicing medical doctors than practicing chiropractors. Likewise, many more people go to medical doctors than to chiropractors. And yet, if you were to compare how many visits each patient makes to a chiropractor versus to a medical doctor, the statistics would overwhelmingly favor the chiros. Patients seem to develop undying faith in their chiros and usually make regular visits, often over months and years. The relief they get at most visits is usually very short-term, a period of hours or days, with little long-term healing benefit for the underlying condition. I'm convinced that along with their practice, chiropractors are trained in how to convince patients of the need for multiple treatments. They speak a sort of foreign language, different than that of medical doctors, but it sounds quite important and very scientific to the patient. For instance, a medical doctor may take a spine X-ray that a trained radiologist would read as being totally normal. But the chiropractor would show the same X-ray to a patient with a backache and find spinal misalignments, vertebrae that need to be put back in line, and conditions labeled with sophisticated terms, such as subluxation. So starts a lengthy and often very expensive course of electric stimulation, massages, and spinal adjustments.

This cynical opening may sound like I am a hater of chiropractors. Not really, as I have had good and bad interactions with chiros over the years. As I will relate, my problem with the profession—and I will call most of them professionals—is that for every competent chiro who tries to help patients there is a charlatan in it for the money paid by patients and their insurance companies.

I'll start by relating my favorable experience. I bought my first home in 1974, a two-bedroom suburban rambler with a one-car garage. I decided that the basement laundry room was large enough for a second bathroom and a cedar paneled sauna (for, as we Finlanders from northern Minnesota know, everyone needs a sauna). To accomplish this I had to install a new floor drain from the existing drain near the washer to the new toilet drain location. This meant breaking up about ten feet of the thick cement floor. Being strong and not afraid of heavy work, I started cracking cement with a sledgehammer. Sometime during this arduous task my lower back at about belt level started to ache and soon forced me to walk in a stooped-over position. My regular doctor found no skeletal problems in an X-ray and suggested medication. I don't remember who suggested a chiropractor or how I found Dr. Sue. (I am happy to use her real name, as she has been a friend and has helped me a lot over the years. I have referred many patients with backaches to her.) Whatever the number of treatments I had with Dr. Sue that first time—probably no more than five—my back pain, described as a muscle strain, was relieved and I was able to complete the bathroom and sauna project.

Since that initial abuse of my body over forty years ago, it's seemed that about once a year I lift something too heavy, overdo working in the yard, or engage in excessive exercise or sporting activity, and I suffer another low-back strain. Dr. Sue manages to get me in for treatment almost any day that I call. Without expensive X-rays and with about five minutes of friendly chit-chat and an explanation of what I did, she diagnoses another sprain and starts the treatments. More than twenty of these back strains over the years have been resolved in one or two treatments. I remember one time, a few days before an expensive ski trip out west, I developed another low-back strain while exercising hard at the club to get my body in shape for skiing. With me stooped over in pain, we seriously considered canceling the ski trip. But again, after a couple of Dr. Sue's treatments, plus sitting in a Colorado hot tub before skiing, my back gave me no problems even on the black diamond runs. Perhaps the impressive part about Dr. Sue, in addition to her very reasonable charges, was the complete lack of pressure to schedule a high volume of palliative treatments.

Now the other side of the story. During my years as an insurance defense lawyer a high percentage of my cases were injury claims related to automobile accidents. The infamous whiplash injury to the neck or low back is the natural result of a rear-end collision, a frequent occurrence on icy Minnesota streets. Many of these claimants commence treatments with chiros for these soft-tissue injuries. It is a consistent belief among the insurance companies that pay for these treatments as well as their defense lawyers, including myself at that time, that chiropractic treatments are unnecessary and excessive, and that the chiros providing the treatment are dishonest quacks helping patients to build up their lawsuit claims. This is where many chiropractors fail the test of integrity. Unlike Dr. Sue, who does not push patients into ongoing chiropractic treatment, most of these chiros see in an auto accident patient a fat cow that they can milk for thousands of dollars. Chiros routinely treat these soft-tissue neck and back injuries three times a week for two or more months. Then they reduce the recommended frequency to two times a week and then once a week, but they still encourage ongoing preventive care to keep the patient coming back forever. Two years after an accident, when the lawsuit reaches the trial stage, there may be $10,000 or more in chiro bills even though the patient still suffers most of the back and neck pain.

Trying these cases presented me with interesting challenges in cross-examining the chiros. At defense lawyer conferences and in publications we learned how to aggressively cross the chiros. I took particular pleasure in going after the worst offenders, often successfully convincing the jury that the treatments were unnecessary and just padding the pocket of the chiropractor. In every case the chiro had rendered opinions that his or her patient, now the plaintiff in the lawsuit, had a permanent injury from the collision and would need ongoing treatment for the rest of his or her life. Under questioning, the injured plaintiff would readily admit that the treatments gave no permanent relief, just a few hours or days of benefit. Usually the chiro would make the return appointments and the patient would have no idea how much was being billed to the insurance company.

At least twenty years ago there was a show on *60 Minutes* or a similar news-investigation show about a fellow in Florida who held seminars for chiropractors. The seminars were not related to new treatments or professional education. They were advertised as teaching chiros how to make money. I seem to remember this fellow would charge attendees $6,000 for the week's training and guaranteed that if the listeners followed his methods they would make over $100,000 a year. The seminars were making this instructor a millionaire. The story quoted some traditional chiros who were openly critical of the methods being taught. Nonetheless, the seminars were obviously well attended, and we started seeing that instructor's methods being used by the younger generation of Minnesota chiropractors. In its simplest form, the plan for patients with pain problems was a several-step method of treatment. First, diagnose the injury and source of pain with expensive X-rays, scans, and examinations; then treat the pain; then correct the source of the pain with months of treatments; then schedule regular "maintenance" forever to keep the problem from recurring. One can readily see how people with available financial resources or a paying insurance company can get sucked into this money machine.

When I started my plaintiff's practice, with my fair share of auto accidents and whiplash injuries, it was inevitable that I would need some of these treating chiros as expert witnesses on behalf of their patients who were my clients. In most cases a big hurdle to overcome in the Minnesota no-fault insurance system was meeting a threshold confirming the seriousness of the motor-vehicle-related injury. We needed from the treating chiros an opinion that their patient had a permanent injury from the collision and that there were legitimate medical bills (including the chiro bills) in excess of $4,000. These thresholds were usually jury issues requiring an affirmative jury finding in order to win the case. After the no-fault system was passed, the chiros quickly caught on to the needs of their patients and their lawyers for litigation success. For $300 they would happily write a report for a lawyer justifying the chiro treatment bills and rendering opinions of permanent injury. After personally meeting some of these chiros before a trial, I cringed at the need to put them on the witness stand to be pummeled by an experienced defense attorney. I lost my share of these cases with a chiro as my main injury expert.

During my career as a plaintiff's personal injury attorney, I became at one point the chosen attorney for accident victims from the Native American community and at another for the Southeast Asian community. For a few months I was broadcast as the best lawyer to help accident victims from these minority populations in their fights with insurance companies. At first this seemed like a great source of business. For a variety of reasons, members of these minority groups have a much higher incidence of motor vehicle collisions, many of them sending drivers and passengers to the county hospital ER followed by lengthy chiro treatments starting soon after. If more than one occupant in a vehicle collision claimed injuries, they all would be treated at the same office, undergoing the same regimen of months and months of treatment. Even though the majority of these victims had little or no money to cover the treatments, the no-fault insurance for one of the vehicles in the collision would pick up the expenses, at least for a period of time. It was amazing how quickly a busy chiropractor's treatments would add up to more than the $4,000 no-fault threshold. After seeing how this system operated in these two minority communities, I could not see myself continuing to work cases in which I had to rely on those chiros as my principal injury witness. Before abandoning the business, I settled a few cases cheap and never took one to trial.

I must relate my most egregious encounter with a chiro. When the no-fault insurance system was set up in Minnesota, insurance companies were given the right to challenge payment for medical treatment deemed not to be reasonably necessary. Usually this required the insurer to schedule and complete an examination of the injured claimant with a doctor or chiro of its choosing. As could be expected, the insurers used a whole stable of practitioners who were paid well to complete a short exam of a plaintiff and then render an opinion challenging the need for chiro treatment. The no-fault system had thus created a new and profitable area of work for medical doctors. A procedure of binding arbitration was established to decide the reasonableness of required payments for the medical and chiro expenses, the lost wages of the injured person, and the replacement services claimed by the plaintiff. Like many injury lawyers, I qualified as a no-fault arbitrator to assist in resolving these issues. With a background in representing both plaintiffs and defendants, I was frequently found acceptable by both sides in these arbitrations. Even though the arbitrations only paid $300, often for several hours of work, I enjoyed doing them as it resembled somewhat the decision-making process of a judge, a full-time job that I never considered pursuing.

I was nominated as the arbitrator on a rear-end motor vehicle case with routine neck and back injury claims. The claimant was an unemployed black woman from St. Paul. The insurer was Liberty Mutual, which had stopped paying her chiro bills after paying somewhere over $5,000. As the story unfolded, not only did the lady claim injury, but her four children, ages five to fourteen, who had been passengers in her van at the time of the accident, were also claiming the same type of injury. Liberty Mutual found that it was paying chiro bills for all four children in amounts remarkably similar to those for their mother. The same chiro had been treating all five claimants, even the five-year-old, for the same type of neck and back strains. The treatment bills all looked the same and claimed that each victim had received the same chiropractic "modalities." The chiro was coming to the victims' home and providing the treatments for all five on a portable table.

At the hearing, on just the mother's claim, Liberty Mutual claimed as its defense that there was fraud by the chiro. The insurer had sent a claims person to sit outside the family home and wait for the chiro to arrive. At the hearing they presented an affidavit by the claims person stating that the chiro was inside the home with his portable table for a total of twenty-eight minutes, supposedly treating all five victims. Liberty Mutual had received bills for that day for treatments for all five claimants. The insurance company lawyer stupidly did not present to me a signed affidavit, which in the unsigned form I could not receive as evidence at the hearing. After listening to the claimant's testimony about how much she hurt, just like all of her children, and that the chiro's treatments were really helpful, I thought the whole case smelled so bad that I just had to see and hear this chiro in person. So I continued the hearing for a second day and required the chiro to appear live as a witness, along with the Liberty Mutual employee who did the spying.

The follow-up hearing was fascinating. The first witness was the claims person, a very pleasant, experienced, middle-aged lady whose testimony was totally credible. She brought her notes documenting the time of the chiro's arrival at the home and her observation of him removing the portable table from his car, entering the home, and returning to the car after twenty-eight minutes. Next to testify was the chiro. He was a young man, just a year or two out of chiropractic school, who worked for an established practice in St. Paul. The young chiro's job was to travel daily to patients' homes to provide these in-home treatments. Even though he billed regular chiro charges, he was paid only a small portion by his employer. This young fellow was incredibly nervous as the questioning, and the story unfolded further.

The insurer had subpoenaed the chiro's records for several weeks of the in-home treatments. I had solved the patient confidentiality issue by having all names deleted from the billings. The insurer also presented chiro standards showing how the various modalities of treatment were to take a certain amount of time, such as fifteen minutes for muscle stimulation and eight minutes for each spinal adjustment. Applying these modality standards to the chiro's treatment of the five family members, he should have been inside the home for something like two and a half hours. Further, his billing for that day claimed that he made some ridiculous number of in-home visits around St. Paul. When questioned about his driving time between stops, he admitted to an average of over ten minutes. When all of his driving time plus his supposed treatment time that day was added up, he should have worked more than twenty-four hours. That day he had billed for his employer a total of several thousands of dollars. The poor schmuck committing this fraud was paid only something like $300, and he was probably going to lose his license. When the questioning was done, I advised this young man that he should get his own criminal lawyer as bad times were ahead.

In these no-fault arbitrations it is recommended that the arbitrator just award dollars (or none) and not write an opinion as is usually done by a judge. In this case I chose to write a rather strong opinion. First, I denied all unpaid bills for the mother and recommended that Liberty Mutual had no similar obligation to pay any more of the children's chiro bills. I went on to say there was more than credible evidence of fraud having been committed by the employer and his young associate, and that this should be reported to the county attorney and the chiropractic licensing and discipline board. I should have followed up to see if Liberty Mutual did prosecute, but I got busy with other things. I suspect those chiropractors are no longer in business. At least, I hope not.

The latest chiro gimmick is promoting chiropractic treatment for animals. A recent website article reports, "A growing number of horses and dogs—along with cats, goats, birds, zoo animals, and other creatures great and small—are seeing chiropractors as part of a comprehensive treatment plan." I would really like to see a chiro give a spinal adjustment to a canary. Perhaps the world is still dumb enough to support this kind of nonsense.

CHAPTER 46

REVEREND M AND Z

In the many interesting cases I handled, one stands out as not only fascinating but downright bizarre. My client was Z, a lady from Ethiopia. I don't remember how the representation started, but it was likely a result of my defending Z and her insurance company in a motor vehicle accident case. Z was a beautiful, dark-skinned lady with a perfect figure and a wide grin. Her story and the basis for her lawsuit related to being sexually abused by a prominent black Baptist minister, whom we will call Reverend M. As the story unfolded, it seems that Z had been a parishioner at Rev. M's church and had sought counseling from him for emotional problems caused by separation from her parents and trying to control a younger brother who resided with her. Like many of the Catholic priests who supposedly gave counseling to their flock, Rev. M soon convinced Z that the way to get past her emotional problems was to trust the reverend and to go to bed with him. After months of this affair and several bizarre intervening events, Z was ready to break away. Feeling that she had been abused as part of her counseling experience, Z came to me to sue Rev. M and his church.

As the case developed, a lot of fascinating information about Rev. M came to light. He was very handsome, married with two kids, a prominent member of the local and national Baptist communities, and had acted in several local theater productions. But it seemed that his extracurriculars with several other church ladies besides Z had some of the church fathers quite riled up, and some were pursuing his dismissal. The congregation was divided, and Rev. M had a strong group of supporters. This all came to a head when Rev. M had a shouting match in the church parking lot with one of his mistresses, who was apparently pregnant with his child. Several bystanders heard the shouting and then watched as Rev. M slapped the lady and knocked her to the pavement. This incident prompted a full-scale church meeting over the dismissal of Rev. M. As reported to me, the meeting was total chaos. When the "fire Rev. M" group as well as the victim of the parking lot assault tried to speak, they were shouted down by Rev. M's followers. The meeting turned to uncontrolled shouting and apparently some physical confrontation. Rev. M's loyalists outshouted those favoring dismissal, and the meeting ended without a formal vote. Rev. M was back in the pulpit preaching on Sunday.

My lawsuit on behalf of Z was defended by Bill Flaskamp, a blustery old defense lawyer who was one of the partners at the Meagher, Geer firm where I had worked in my first two years of practice. The Baptist church had a $100,000 liability insurance policy that provided a free defense for the church and Rev. M, so Flaskamp, in his typical posturing, blew the case off as my client's fantasy of trying to extract money from this pious, prominent minister and his church.

In putting together the case, Z led me to two other ladies who had past sexual relations with Rev. M. Although initially embarrassed during my interviews, the ladies eventually opened up and willingly—and sometimes quite graphically—described their activities with Rev. M. Z also put me in touch with one of the most outspoken church members in the dismissal effort. My meeting with this fellow was most interesting. He was in his mid-forties, well-educated and working in some professional field that I do not now recall. I sat for two hours in his home as he spoke very knowingly not only about the local church's problems but also a long history of the denomination's problems going back to slavery days. I do not mean here to malign the Baptist church, but only to repeat the rather astounding story told to me by this fellow. He told me that historically, when black people were enslaved and had no freedom and limited individual rights, the one prominent person in the black community was always the minister. The slave owners tolerated this one man of prominence and even encouraged church attendance and obedience to the minister because it assured peaceful behavior among the slaves. The community looked up to preachers and provided quite well for them. In many cases this support included offering sexual favors to the minister. Not only were single women made available, but often married women considered it their duty to take care of the minister's needs. As the decades passed and slavery was abolished, many black Baptist ministers continued to consider it part of their right to receive, and their parishioners' obligation to provide, sexual favors.

He continued to describe that Rev. M had the same arrangement when he went out of town to attend church meeting; the local congregation was expected to supply a woman to satisfy his sexual needs. Similarly, when out-of-town ministers came to the Twin Cities, Rev. M had arranged similar services for them. Z and the two other ladies I had interviewed confirmed that when a group of high-ranking Baptist clergy had come for some big meeting, the three of them were among the women solicited to be available to "take care of" these dignitaries. As best as I can remember, two of the three had felt obligated to do so. Such abuses had been tolerated for decades by the church, the congregation, and its clergy. So it is hardly surprising that Rev. M. felt free to spread not only the gospel but his sperm among his flock.

At some point well into the lawsuit, Z advised me that she had some pictures of her times with Rev. M. Once again, a picture proved worth a thousand words. Z had pictures of her and Rev. M together in Atlanta, Seattle, and other places where they had traveled to attend church meetings. In these pictures they had handed the camera to a passerby to take a memorable picture of the two of them before some city monument. They were always hugging or kissing, with huge grins on their faces, looking like happy honeymooners. But these pictures were only the beginning. In apparent moments of bravado, Rev. M had allowed Z to take pictures of him in her apartment, lying totally nude on her bed. In several shots he lay there with a big grin on his face and his exhausted phallus clearly visible. His face in the pictures was not as clear as it could have been, but he had a very distinctive, wide scar on the front of his shoulder. (I can only speculate that after some disrupted sexual affair, some angry mistress or husband had chased Rev. M and caught up to him for one good slash with a knife.)

Taking an opposing party's deposition can sometimes be a real pleasure, especially if you have the goods on the witness. Deposition day arrived, and defense attorney Flaskamp took Z's deposition and I followed with Rev. M's deposition. Up to that point I had not had to disclose to Flaskamp in response to discovery any of my client's pictures. Rev. M, being a very smooth and believable talker, had obviously convinced Flaskamp that he was innocent, that there had been no sexual involvement, and that this whole lawsuit was to extort money from the Baptist church.

A side comment is in order. Early on I concluded that my own clients seldom told me the whole story, no matter how much they trusted me as their lawyer. As a result I would emphasize in our first client meeting that I needed to know everything, good and bad, about them and their case. I stressed disclosing every "skeleton in their closet." No matter how bad it was, I wanted to know about it, because then I could deal directly with it and not be surprised down the road. With that admonition, clients would often spill their guts, revealing past alcoholism, drug abuse, domestic battles, and prior accidents or injuries. Even with this type of so-called full disclosure, I have always proceeded under the skeptical assumption that there would be surprises ahead as the cases progressed. In a good percentage of the cases that proved to be correct. Obviously, Flaskamp had not gotten the whole story from his client.

Back to the deposition day. Flaskamp, in his usually boisterous manner, aggressively attacked Z and her story. I had warned her to expect this, and she held up quite well. Then it was my turn with Rev. M. In cross-examination you always want to ask lots of foundation and background questions before you drop the bombshell. The witness is under oath, and you want to put him solidly into cement in his own words before you bury him. Rev. M smoothly and repeatedly denied having sexual relations with any of his parishioners. He denied the first sexual event during his counseling of Z and steadfastly denied any sexual involvement with her. He denied ever having been out of town with her or in her apartment. To make sure he was knee-deep in cement, I re-asked the questions in slightly different ways to get repeated denials. Flaskamp objected loudly, accusing me of not only being repetitious but also abusing his client. Ho-hum, I felt sorry for the poor fellow.

The first pictures I revealed were the travel shots of Z and Rev. M in their affectionate poses in various cities. Rev. M denied recognizing where these shots were taken but admitted that Z was in the picture. When I pushed him, he changed his story to say that Z had accompanied him and his wife on one or two church trips to babysit the couple's children, still claiming total innocence of sexual involvement. We then took a look at the bedroom pictures. The defense lawyer is always entitled to see an exhibit before using it in the questioning. When Flaskamp looked at the pictures he seemed to deflate; he leaned back and did not interrupt the remainder of the deposition. When Rev. M looked at the pictures, he said, "I don't know who this is and where the pictures were taken." He claimed total ignorance about what was shown in the pictures. He denied that was him bare-ass naked on the bed. I then asked him if he could see the large scar on the shoulder of the person in the picture. He had to say yes. When I asked him if he had such a scar, he did not want to answer. I asked Flaskamp to have his client take off his shirt and tie. When Flaskamp made a weak objection, I said, "We can either do it now, or I obviously can get a court order to have him do so." Flaskamp called a recess and took his client out of the room, obviously to check for himself if there was a scar. They returned in a few minutes and Rev. M, without removing his shirt, admitted on the record that he had a scar in that location. I believe my last two questions to him were, "Your scar is about the same size and shape as the scar on the person in the pictures, right?" The answer was "Yes." "You still deny that that is you in the pictures and that you were having sex in Z's bedroom?" The answer was, "I deny it."

I don't remember how soon thereafter the case settled, but Flaskamp paid his insurance company's full $100,000 policy limit for a dismissal of the case against Rev. M and his church. I later had several humorous conversations with Flaskamp about his client and the pictures. Flaskamp knew that I knew that he was also quite the ladies' man, so I could openly kid him whether he was as good a man as Rev. M and whether he could satisfy his girlfriends as well.

Some clients and opposing defendants disappear after a case is resolved. Not so for Z and Rev. M. Z kept in touch with me for a few years after the settlement. She had been in a typical whiplash-type rear-end motor vehicle accident. On the phone I had explained to her that her no-fault insurance would take care of her medical bills, that she should seek appropriate medical treatment, and that there was nothing I could do for her until she met a no-fault threshold of more than $4,000 in medical bills. Several months went by with no contact from Z. She then came in with another bizarre story. She had chosen a chiropractor in northeast Minneapolis for her neck and back treatment. As usually happens, the no-fault insurer became upset after a few months of paying chiropractic bills and took the steps to terminate their payments for the chiropractor's treatments. Z had continued to see the chiropractor but had no money for the treatments.

When I inquired about how long this had gone on and the amount of the outstanding bill, Z told me with little hesitation that she was not being billed, as she would give oral sex to the chiropractor after every treatment. Needless to say, this was a strange way to pay for chiropractic treatment. Clearly the chiropractor was getting the best of the treatments. Z not only now wanted to start a car accident lawsuit but wanted to sue the chiropractor for malpractice. I don't know if complicity would be a defense to a chiropractic malpractice or sexual abuse claim, but Z clearly had been a willing participant in providing payment in kind for her treatments. Fortunately my better judgment told me to stay clear of this one. I told Z that I could not handle either lawsuit for her and recommended that she contact the state chiropractic board if she wanted to make a complaint against the chiropractor. This was, happily, the end to my Z stories.

But Rev. M surfaced again after another parishioner accused

him of sexual abuse. This woman in her early twenties, whom we will call D, was the daughter of one of the two women I had previously interviewed. Her story was that when Rev. M was in their house to see her mother he cornered her in the bathroom and raped her. I don't remember all of the circumstances, but the rape story was quite credible and D became my client. At that time Rev. M had left his position at his Baptist church. It seems that the ongoing division of parishioners over his philandering had resulted in Rev. M and all of his supporters, about half of the congregation, leaving the church to set up a new congregation in a St. Paul suburb. The new congregation was small and just getting going with Rev. M as their leader. My lawsuit for D was against Rev. M and the new church. For whatever reason, the church and Rev. M. ignored the lawsuit and never answered. I moved for a default judgment and had to serve the default papers on the church. At the hearing to prove up $100,000 in damages for D, a lawyer showed up for the first time, along with Rev. M, and claimed to be representing Rev. M and the church. The lawyer never really tried to contest the rape claim. Instead he wanted to talk settlement, claiming that the church had no money and its building was fully mortgaged. Likewise he claimed Rev. M was paid only a modest salary. A settlement was reached, with the church and Rev. M. agreeing to pay $200 a month to D for as long as Rev. M was associated with the church. If he regularly made his payments, we would not enforce the $100,000 judgment against the church.

Rev. M made the regular payments, though some of them were late and required a reminder letter. Sometimes Rev. M showed up at my office to drop off the checks. If I saw him at the office I would go shake his hand, and he'd pleasantly say, "Mark, how are you?" Aw, the friendships we make in this business! From each $200 monthly payment I extracted $66.67 (about the amount for a nice dinner for two with a bottle of wine) as my attorney fee.

My final involvement with Rev. M was a fortuitous event. Rev. M called me in December of 2008, expressing an interest in settling the remaining balance owing on D's judgment. He was retiring down south and was planning to sell his St. Paul home. My judgment against him had created a lien on his home, disrupting his sale. He had a lawyer who was helping to clear title to his home. When I looked at my judgment papers I was amazed to find that we were about one week short of the ten-year anniversary of the date of the judgment. I had totally lost track of how many years had passed. Under Minnesota law, after ten years a judgment becomes unenforceable unless it is formally extended with a new court proceeding. If more than one week had passed after Rev. M's call my judgment would have been worthless and Rev. M could have walked away from it. Obviously, neither Rev. M nor his lawyer had looked at the judgment date, or they would have waited one more week to discuss settlement. I hurriedly prepared the appropriate papers and had a judge sign an order to extend the judgment for another ten years. With a new judgment intact, I negotiated a lump-sum payment of $50,000 for a satisfaction of judgment. That amount came right out of the proceeds from the sale of Rev. M's house. My client, D, was very happy with the result.

CHAPTER 47

TWO TOUGH CASES THAT I WON

Two of my wins for clients involved particularly memorable and difficult challenges in selling the case to a jury. The first was called *Wells v. Gay Nineties*. This fine downtown watering hole had become an accepted hangout where gay men could safely congregate to drink and dance and be entertained by a raunchy, transsexual comedian. My client, an openly gay fellow about twenty years old, had gone to the Gay Nineties with three friends. After drinking heavily in the main bar area, the client's buddies went into a back room where dance music was playing. After more drinks, my client went looking for his friends. He somehow took a wrong turn and came across an open elevator shaft. As he turned right, thinking it was the room entrance, he went airborne and landed over a floor below at the bottom of the elevator shaft. Until the loud music shut down about two hours later, no one heard his cries for help. He was trapped there, covered with oil, lying on broken glass, and enduring pain from several orthopedic fractures.

One of our associate lawyers brought his injured friend in as a client. He asked my help in representing the plaintiff's case. We sued the elevator company for failing to have appropriate self-locking gates on the elevator. When the elevator was at a different floor there clearly should have been a gate across the open shaft, but this one had failed. We also sued the Gay Nineties for allowing this dangerous situation to exist as a serious hazard to its customers.

The trial and its preparation were most interesting. I was quite concerned about how a jury would react to the gay client and his friends. In meeting with the four friends before trial I was stumbling over my words, trying to be polite but forceful in my recommendations to downplay the gay aspects of this situation. Sensing my nervousness on the issue, one of the guys made a memorable comment: "Mr. Stageberg, what you are saying is you don't want us to act swishy." I laughed with them and responded, "That's exactly right, I just couldn't say it as well." At trial, during my questioning of the prospective jurors, I first explained that my client and his friends were gay and then strongly challenged them to put aside any prejudices they might have about homosexuals. Everyone agreed, but I still had many concerns how my client would be treated by the jury.

One moment in the trial was rather entertaining. The Gay Nineties had some big bruisers as bouncers. One of these fellows looked like a Vikings offensive tackle. When this huge fellow got up on the witness stand, he was initially asked, "Give us your name and address." In a very high falsetto voice he responded, "Oh, my name is Robert [something]." Everyone in the court room had a chuckle.

My injured client was found to have a blood alcohol level of .19, indicating that he was heavily intoxicated when he stumbled around towards the elevator shaft. But to counter this I presented some forceful evidence that the Gay Nineties bartenders routinely poured "heavy drinks." We actually used bar glasses with Coke to show how much liquor was poured into each drink.

My client and his friends turned out to be very likable witnesses. Since we were suing a gay bar, there was no prejudice our way as both sides were equally offensive to any homophobes on our jury. The jury swung our way on both liability and damages. Because of the heavy drinks served by the bar and the failures of the elevator company, both were found at fault. My client was not found negligent to any degree and was awarded $414,000 for his injuries. After the jury verdict was read, several of the jurors walked up to my client, smiled, shook his hand, and wished him well. My thought was that these jurors had actually done a guilt trip on their own biases. That is something I have seen before in trials. Rather than admitting to being biased, they will bend over backwards to demonstrate the opposite, especially in a mixed group in a jury room. This can really benefit a minority client if guilt about being biased can be called out during the jury questioning.

The second fun case, called *Rider v. Spring Lake Park,* had similar potential problems to overcome with the jury. My client was a bearded, thirty-year-old motorcycle operator. Prior to his accident, he had been drinking with buddies and left after dark. On his way home he missed his turn and was proceeding on a service road to get back onto the freeway. Where the service road should have continued straight, it instead made a sharp 90-degree turn to the left because for some strange reason a church had been built directly in the path of the service road. The City of Spring Lake Park had one small 90-degree warning sign a ways back from the turn. After many motorists had missed the poorly signed turn and driven onto church property, the good church fathers had dumped a large pile of dirt next to the turn, supposedly to discourage the trespassing motorists. Along came Mr. Rider, after leaving the bar, believing that the service road would continue straight. Hardly slowing down at all, he missed the turn, hit the dirt pile, and launched into the air, flying off his motorcycle.

His injuries were impressive. He actually landed on his feet, but the impact was so severe that it drove the balls of his hip joints right through the sockets on both legs. The X-rays graphically showed the injuries. After complex surgery and a long time in rehab, Mr. Rider had a fairly good recovery but was left with permanent disabilities.

The lawsuit was against the city and the church. I distinctly remember deciding to make a frank presentation to the jury on the tough issues during my questioning. I said something like, "There are several parts of this case that make my client's severe injury case difficult. They are as follows: He looks like a Hell's Angel; he was driving a motorcycle; he had been drinking some beer before this happened; and we are suing a city and a church. How could we possibly prevail?" I actually started laughing, as did most of the prospective jurors. One actually said as he laughed, "Yah, you really got a tough one." But with further questions focusing on what was really important to the outcome, I felt pretty good as the final jury was seated.

My discovery showed a string of accidents or near accidents as many motorists missed that turn. Both the city and the church were well aware of the hazard. Some of the church's council meeting minutes even discussed the problem. Before the church removed the dirt pile and added lots of signs and barricades, I went out and took pictures and measured the dimensions of the dirt pile. I hired an accident reconstruction expert to try to determine the speed of the motorcycle. The police investigators had found a gouge some feet past the dirt pile and concluded that it was the first landing place of the flying motorcycle. Using some launch physics, my expert calculated the launch speed of the motorcycle as it flew to its first landing place as something like thirty miles per hour, or within the speed limit. The city and the church had nothing to challenge this expert opinion.

This jury was also able to put aside their biases and came back with a favorable plaintiff's verdict. Both the city and church were found at fault, 40 percent for the city and 50 percent for the church. My client was found 10 percent at fault and was awarded $277,000 in damages. I am quite sure that the jury's believing that both the city and the church had liability coverage (which they did) played a big role in the finding in our favor.

Some good lessons were learned from these cases. One can overcome difficult clients and issues by being straightforward with a jury. Trying to sugarcoat and downplay the problems in a case will usually backfire; the jury will not like you for doing so.

CHAPTER 48

COURTROOM DEMONSTRATIONS

This is one of those fun subjects that make trial work fun. There is an abundance of stories of attorneys presenting before a jury some type of courtroom demonstration that fails miserably and hurts rather than helps the lawyer's case. Most recently the advent of electronically equipped courtrooms has led too many lawyers to believe they are tech geniuses capable of making presentations without any real training in the technical side of things. I have seen too many time-consuming electronic glitches that have distracted a jury's attention from the real issues to be decided.

I do like demonstrative exhibits in the courtroom. A visual has a much greater impact on a jury than the words spoken from the witness stand. Bland, technical medical testimony in a videotaped deposition can really be jazzed up with a model skeleton and X-rays and films on a shadow box. There are plenty of medical illustrators who are happy to prepare, for a healthy fee, beautiful multicolored illustrations of a client's injuries. For some twenty years now there also have been animators available to produce a computer simulation of any type of an accident. These often can cost $25,000 or more, but they are most impressive if done right (that is, if they do not remind viewers of a cartoon show).

In the preparation of Mary's double electrocution case, I wanted to recreate the three-story farmhouse next to the high voltage powerline where the two painters were electrocuted. Rather than using one of the high-priced professionals to create a replica farmstead, I called the University of Minnesota architectural school and asked them to put a note on the bulletin board requesting assistance on an architectural model issue. The first call I received was from a third-year landscape student who sounded as if he really needed the job. He turned out to be a most personable Iranian named Asharjavan. I gave him pictures and a tour of the farm site, and he went to work. He came back with a perfect styrofoam model of the farmhouse with the trees and the high-voltage power line in perfect position. His creation allowed us to raise and lower the power line to demonstrate to the jury how the power company had let the line sag and come too close to the building. Every demonstrative exhibit needs foundation to convince the judge that what is being presented is an honest and reasonably accurate representation of the real thing. My first witness in the trial was Asharjavan, who testified exactly as planned. With his boyish smile, no jury could possibly doubt his honesty. Asharjavan's work cost me a total of $500, plus a bonus on top.

Mikey's case is another that brings back memories about some fun demonstrative exhibits. Mikey was a very handsome young lad who participated with my son and me in a YMCA Indian Guides troop for adolescent boys. For several years we fathers and sons engaged in Indian rituals and entertaining activities. I developed a real liking for Mikey, who always seemed to be smiling. During the summer after Mikey's first year of college, he was working for a home building contractor as a helper and gofer. One day, on the job on a home under construction, a carpenter was using a pneumatic nail gun to attach sheetrock around a door opening. As he rapidly drove in nails around the door, one ten-penny nail shot through the door opening and struck Mikey in the eye as he was walking past. Needless to say, this handsome young man lost the vision in that eye.

My case against Senco, the nail-gun manufacturer, was just one of many across the country. These nail guns were designed to enable the user to hold the trigger down and bounce the spring-loaded end of the gun on a surface; with each bounce, an air-driven nail was ejected from the gun. One fellow had raised the gun to scratch his ear, still holding the trigger down, and drove a sixteen-penny nail into his brain. (He survived the injury.) A few years later I had second nail gun case with a carpenter who bumped his leg with the gun while the trigger was pulled and drove a sixteen-penny into his knee. In Mikey's case, as in many others, the claim was that a safer design for the nail gun was available.

One of Senco's defenses was that Mikey should have been wearing OSHA approved safety glasses on the jobsite. Of course, on home construction no one ever did, even if OSHA required it. I hired an engineering expert to help me disprove the defense and show that the power driven nail from the Senco gun would have penetrated even a safety lens. We set up an air compressor and a similar Senco nail gun in my driveway. We began shooting nails at a target from a few feet, then ten feet, twenty feet, and amazingly, fifty feet, to test the power of the gun. One shot sent a nail right over my garage and into my neighbor's yard. A few minutes later my neighbor came over, wondering what was going on. He explained that a nail had fallen from the sky onto his driveway— about 150 feet away from its launch point! The expert and I then shot some nails at OSHA-approved safety glasses from different distances, producing some fantastic court exhibits. We had two pairs of OSHA-approved glasses with nails driven right through them by the Senco nail gun. All of this, of course, was carefully photographed and videotaped.

The fun was yet to come. The case, by agreement, was to be decided by a three-person arbitration panel. After we presented our case, the defense for Senco brought its expert in to present a videotape of their testing of the benefit of safety glasses. The first videotape showed a styrofoam head, such as a wig-seller might use, with a pair of dark OSHA glasses attached. Then, in impressive super-slow motion, they showed nails from the Senco nail gun bouncing off the safety glasses several times. On first viewing it was very impressive. The expert described the many people who were present and witnessed this videotaped experiment, including technicians, company representatives, experts, and defense lawyers. I watched carefully and saw a small gray circle in the bottom of one lens of the safety glass being used in the video. Following up on that observation, during my beginning cross of the expert I had him confirm that he had shown an edited version of the original tape of the total testing. Upon inquiry, the expert acknowledged that the full tape was in his hotel room near the courthouse. The arbitrators agreed that the expert had to produce the full videotape for my review over the noon recess. Much to my delight, footage of the very first test they had run showed a nail clearly penetrating the safety lens, producing the little gray circle I had seen on the safety lens. The edited version had eliminated this first sequence and the sound accompanying it. I prevailed on our arbitration panel to view the full, unedited version of the Senco testing. Playing that first test, with full recorded sound, was one of my most fun moments in court. As the film showed the nail, still in super-slow motion, penetrating through the safety lens and right into the styrofoam head, the soundtrack captured the unanimous outcry of "Oh, shit!" from the Senco observers. I had a lot of fun cross-examining the expert after that. Two great lessons to be learned from this example are to never record sound, and never film a demonstration the first time through.

A final example of a fun demonstration was one where I kept my fingers crossed when we did it in court. A client had a hand drill with an automatic "on" button placed right where an operator would wrap his or her right hand while operating the drill. My client had been using this drill, with a metal-cutting bit, to drill a hole in a piece of metal. The bit caught, pulling the drill out of the client's right hand, while continuing to operate because of the engaged "on" button. When the drill bit caught, there followed an amazing sequence: The drill whipped around, wrapping the cord tightly around the drill and my client's right thumb, which remained caught around the spinning drill. Unable to let go, the drill cord tore my client's thumb right off. In my product liability lawsuit I sought to prove that the placement of the "on" button on this drill was inappropriate and contrary to industry standards. I sent a memo around our office to all lawyers and staff asking them to bring in their handheld drills. The response was great. I obtained as trial exhibits ten or twelve drills, each with the "on" buttons placed in much safer locations.

I had to admit that the spinning drill tearing off a thumb was going to be hard for a jury to believe. My twelve different drills with switches in better locations did not prove that the drill in question was defective. My engineering expert and I played around with the poorly designed drill and a drill bit embedded in a two-by-four. We started drilling a hole in the wood, then pressed the "on" button and let the drill go. In most tests the cord wrapped tightly around the drill, just as the client contended. Taking this demonstration before a jury was still cause for real trepidation. With no assurance of success, my engineer and I set up the drilling demonstration in the courtroom in front of the jury. My engineer started drilling into the wood, punched the "on" button, and released the drill. In a split-second the drill whipped around faster than the eye could follow and wrapped the cord so tightly around the drill that it pulled the plug out of the electrical outlet. My engineer and I could not help but smile, as we had completely convinced the judge and jury that any finger, including my client's thumb, could have been squeezed off in an instant. Demonstrations are great . . . when they work.

CHAPTER 49

THE NOT-SO-SPECIAL OLYMPICS

We all know about the Special Olympics (SO). Seeing the happy, smiling faces of disabled adults and youngsters competing for ribbons and trophies, we cannot but have a warm feeling for these athletes and their achievements. However, I had a case that illuminated the other extreme, involving serious damage to a youngster who wanted to be an athlete at the SO.

My client was a very friendly eleven-year-old who since birth had suffered from Prader-Willi Syndrome. This is a rare metabolic condition involving mental retardation and an excessive appetite resulting usually in extreme obesity. My client, whom I will call Joey, received special education help and was slowly progressing through grade school. He had a very caring mother who spent many hours trying to control Joey's food compulsions and keeping his weight down through regular athletic activities. Joey's father had pursued a divorce because, as he relayed to me, he just could not deal with his son's disabilities. When I met Joey he had a big smile on his face and always was a joy to be around.

Throughout the litigation, and for years after, he and I got along very well. His speech was affected by the syndrome, and he had trouble saying words with the letter *R*, so he regularly called me "Mawk."

Through his school years Joey became involved with the SO. He was very enthused about participating in several upcoming events at the University of Minnesota. The group of youngsters with their chaperones planned to spend the night before the competition at a hotel in Minneapolis. Joey was assigned to a room with his friend Danny, also about age eleven. No chaperones were near the room when a husky sixteen-year-old disabled boy named Fred entered Joey's room. (Joey always referred to his attacker as "Fwed.") Fred took Joey into the bathroom, threatened him with a knife, and anally raped him while Danny waited outside the bathroom. I don't remember how the rape was reported, but Fred was taken away and Joey's SO trip was cancelled.

Through his mother and social workers Joey had already had a good deal of psychological counseling to deal with the rape. By the time he became my client he had adjusted fairly well and could describe the events at the hotel. My lawsuit was against several parties, including the chaperones, the local SO organizers, and the hotel for not having secure rooms. Discovery established a solid case of negligence on the chaperones and organizers for not supervising these youngsters in the hotel. We also found out that Fred had anger problems and dangerous tendencies that were known to the defendants. He never should have been allowed to roam unattended in the hotel.

Probably some of my most memorable deposition moments occurred in this case. A deposition of Danny happened first. Although he was never in the bathroom, he knew exactly what was going on and freely described the events. His speech ability was at about the same level as Joey's and was mostly understandable. He claimed to have seen Fwed's knife. Before the deposition Danny described to me that the knife was about five to six inches long. When questioned by the defense lawyers, however, he held his hands apart about twelve inches to describe it. When it came my turn to question, there was no sense in my trying to correct Danny's description of Fwed's saber.

The defense lawyers were hesitant but knew they had to take Joey's deposition. In preparing for the deposition, his mother and I decided that Joey's favorite psychologist should attend the deposition with him for support. I spent a long time with Joey getting him prepared for the questioning. Our conference room had all the defense lawyers and several insurance claims people in attendance to hear Joey's story. To try and quell his appetite, Joey's mother had him drink Diet Coke. Whenever he was with me, there always was a Diet Coke handy. During the deposition he consumed at least three Diet Cokes, and of course that meant numerous bathroom breaks were required. The questioning lawyers were appropriately polite and kind to Joey. When they reached the critical testimony of what happened in the bathroom, I held my breath. How would Joey handle it in front of about ten strangers? In response to the question, "What happened next?" Joey turned to me and said, "Mawk, can I say it?" I responded, "Go ahead, Joey." Without hesitation, Joey said, "He fucked me up the ass." If there ever was stunned silence in a conference room this was it. I don't remember what the next question was, but it took a while for the lawyer to get it out. If I have to look back at my total legal career, this moment and Joey's response was my single most unforgettable event.

I was successful in negotiating a settlement somewhere over $500,000 for Joey. Putting this into a structured annuity guaranteed him a lifetime income even if he never was able to have gainful employment. For several years after the case closed I would take Joey to Twins games or other fun events. At the Twins games his favorite was the large Walkaway Sundae with ice cream and lots of chocolate sauce. At one game I remember he somehow lost his spoon, and by the time I finally noticed it he was eating the gooey sundae by the handful. I somehow never seemed to take enough napkins. As a Christmas present one year I took Joey down to see the Holidazzle parade on Nicollet Mall. We went to a nice restaurant afterwards. How could I refuse him when he spoke up and ordered steak and lobster from the waitress?

Joey and his mother eventually moved to Arizona, and one time I went to visit them at their new home. Joey was then about age twenty-one and was doing well. He was active in handicapped bowling, horseback riding, and softball. With the monthly annuity payments Joey and his mother were doing just fine. We still exchange Christmas cards, and their future still looks good.

CHAPTER 50

OWNING PINE RIVER

I'll say it again: No matter how much potential a case has in liability and damages, you still need lots of insurance coverage to make it a good case. Minnesota has a statute requiring only $30,000 in automobile liability coverage for drivers, leaving many seriously injured accident victims with inadequate compensation, even with a clear liability and serious injury case. Fortunately, Minnesota made it mandatory for auto insurance policies to have under-insured motorist coverage to fill at least some of the gap between low liability coverage limits and the true value of a personal injury. Outside of the motor vehicle accident arena, however, the limits of defendants' liability insurance coverage governed the outcome of many a good liability and damage case. Such was the dram shop case against the City of Pine River, a small community in central Minnesota.

I will call my client Susan. She was a lovely blonde in her early twenties with two cute girls, ages four and two. Susan was a Pine River local, married to a jovial hometown fellow, who I will call Chad, also in his mid-twenties. Chad was well liked at happy hour at the Pine River Municipal Liquor Store. He had never accomplished much in his lifetime except snaring one of the prettiest ladies ever to process through the Pine River school system. Chad's work was primarily physical labor, having worked in logging, then at a local sawmill, and then for a house-moving company.

Chad and Susan's story begins with a serious industrial accident that occurred when a fellow employee at the house-moving company allowed a steel beam to fall across Chad's lower leg, resulting in a serious compound fracture of both bones. From a financial standpoint, the resulting workers' compensation paid to Chad and Susan during his disability, which always is tax-free, was steady and almost equal to his wages. The injury, however was very serious and required two attempted reconstruction surgeries by an orthopedic doctor at the Brainerd hospital. Whether that doctor committed malpractice is immaterial to the story, but even several months later Chad's femur bone had not yet knit itself back together. X-rays of the leg showed nearly an inch separating the two fractured ends of the femur. After seeking out a second opinion, Chat was referred to the orthopedic department at the University of Minnesota. The university doctors recommended a complex procedure over several months involving the application of an external metal brace around the lower leg with adjustment screws that would be tightened weekly to gradually pull the two bone ends together until union and healing took place. Chad scheduled the surgery, with the blessing of the workers' compensation insurance company, as the last hope for mending his leg and returning him to work.

The day before the scheduled surgery, Chad, anticipating many months of recovery, limped on his crutches into the Pine River Municipal Liquor Store to toss down a few with his drinking buddies. As is often the case, as the afternoon hours passed, a few became a few too many. Chad was a steady customer of the muni, as witnesses later testified, and the bartender regularly poured him heavy hits in his chosen mixed drinks. Picture if you will the following: Chad, quite intoxicated, sitting on a bar stool, demonstrating to several onlookers how he could flop around his fractured lower leg. Witnesses later described that Chad was laughing during this gory exhibition and "obviously feeling no pain."

In theory, or at least in every case of claimed dram-shop liability, bartenders contend that they are well trained to "cut off" customers showing visible signs of intoxication. That at least is the statutory standard in Minnesota for holding a bar and its bartenders and servers liable for damages caused by any intoxicated person. To succeed in a liquor liability violation claim, commonly called a dram-shop claim, it is the burden of the party damaged by the intoxicated person to prove that the person was served at least his or her last drink while showing visible signs of intoxication. Visible signs may include slurred speech, blurry eyes, staggering or weaving, incoherent thoughts, rowdiness, or any other loss of control, coordination, or thought process. Invariably, the bartender and serving staff will have no memory of the drunk's condition or will testify to no visible signs of intoxication. A high blood-alcohol reading is helpful proof but far from conclusive. Eyewitnesses, if not themselves too intoxicated, can best prove the condition of the drunk at the time of last serving. In our case, several of Chad's afternoon imbibers were easily found by our investigator and, while claiming themselves to be less than intoxicated, contradicted the bartender by giving sworn statements that Chad was allowed to become very intoxicated prior to leaving his barstool at the muni. But Chad was not done. The friendly bartender had sold Chad a six-pack of beer for the road.

Chad and Susan's home was two miles north of Pine River.

Chad, however, headed east in his Jeep, an open can of beer from the six-pack as his companion. Witnesses speculated that he was heading to a coworker's place for more partying. About a mile east of town the Jeep left the roadway and went into the right ditch, proceeding several hundred feet until it hit a farm driveway, flipped, and rolled several times before grinding to a halt. After emergency treatment at the local hospital, Chad was airlifted to North Memorial hospital in the Twin Cities. Several days later, after receiving a call from a referring lawyer, I found Chad in body traction at the hospital, Susan at his side. X-rays and scans showed that Chad had an inoperable severed spinal cord and would be a paraplegic the rest of his life. My review of his hospital chart revealed that a blood sample had been taken and analyzed upon his emergency room admission some four or five hours after he had been served his last drink. I recall only that the blood alcohol reading was quite high, somewhere in the area of .20, or at least double the legal driving limit (.10 at that time). After several months of hospital rehab and physical therapy, Chad returned home in a wheelchair, never again to have functional use of either leg.

Susan and her two children became my clients. Under the Minnesota dram-shop law, these three innocent victims, even though closely related to the intoxicated person, had suffered pecuniary loss because of the illegal sale by the Pine River Municipal Liquor Store to an already intoxicated person. Each of the three could be individually named as a plaintiff in the dram-shop case against Pine River. Even though Chad's work record was sporadic, he still was the primary provider for his family. The financial loss to the family was calculated at well in excess of half a million dollars. Because of his paraplegic condition, Chad needed daily and often hourly nursing assistance, another large calculated future damage expense as part of the family's claim. In addition, Chad's paraplegia and wheelchair confinement eliminated from his life many normal functions and activities of a husband and father. One ironic outcome of Chad's severed spinal cord was the elimination of the need for any further leg surgery. With his loss of all feeling below the waist, the doctors let the non-union of the leg fracture continue, as it presented Chad with no serious pain or additional limitations. Unfortunately for Chad and the family, the workers' compensation insurer had agreed to pay lost wage benefits for the leg injury for only six months or until the predicted healing period from the leg surgery was completed, presuming that Chad would have then returned to employment. The damage potential of the case that I started for the family, even in a rural Minnesota courtroom, was well in excess of a million dollars.

I set out to establish my trifecta of good liability, good damages, and lots of liability insurance. An investigator dispatched to interview Chad's drinking companions obtained statements about Chad's intoxicated condition as he left the muni with a six-pack under his arm. These witnesses' statements, together with the high blood-alcohol reading, made for a solid liability case against the Pine River Municipal and its bartender. As is way too often the case, the very sympathetic plaintiff's high-buck damage case confronted a defendant with limited liability insurance coverage. So, too, for the City of Pine River. For whatever reason, the city's mayor and council had agreed to purchase only $100,000 per claim of liquor liability insurance for its municipal liquor store. When questioned about this in depositions, these officials claimed the tax base for the one thousand low-to-middle-income Pine River residents did not allow a budget expenditure for more than this minimal coverage.

As would be expected, when the city's insurance carrier and its defense lawyer reviewed our liquor liability evidence and comprehended the damage potential of the case, they agreed to offer the full $100,000 in settlement in exchange for a release of the city, its liquor store, and its bartender. In many such instances, we lawyers have no choice but to advise our clients to fold the tent and accept the available insurance policy limit. Unless the target defendant is a wealthy individual or a corporation, pursuing an excess claim against the assets of the defendant is usually a futile effort. Even if the target has assets, a significant personal judgment above the insurance coverage may result in a bankruptcy filing by the defendant, again leaving no recovery for the client after a lot of legal effort. A city, however, is a slightly different animal. It does have assets: Buildings, parks, playgrounds, fire engines, police cars, and even a budget that may be subject to attachment. Furthermore, the governing body of the city has the power to borrow money or to levy increased property taxes on its residents to pay off a judgment, just as it pursues revenue for other municipal improvements.

Refusing to close this case for the insurance limits, I explored the budget, resources, and assets of Pine River. As anticipated, Pine River had assets: Two parks situated on valuable land, two fire engines, two police cars, an ambulance, a snowplow, and several municipal buildings. At best these assets comprised another $200,000 of potential recovery. We soon heard moaning and gnashing of teeth from the city officials and their attorney about how the low-income Pine River citizens could never be taxed more than their present amounts, and the only option for the city was bankruptcy (difficult for a municipality because of the destruction of its borrowing power, but not impossible). Even the most hard-nosed plaintiff's attorney would have some compassion for city officials facing this predicament. My sympathy for the city was tempered by their stupidity in not securing more insurance and the severity of the liquor violation by the bartender in continuing to serve the badly intoxicated Chad. Although halfway kidding, I told Susan that she could become the owner of Pine River and Chad could manage the municipal liquor store from his wheelchair.

A mediator was chosen and two days of mediation ensued, with the mayor and city council members actively involved. At the second mediation session, the mayor came forward with a workable and creative solution. The local bank had wanted a portion of some city land for a drive-in bank expansion. In exchange for the land, the bank agreed to loan the city $200,000 on a twenty-year payback at a very low interest rate. The city would levy increased property taxes on its citizens over the next twenty years to pay back the loan. As this $200,000 offer matched our valuation of the city's net worth, we concluded we could do no better. We finalized a total settlement of $300,000.

After the deduction of attorney's fees, case expenses, and the payment of a portion of a large medical assistance lien, the balance purchased structured annuities for Susan and her children. Although it provided nice monthly payments, the settlement covered only minimal living expenses for the family. Susan was unable to work and was providing the day-to-day care for Chad, a major responsibility. I always questioned how long beautiful Susan would hang in there, tied to her suddenly dismal existence. The last I heard from them, they had moved to Arizona to live with Chad's mother. One question remains: How many Pine River residents ever got the full story of why their property taxes increased by several hundred dollars a year?

CHAPTER 51

JOE, HOW I WOULD LIKE TO FORGET

Every lawyer probably has a client in the past that he or she wants to forget, whose name should never be mentioned again in any context. Well, Joe is mine. And not just because I once foolishly appeared as his lawyer, but because I was stupid enough to do it two more times.

I first encountered Joe in the first five years of my career; he appeared at a friend's house as a dashing ladies' man. After a few social interactions, my wife and I decided to participate with Joe in a weekend sailing trip on Lake Superior. Joe brought along a naïve young date who fit our group like a bad slipper. It was soon clear that he had no respect for his date, who was retching with seasickness. Joe called her his "dinghy." The trip was less than glorious.

I had learned that Joe was running his own company, recycling plastic waste material and turning it into reusable pellets for the plastic industry. Not having much interest in Joe at that time, I considered his motives and business plan fairly sound. It didn't matter, because Joe disappeared until about ten years later.

Then my agony started. He was referred to me by a friend we had in common. Joe claimed his booming plastic recycling business had tanked because of the failure of the Chinese to accept two container loads of his scientifically designed plastic material, which was radiation-resistant and would revolutionize the plastic syringe business. Joe claimed the shipping company was at fault because the Chinese import officials had opened the containers, destroying the sterility of the plastic. I was fortunately not involved in the complex case against the shipping company. Joe had hired a good lawyer in town, but after huge expense and a lengthy trial, the case had been thrown out at both the trial and appellate level. When Joe came to me, his complaints were against not just the Chinese and the shipping company, but also his lawyer for failing to make all of the correct arguments at trial.

As I look back I wonder, how many signals of a pending disaster in a client's case must explode in front of you before you refuse to accept a client's case on a contingent fee? In this case I ignored all of the warning signs. One of my partners at the Lommen, Nelson firm, appellant specialist Kay Hunt, had represented Joe on his appeal, trying to resurrect his federal court lawsuit against the shipping company. Kay confirmed that Joe's lawyer had not done a very good job for him. With that little bit of hope, and Joe's insistence that his lawyer was very negligent, I agreed to represent him in suing his lawyer for legal malpractice.

I flew down to Chicago to talk to the lawyer who had represented the Chinese shipper in the original trial. He told me in confidence to read the trial transcript about Joe's testimony in front of the jury. He said that even if Joe was right, the jury just hated the guy. The transcript further showed that Joe, after sitting in court for four days hearing the defense lawyer impale him right and left, ended up in the hospital with a bleeding ulcer. The trial had been delayed a few days before Joe returned to court to hear the jury return the total verdict against him. A follow-up appeal to the federal court gave Joe no help. With that background on Joe's disastrous trial, I was going to try and blame his trial lawyer for the defeat and the demise of Joe's plastics business.

A lot of legal time and several depositions followed to support my weak accusations of malpractice. Although not of great import, the eventual outcome was that the lawyer's malpractice carrier did pay some amount, maybe about $100,000, to get rid of the case. On this one I did get my one-third fee.

But hardly was I done with Joe. During the course of this first case he suckered me into representing him on two more cases. One involved his attempts to sell his plastic syringe technology to a company in California. Without legal help Joe had negotiated his own contract with the California company, supposedly securing a guarantee for an employment position in marketing with the company after the sale of the technology. As would be expected, once the company met Joe, the offer of employment changed. As Joe put it, instead of an executive position he had a job as an office boy, emptying wastebaskets. Again, he somehow convinced me that he had a valid claim against the California company for breach of contract as well as fraud in inducing him to sell his company and the technology. After involving co-counsel in California and doing all of the preliminary work, I traveled to San Diego for trial. Shortly before trial, it became known that the California company had just been bought out by a big national drug appliance manufacturer. Now our claim needed a two-step recovery to succeed. Midway through this trial, we reached a settlement and the California company paid Joe and his lawyers some dollar settlement plus a promise of stock in the new parent company. We attorneys did get a few dollars out of the deal, but when Joe got a check for the stock part of the settlement, he cashed it and forgot about the 40 percent share, worth $50,000, owed to his lawyers. It is probably over ten years since this happened and we lawyers still have a judgment against Joe for the 40 percent stock value. As Joe has since slipped away to California, we have no way of recovering anything from this bum.

I do not remember the details of the third case Joe suckered me into as his lawyer. Perhaps I have succeeded in blocking it out of my recollection. It, too, started during the Chinese shipping case mess. After the case was concluded with some favorable result for Joe, he disputed my entitlement to a $13,000 attorney's fee for my representation of him in the legal battle. He agreed to have a neutral mediator of the bar association's fee arbitration board decide the fee dispute. In a two-hour hearing I had to sit and listen to Joe blatantly lie about numerous parts of the case and my lawyering for him. Fortunately, the arbitrator saw what a jerk this guy was and awarded me the total fee. Fortunately, again there had been enough money secured in an escrow account to cover my $13,000.

To somehow reset the clock and stay away from a client like this would be every lawyer's dream. Joe was a disaster for me. But as we found out from searching court records, he had screwed over many of his prior lawyers by disputing their fees and even claiming legal malpractice. Several lawyers had pursued uncollectable judgments against him. At least I did better than most of his lawyers and got a few bucks. The only good part was the lesson I learned: Never believe everything your client tells you, and don't accept a client without investigating his or her background.

CHAPTER 52

TWO FAILED LIBEL CASES

I would like to contend that all of my trials were successful, but like any trial lawyer, sometimes I took it on the chin in a case I thought was in the bag. I became involved in two different libel cases that looked good from the start right through the jury trial. All was well except the jury results in both cases, which were complete losses. It is of course much more fun to brag about your wins rather than to fess up to your losses, but these two losses were something out of the ordinary.

First, a little legal lesson about libel and slander. Libel deals with written statements, and slander concerns oral statements. Both center on the concept of defamation. A statement is defamatory if it is untrue and disgraces or degrades a person or holds that person out to public hatred, contempt, ridicule, or embarrassment, and is damaging to his or her reputation. To be actionable, the statement must have been broadcast to some number of listeners who might be affected by it. Truth is always a defense. As you can imagine, damages to a person libeled or slandered are very nebulous and can be very large or small depending how egregious was the defendant's conduct.

I was hired by a Middle-Eastern OB/GYN doctor who had been accepted into a cancer fellowship program at the University of Minnesota medical school. The head of the department was a large, loud, and outspoken tenured professor who was not well liked in the department. He was notorious for bringing nurses to tears in the operating room with his swearing and abusive behavior. Although my client was progressing well in the program and had been accepted by other doctors and professors, he somehow got on the wrong side of the department head.

During the second year of the three-year fellowship, my client took his specialty board tests. They consisted of two parts, a written exam and an oral question-and-answer session. It was not unusual for those testing for the first time to fail one or both parts of the boards. My client had failed the oral portion, due in part perhaps to a minor language problem. Under the rules of the specialty boards, failure of an exam is confidential information not to be disseminated. The client retook the failed portion and successfully passed it two years later.

During the third year of the fellowship program the doctors, including my client, were pursuing academic jobs at various universities and hospitals. The client's first choice was a position at a large medical complex on Long Island with a projected annual salary of about $600,000. As would be expected, the head of the department had to write a recommendation letter for those graduating from his fellowship program. Taking out his anger on my client, the head wrote a totally negative letter revealing the failed board exam and, using strong language, recommending against his acceptance into any academic position. The letter was sent to the Long Island facility and broadcast throughout the University of Minnesota medical school, and no doubt reached every place where my client sought employment. Needless to say, the Long Island position disappeared. By the time my client graduated he had not been accepted in any academic position and was working with a St. Paul doctor, doing mostly surgical work, at a salary of about $250,000 per year.

To me this looked like a good libel case with not just reputation damage but also a huge wage loss from the loss of the Long Island position. The case was sued out with absolutely no offers of settlement or apology from the department head or the U of M medical school. To prove the significance of the disclosure of the failed exam, I took the deposition for trial of an officer of the national boards. He strongly confirmed the confidentiality of failed exams and stated that all department heads were well aware of the restrictions. My client was not a particularly likeable witness, and it appeared that the Minneapolis jury (none of whom probably made more than $50,000 a year) were offended by and not at all sympathetic to someone complaining about only making $250,000 a year. The defense lawyer had cleaned up the defendant so he came across as a well-respected university scholar who was justified in his criticism of my client. After about a week of hard-fought trial, the jury came back finding no defamation and no damages being suffered by my client.

My second venture in libel cases was equally unsuccessful. On the north side of Minneapolis was a black general practice doctor by the name of Dr. Thomas Johnson who operated the Plymouth Avenue Medical Center. All of his patients were residents of North Minneapolis, a mostly low-income area with a predominately black population. "Dr. Tom" was notorious among defense lawyers for helping out victims of car accidents, building up their cases and testifying on their behalf. When I was defending cases, I probably attended five to ten of his accident lawsuit depositions. I always felt he was exaggerating the injury cases of his patients, and I aggressively cross-examined him whenever he appeared in my cases. Most plaintiff's lawyers would settle rather than go to trial with Dr. Tom as their main medical expert.

As Dr. Tom was into his early seventies, he was going to sell the Plymouth Avenue Medical Center and retire to California. About that same time his son, Tom, Jr., was running for the Minneapolis city council for the Fifth Ward, the North Minneapolis area. The incumbent councilman was a crusty old fellow named Van White who had been the first African American elected to the Minneapolis city council. He had been reelected over and over for years. When Dr. Tom's medical center was put up for sale, one inquiring buyer was a well-known porn king who already ran several adult businesses in Minneapolis. Dr. Tom and Tom, Jr. entertained no thoughts of selling to this man, but somehow word got out about the offer to buy the building. Councilman Van White put out in a newsletter that was quickly passed throughout the north side that the Johnsons were selling to the porn king and a porn business was soon to open on the north side. I recall Tom, Jr. going to a neighborhood rally about the accusation, and no matter how he tried to deny the allegations, his protests were shouted down. Dr. Tom quietly slipped off to California, happy to leave the north side where he had helped most of the residents for over forty-five years. Of course, Tom, Jr. lost the election.

I was asked by a lawyer, who was a friend of Tom, Jr., to sue out the libel case against Councilman White. After listening to the story and looking at the newsletter I thought it looked like a good libel case. The accusation of selling out to the porn king was false, defamatory, widely broadcast, and clearly damaging to the reputation of both Johnsons. The City of Minneapolis had an obligation to defend the lawsuit against one of its council members. Unfortunately, my lawsuit then turned out to be seeking money damages against the City of Minneapolis. I remember well the cross-examination of Van White on the witness stand. He had to admit that the Johnsons had never sold out to the porn vendor, but in his slow drawl he spoke of his sworn duty as the representative of the people to put a stop to even the threat of a porn business coming into his northside ward. He actually claimed proud success in halting the sale of the building.

As probably could have been predicted, the Minneapolis jury was all white and obviously city taxpayers. Their verdict was for the city, finding no defamation by Van White and no damages to the Johnsons. This white jury clearly did not want to spend any city tax money on a dispute among north-side blacks.

So, there are my two unsuccessful ventures into defamation law suits. I vowed afterward to never again pursue a libel or slander case, and I never did over the last years of my practice. If you follow some of the highly publicized libel and slander cases in the news media, you'll see that those cases, like mine, seldom end with a large verdict for damage to a reputation. In the eyes of a jury, a person's reputation is not worth a heck of a lot.

CHAPTER 53

GOLF IS A DANGEROUS SPORT

Most people would not consider four hours of chasing a little white ball around a pristine golf course to be a contact sport with risks of serious personal injury. Occasionally you hear about a golf cart accident where some intoxicated player tips a cart over, injuring a buddy in the passenger seat. If someone takes a practice swing with a club and creams another golfer standing nearby, it would be a good negligence claim, but also with some contributory negligence on the victim for standing so close. With golfers of all skill levels sending high-speed balls in many directions, striking another golfer with a ball might seem to be a basis for any injury claim. But not so. Generally, golfers on the course assume the risk of stray and misdirected shots from other golfers. And if the shooting golfer, after hitting a misdirected shot towards other golfers, yells out a loud "fore," he or she has basically done all duty necessary to avoid injury to others. There are, of course, a variety of situations in which a golfer should never have hit in the first place. For instance, if you are within range of a shot reaching the green, you must wait for other golfers to clear the green before hitting.

I had a most interesting golf ball injury case. In St. Paul's north suburbs there is a private country club called Dellwood Hills that has been in operation for many years. I have played Dellwood and never thought it was a great course, but it was fun to play. Much of the course is quite low, soft and boggy, with creeks and ponds around many of the holes. I later found out that several of these water hazards are connected by creeks and waterways to a string of small lakes outside of the course. At various times of year, especially in springtime, fish find their way from adjoining lakes into the ponds and creeks on the course. For years it had been accepted that club members could fish in the ponds. Somewhere in the clubhouse or in one of its newsletters was a picture of a member holding about a fifteen-pound muskie hc had caught in one of the ponds on the course. And as could be expected, fishing ponds and the prospect of catching a few fish are a great attraction to neighborhood youngsters. Although the club tried to shoo the kids off, there weren't any No Fishing signs, fences around the ponds on the course, or other deterrents to the fishing youngsters.

My clients were the parents of a really cute eight-year-old fisherman, whom I will call Tim. The Dellwood course had been originally built around the homestead of a relative of my clients, and the family still had driveway access to the home on the course near the fifth, sixth, and seventh holes. The homeowner had some project to do, and Dad went to help, while Tim planned to do some fishing. On at least one prior occasion Tim had fished at the pond near the fifth hole. With a bright orange life jacket and his fishing pole and tackle box, Tim walked from the house about two hundred yards back towards the fifth tee to fish in the pond. I don't remember how long Tim had been fishing before his dad became worried and walked towards the fifth-hole fishing pond.

As Dad reached Tim and was helping him gather his fishing gear, four golfers were on the fifth tee waiting to tee off. They had seen Tim's dad walking towards them and had held off hitting their shots until he left the fairway and was standing with the boy by the pond. When Dad reached Tim, the first fellow teed off.

The first hitting golfer was the president of a bank in St. Paul. As I remember it, he was no better than a plus-20 handicap golfer whose shots could spray all over. He wound up and hit a low curving hook shot to the left (golfers call it a duck hook) that hit Tim directly in the eye. Realizing that his son was seriously injured, Dad picked him up and ran towards the house. The golfers, who knew there was a big problem, did not try to cover up the incident; they quit playing for the day and reported it to the clubhouse.

Tim lost something like 90 percent of the vision in his injured eye. He was quite the personable youngster, and I developed a good friendship with him. My lawsuit for Tim was against the bank president and the Dellwood Hills Golf Club. I had been out to the accident scene twice, both times sneaking onto the course from the backside, where Tim had previously entered to go fishing. As I stood on the fifth tee, I had Tim first stand alone, then with his dad, at the place where he had been fishing. We measured the distance and, as I remember, from tee to boy it was about eighty yards. The pictures I took of Tim were dramatic. With his bright orange life jacket it was impossible for the golfers on the tee not to see him.

I had retained as a golf course expert a sharp golf pro named Jeff from a competing country club. He was highly critical not only of the bank president, but also of the country club for allowing anyone, club member or not, to fish on the golf course. I took Jeff out to the fifth tee for a firsthand view of the area. He brought along his driver, and I asked him to tee one up and try to hit toward where Tim had been fishing eighty yards away. Being

capable of hitting not only long, straight shots but also intentionally misdirected hits, he hit a low, screaming duck hook towards
the pond. I was amazed that the speeding ball reached the pond
in something like two seconds. There would have been no way
for the boy, his dad, or anyone else to duck or avoid getting hit by
that shot. Even if the golfers had yelled "fore" or something else,
Tim or his dad still would have been hit. The only way for Mr.
Bank President to have avoided this bad injury was to have waited
on his tee shot until father and son were a long ways away.

It was not too difficult to reach a settlement with the insurance company for the negligent golfer. After I consulted with the
plaintiffs' records of past eye-out verdicts and recoveries, a settlement for Tim of $375,000 was very much in line with past
precedents. Minnesota has a procedure called a *Pierringer* settlement in which a plaintiff can settle with one defendant and
reserve the right to try the case against another at-fault defendant. The case is tried to a jury as if there were no settlement, and
the jury is to apportion negligence amongst the settling as well as
the non-settling parties. In this case the jury would decide the
percentage of negligence on the golfer, the country club, and
Tim's dad. Tim, being only eight years old, was too young to be
found at fault under Minnesota law, so no percentage of negligence could be apportioned to him. In a *Pierringer* case, the jury
is not told about the amount already received in settlement and is
asked to award a total damage sum for the injury. Depending on
the total damage award and the negligence percentages between
the settling and non-settling parties, the end result for Tim was
potentially much greater than the $375,000 already in the bank.

The case went to trial in Stillwater. With the *Pierringer* settlement wrapped up, my trial strategy changed. I argued strongly
for negligence on Dellwood while downplaying the golfer's negligence. The Dellwood defense lawyer emphasized the primary
negligence of the golfer and Tim's dad. In quite a surprise to me,

the jury let Dellwood off with a finding of no negligence and found the golfer primarily at fault, with a lesser percentage to Tim's dad. Also quite amazingly, this jury calculated the total damage to Tim not at the million dollars that I had suggested, but at an amount within $10,000 of our $375,000 settlement amount.

Even with that disappointing jury result, my clients and I were still quite happy with the $375,000 settlement, which was already signed and sealed and not affected by the trial result. I was able to set up a structured annuity amount for Tim with payouts starting when he reached the age of eighteen. The annuity would earn interest for ten years and then provide Tom a nice monthly payout for many years of adulthood.

CHAPTER 54

AIRPLANES FREQUENTLY CRASH

A most interesting and often quite lucrative area of personal injury legal work involves airplane crashes. When one of those flying machines descends to earth at some place other than a designated airport, the consequences are usually tragic deaths for all aboard. Quite obviously, an airplane is supposed to leave and return to an airport in the normal way and stay in the air in between. If the airplane doesn't do these logical things and someone dies, there is in most cases some reason that will be the basis for a good wrongful death lawsuit. There are four primary potential causes for airplane crashes: (1) Some mechanical failure in the plane itself leading to a product liability claim; (2) Some inaccurate or incomplete information from air traffic controllers (including weather-related forecasts); (3) A maintenance or service error by a mechanic; (4) Pilot negligence, more commonly called pilot error. Statistically, the vast majority of small aircraft crashes are the result of pilot error.

Kids in northern Minnesota did not get much exposure to

the worldwide aviation experience. I remember being almost overwhelmed as a youngster when the word spread that the one wealthy guy in our town had taken the Royal Hawaiian Champagne Flight on a vacation to Hawaii. We used to see this luxury advertised on our seventeen-inch oval television, but reaching that ideal of the rich and famous was so far out of my world it was a barely a dream. At one point in my teen years, my father took my brother and me on a float-plane fishing trip into a remote Minnesota lake. The pilot pointed out a black bear and swooped low so we could see it. I was impressed with his flying ability. Other than that one in-flight experience I was never in an airplane until the invitation to New York for the job interview during my junior year of college. Looking back now, I can calculate dozens of times that my kids flew with me to destinations around the country and even overseas, all before they reached college age. I feel fortunate to have given them such worldwide exposure, which wasn't an option in my youth.

Some fine mentoring from my friend and senior partner, John Lommen, had convinced me that a big part of being a trial lawyer involved aviation accidents. John had never gotten his pilot license but was an avid reader of aviation magazines. He was quite conversant about a multitude of private aviation planes and the problems that contribute to their crashes. Because I saw the potential for involvement in aviation crashes cases, and with John's encouragement, I obtained my private pilot license.

Aviation cases are really fun to work on. A big supporting factor is that the government, through the National Transportation Safety Board, does a thorough investigation of every accident and publishes a report from its experts identifying the probable cause of the crash. Thus, much of the case investigation is done by the government. But the NTSB people cannot be witnesses in a civil trial, so the case must be put together with privately retained experts. For instance, an experienced pilot or flight instructor who flies the same type of aircraft involved in the crash could be an expert witness as to a pilot error. When Minnesota Senator Paul Wellstone and his wife died in a twin-engine plane crash on the approach to the airport in Eveleth, Minnesota, it was an easy task for pilot experts to conclude that the pilot approached his landing too slow and too low and had hit the ground short of the runway. There had also been some bad weather with low cloud ceilings at the time, but evidence showed the pilots had received appropriate weather forecasts from the air traffic controllers.

The tougher, and from my standpoint most interesting, cases are product liability cases involving claims of defects in manufacture or design of the airplane. There is no shortage of well-qualified expert witnesses available for hire to help develop design theories. If the case merits such expenditure, it might extend to modifications and redesign of aircraft parts, accident simulations by test pilots, or sophisticated teardown and testing of engine or structural parts. One case in our office dealt with an engine carburetor problem that stopped a small plane engine, sending it to the ground. Careful teardown of the engine showed that the float in the carburetor had stuck in a closed position, cutting off fuel to the engine. A small ball of shellac-type material had stopped the movement of the float. Further digging showed that the assembly-line worker who installed a small screw in each carburetor, instead of applying sealant with a finger on the threads of the screw, had been dipping the screw into the sealant, leaving a blob of sealant on the end of the screw as it entered the carburetor.

Over the years I was personally involved in several aviation death cases. Each case had some most interesting aspects. The first case involved a midair collision of a North Central Convair plane and a smaller passenger plane flown by Air Wisconsin. On a clear day, with both pilots flying with unrestricted visibility and without instruments, the planes collided over Lake Winnebago in central Wisconsin, resulting in the deaths of thirteen crew and passengers. A variety of lawsuits ensued. The big issue that went to trial was which pilot was more at fault. Our office represented the wife of the North Central pilot, and our task was to put the majority of negligence on the Air Wisconsin pilot. I was working with the lead North Central lawyer, a fellow from Chicago who had been hired by the insurance carrier for North Central. He was about thirty-two years old and smart, with some aviation law experience, but obviously lacking in trial experience. By this time I had probably tried twenty-five jury trials, but I had to sit frustrated most of the time while my colleague floundered in the courtroom. The venue for the trial was a disaster. The seat of the county in which the crash occurred was Appleton, Wisconsin, which also happened to be Air Wisconsin's home base. Their trial lawyer was a gray haired, well-respected Appleton attorney. From the start I knew our side was in trouble. The old guy ate up my young colleague from Chicago. The interesting issue of a midair crash is that the right-of-way rules are just like those for two vehicles approaching an uncontrolled intersection. The plane on the right has the right of way over the plane approaching from the left. Even though our North Central pilot was looking into the sun, the Air Wisconsin pilot had the right of way. The jury agreed and stuck the vast majority of negligence and fault on our pilot.

One sidelight was my experience in flying Air Wisconsin back to Minneapolis for the weekend. The pilot took off from Appleton, and shortly after becoming airborne I could tell something was wrong, as he was circling in a tight turn back to the airport. After several days of being highly critical of these pilots in court, I was sure that Air Wisconsin was going to do me in. We did get back to the airport, at which point the pilot reported that a warning light had come on, necessitating the emergency landing.

I had occasion to participate with some very good aviation

lawyers in a multiple-death case in Minneapolis. A twin-engine Cessna had taken off from the Minneapolis St. Paul International Airport and lost one engine shortly after liftoff. If the pilot cleans up the plane (lifts the wheels), the Cessna is supposed to stay afloat on single-engine power. This pilot, however, tried to make a quick turn back to the airport, stalled out, and crashed in the backyard of a Richfield homeowner. All passengers and crew died, resulting in several lawsuits. One interesting claim was for severe emotional distress from the homeowner who was working under his car when the plane crashed a few yards away from him. A lot of lawyer time went to fighting issues of pilot error or product liability defects in the failure of the Cessna's single-engine operation. What I remember most was being very impressed with our lead lawyer, a Los Angeles attorney named Cathcart. He flew his own twin-engine plane, and in the end he was the winning lawyer.

One fascinating aspect in the case was a simulation done by the Cessna people in an attempt to demonstrate the single-engine capability of their plane. They set up a video camera behind a test pilot in the same type of twin-engine plane. The pilot took off and shut down one engine shortly after takeoff. To the dismay of the Cessna people, instead of continuing to climb, and despite the pilot's frantic efforts, the Cessna gradually settled onto the ground past the end of the runway. All of this was nicely recorded on film. For our side in the case it was pure enjoyment to see fenceposts, dirt, and debris flying as the test pilot struggled to bring the plane to a halt. So much for Cessna's claims of single-engine flight capability!

The air crash that took the lives of the greatest number of Minnesotans in aviation history happened on January 21, 1985, near Reno, Nevada. A gambling junket charter flight operated by Galaxy Airlines crashed shortly after takeoff from the Reno airport, killing seventy, including six crew members. Only a single young man survived. A multitude of wrongful death claims and lawsuits followed. My representation of a widow resulted in the very first settlement, which was big news in the local media. I was interviewed for the six o'clock news by every local television station. My media presentation must not have very been good, as no new cases streamed in my direction. At least my kids liked seeing their dad on television.

The pilot of an aircraft always sits in the left seat in the cockpit and the first officer, or copilot, sits in the right seat. The left seat pilot is the one in charge and bears final responsibility when something goes wrong. An interesting complication arises when a flight instructor has a student pilot in the left seat. The instructor who directs the flight maneuvers is still the pilot in command. One flight instructor got himself in serious trouble in a Learjet crash case I handled. Two Northwest Airlines pilots desired to get checked out by an instructor in order to fly chartered flights in a private Learjet. Together with the instructor they flew eighty miles south from Minneapolis to Rochester to do their maneuvers around the less busy local airport. One of the Northwest pilots, my client's husband, was in the left seat, with the instructor in the right seat.

The NTSB investigators and our experts reconstructed the events of this crash as follows. On the approach to do a touch-and-go (a routine practice maneuver in which the pilot executes a landing on the runway and then, without stopping, accelerates to become airborne again), the instructor initiated an unexpected rocking motion of the plane to test the pilot's response control, expecting the pilot to correct back to straight and level flight. The startled pilot overcorrected and rolled the plane past level into a completely inverted position. They were at low altitude near the end of the runway, and there was no space to correct the condition. An observer on the ground testified that for a good portion of the length of the runway the pilot amazingly kept the Lear flying upside-down until it eventually crashed, killing all three occupants. Our negligence claim was against the instructor pilot, even though my decedent was an experienced pilot with lots of flying hours and had been sitting in the left seat. An eight-day trial produced a very nice damage award for the pilot's wife.

I became involved in three different helicopter crash cases. One had a good result and the other two were busts. As the losses are not much fun to talk about, I'll provide the story about the winner. My client was a thirty-five-year-old fellow who lost power to his engine while spraying swamps around the Twin Cities for mosquitoes. To do the job he had to fly close to the ground to do the spraying and then accelerate upward for his next pass. When his engine quit he was over an apartment building, with his best chance for a landing being on the adjoining parking lot. Most people assume that when a helicopter loses power it descends to the ground like a lead balloon. Not so, as helicopters are designed for what is called autorotation. When the circling blades lose power, the pilot can disengage the transmission so the blades are freewheeling in the wind. Pilots are trained to nose the helicopter down so that the airflow rotates the blades, creating enough lift for the helicopter to make a soft landing and usually avoid structural damage and injury to occupants. In this case my pilot client started his autorotation and aimed for the parking lot. Unfortunately, he had to elevate over a power line, resulting in total loss of his lift. The helicopter dropped hard and fast onto the parking lot, destroying the helicopter and injuring my client's back so severely he was done flying. I don't recall what the engine defect was, but a hard-fought five- or six-day battle in federal court resulted in a very large verdict for my client.

A very funny event occurred near the tail end of this trial. I was also representing a young chiropractor who owned the helicopter that had been leased to the mosquito control folks. I was trying to recover the value of his destroyed helicopter. While we lawyers were back in chambers with the judge, preparing the jury instructions, the chiropractor was sitting in the almost empty courtroom dictating some of his patient notes. He was told by a U.S. Marshal that he could not have the recording device in the courthouse. He questioned this rule but reluctantly agreed to take it out to his car. A group of marshals escorted him to the elevator, where he apparently made some inappropriate remark. A big marshal got right in the face of the much smaller chiropractor. He did what he shouldn't have done, and pushed the marshal away. The marshals roughly put him down on the floor and cuffed his hands behind his back. All of this occurred without my knowledge. Someone came and told the judge about this trouble and that it was my client. I went out and found my client in some kind of lockup secured by the marshals. His sport coat was torn, and he was very shook up as he explained to me what had happened. I had to sign some kind of release to be responsible for him until he made his first criminal appearance. A great way to get myself prepared to give a closing argument in a major case! Despite the ruckus, the end result for the chiropractor was okay. I won for him the damages for his lost helicopter, and my later conversation with the U.S. attorney, describing the excessive, unnecessary force used by the marshals, convinced the government to drop all charges.

The thrill of lifting off from an airstrip and being totally in control of flight through the air is amazing. Except for a few required radio communications to air traffic controllers, you, as the pilot in command, are on your own to keep the plane from hitting the ground. I really enjoyed flying. But I soon discovered that "keeping current" with the number of required flights each month, including touch-and-goes and night landings, was quite time-consuming and expensive. Worse, I no longer found it very stimulating. It gets old fast to fly around the local airport and practice landings and takeoffs every month. To justify being a private pilot, you simply need someplace to go. For several years after I obtained my license, I had lawsuits in Bismarck, North Dakota, and Madison, Wisconsin. These were great places for private flying. At that time domestic fares to these locations were about $350 round-trip. So billing a client for that plus ground transportation time justified my flying and billing the client for the plane rental. Handling cases in those two locations was great fun. I specifically remember making one flight to Madison during the height of the fall leaf color and marveling at the colored landscape below.

When my folks were alive in Orr, Minnesota, about 250 miles from Minneapolis, flying to the Orr airport was also efficient and handy. An in-flight radio call to the Orr airport manager would alert my folks to come out to pick us up at the airport.

In conversations with almost every pilot you will hear tales of their near misses with tragedy. Most live through these traumatic flying events, but many do not. Almost every tale describes some mechanical or weather problem that contributed to a crash. Seldom do you hear from a surviving pilot anything about the pilot error that contributed to a crisis. I openly confess to several errors in my years of piloting, none of which, fortunately, resulted in a crash or tragedy. But the one problem that finally chased me out of flying was truly a mechanical problem.

I still shudder to describe these events. When my father was in his final year of life, after a diagnosis of terminal pancreatic cancer, my brother and I decided to arrange one last Canadian fishing trip for Dad and our children. Roger was a more experienced private pilot with more flight hours and an instrument rating. We each rented a plane and flew with our children from Minneapolis to our family home in Orr. Our plan was to spend the night at our father's home and leave in the morning in the two planes for Red Lake Falls, about three hundred miles further north into Ontario. After I landed and was tying up my Cessna

172 at the Orr airport, I just happened to see a single drop of oil fall from the engine onto the front-wheel cowling. It concerned me enough to ask the local airport mechanic to look at it. With little investigation he reported, "Oh, yeah, this is a common problem with the Lycoming engines on these small Cessnas; the tube connecting the oil dipstick to the engine fractures, allowing the engine oil to leak out." It soon became apparent that if I had taken off in the morning with this Cessna to travel three hundred miles over the Canadian wilderness, the engine would have pumped out all of the oil, leading to a disastrous crash for me and my kids. This shook me so much that I personally flew a small plane only a few more times. Thus ended my flying career.

CHAPTER 55

ETHICS ISSUES

No other profession polices itself as well as the legal profession. We pay a significant portion of our annual dues to support full-time watchdogs that enforce a strict code of conduct on lawyer activity. There is sound logic in doing so. Clients come to lawyers and disclose, subject to strict rules of confidentiality, all types of transgressions, legitimate and illegitimate schemes, and even criminal acts. Clients entrust lawyers with their money as well as their secrets. If a lawyer chooses, there are all kinds of ways to go wrong at the expense, literally and figuratively, of the clients. The vast majority of lawyers tread the straight and narrow and do not cross the line into the black or even the gray ethical areas. But for the few that do, the cost to clients can be great. Even more so, the publicity that usually accompanies a wayward lawyer who absconds with a client's funds greatly damages the profession as a whole.

The importance of ethics in the legal profession is pounded into our heads in law school. We study the various rules of the profession and discuss hypothetical situations in which lawyers are faced with difficult decisions between right and wrong in client matters. A major portion of the state bar exam likewise deals with ethics. Every year, a number of students do not become licensed to practice law because they failed to pass the ethics portion of the bar exam.

In my career I was never disciplined by the Lawyers Professional Responsibility Board. I had only a single complaint filed against me, as recounted in another chapter, and that complaint was dismissed without any action by the board. But in my career I become involved in two ethical issues that caused me concern as I decided how to properly deal with them. The first was when I was a fairly inexperienced defense lawyer representing the insured of an insurance company. This injury case arose in northwest Minnesota when a laborer struck a metal chisel with a hammer and a piece of the chisel top broke off, striking him in the eye. A good lawyer in Hallock, Minnesota, had sued the Minneapolis retailer that had sold the chisel and the out-of-state manufacturer of the chisel. I was hired to defend the retailer. The manufacturer hired a middle-aged, experienced defense attorney from Fargo to defend that part of the case. As my retailer was only a pass-through for the chisel, the manufacturer was to be the primary liable party if the chisel was defective.

The plaintiff's lawyer had done his job by hiring a metallurgist who came forward with the opinion that the metal used in the chisel had not been hardened properly during the manufacturing process. Hardening is done by subjecting the metal to very high temperatures in a process called heat treating. The Fargo defense lawyer denied any such problem and proceeded in a full-scale defense. Perhaps midway through the case, the Fargo lawyer showed me a memo from his manufacturer announcing a recall of a number of different products identified by their serial numbers. The serial number for the chisel involved in this case was on the list. The memo explained that the reason for the recall was that the manufacturer had found inadequate heat treating on these parts, an admission precisely confirming the plaintiff's theory. Astounded by this revelation, I said to him, "You've got to disclose this to the plaintiff, don't you?" To my amazement, he said he didn't have to do that unless the plaintiff's lawyer specifically asked for it. I said that the plaintiff's lawyer's interrogatory questions were broad enough to cover a recall notice. He brought out the interrogatories and showed me that no question specifically mentioned the term "recall." I argued with him that one request had demanded all documents dealing with the manufacture of the chisel. He disagreed and told me in no uncertain terms that he was not going to disclose the recall memo, and since it was his client's primary liability I was not authorized to disclose it either.

Throughout the remainder of the case I was troubled and uncomfortable. During depositions and court hearings before the trial judge, I saw the plaintiff's lawyer struggling to put together a strong basis for his liability theory of inadequate heat treating on the chisel. The Fargo lawyer argued strongly that the heat treating was just fine and that the injured plaintiff had just struck a glancing blow to the top of the chisel with a heavy hammer, causing the metal piece to separate. Never once did the issue of the recall memo get brought up. As I saw the case, the fellow who had lost the sight in his eye was totally innocent and should have received a large settlement from the manufacturer. Instead, just before trial the parties agreed to a modest settlement of about one-fourth of the real value of the injury case if the recall memo had been out in the open. I knew our ethics rules would require a disclosure of this critical piece of evidence. But I was in a predicament. With my more senior defense attorney, whose client was the real party at fault, having refused to do the right thing, I could do little. I never did report the defense attorney to the ethics board, and even today I am not sure if I should have, or would if I had to do it all over again.

The second situation arose in my efforts to put together a Coleman case for two deaths from a propane camping lantern. A lawyer in a big firm in Salt Lake City contacted me about a widowed client who told him that her husband, who ran a carpeting business, and his friend, an airline pilot, had died from carbon monoxide poisoning while hunting elk in Wyoming. They were found dead in their tent with a small, portable Coleman lantern attached to 16.4 oz. green propane cylinder. The lawyer had the lantern in his office, and he wanted me to come out and talk to the wives of the two decedents. I did so and found both widows to be charming ladies who were enthused about the prospects of my suing Coleman on their behalf. The pilot's wife lived in a beautiful log home in southwest Wyoming with her five small children.

After signing up the widows as clients, I returned home to have one of my engineers test the lantern for its carbon monoxide production. Amazingly, this small lantern, about the size of a cantaloupe when attached to a propane cylinder, produced huge quantities of carbon monoxide. It looked like a good case with high damage potential, especially for the widow with young children. I needed to associate with a Wyoming lawyer on the case. After a few calls I found a lawyer located in southwest Wyoming, about my age, whom I will call Jerry. My new associate had a good background in handling injury cases. We planned to sue the case out against Coleman and the tent manufacturer, claiming that this tent, unlike many other tents, did not have any warning about the use of propane devices within the tent.

But before the case even got off the ground it stalled out. In 1998 Coleman had been purchased by the Sunbeam Corporation of Florida. Sunbeam's president was then on a massive takeover campaign, buying out many new subsidiaries. By 2000

Sunbeam was broke and went into bankruptcy, taking all subsidiaries, including Coleman, with it. When a company goes into bankruptcy, all litigation against it is put on hold until the bankruptcy is concluded. The portion of the case against the tent manufacturer continued, but it was clearly a weak claim and hard to get very excited about.

I regularly received documents from the New York bankruptcy court and followed Sunbeam's progress until the case was winding down at the end of December 2002. By that time the statute of limitations in Wyoming had expired, but the bankruptcy law had provided for that contingency. The bankruptcy code provided that we would have thirty days from the bankruptcy discharge to commence a lawsuit against Coleman and we would not be barred by the statute of limitations. I advised Jerry of this fact and even sent him the portion of the code that specified the thirty days. I talked to him on the phone about ten days into the thirty-day period, and he assured me that he would get the case against Coleman started.

The case against the tent manufacturer had been removed from Wyoming state court to federal court in Cheyenne, so our efforts to add Coleman to the case required commencing in federal court as well. Unlike the commencement procedures in Wyoming state court, where the summons and complaint would just be served on the defendant, federal procedure requires that you first file the complaint with the federal clerk and then you receive the summons. Serving the complaint together with the summons on the defendant is the second step. I knew that this was federal court procedure and assumed that Jerry, who had worked in federal court, knew it as well.

Sometime after the expiration of the thirty-day window, Jerry disclosed to me that he had served the complaint on Coleman in a timely manner but had forgotten to first file it with the clerk. I expounded, "What? You've got to be kidding!" He apologized all over the place and said he had already done some research and felt we could undo the problem by bringing a motion before the Cheyenne federal judge. Even before we made our motion, Coleman's attorneys made a motion in federal court to dismiss our claim as procedurally improper and now beyond the statute of limitations. I researched this issue and, contrary to Jerry's optimism, I felt our claim against Coleman was down the drain. Jerry prepared a lengthy "I'm sorry, I goofed" argument and claimed that "It really doesn't make any difference." I attended the federal court hearing on the motion and found Jerry's pleading argument to be almost a pitiful attempt at convincing the judge to not let Jerry be sued for malpractice.

It was a matter of only a few days before the judge's order came down dismissing the Coleman claim. Here comes the ethics issue. Jerry and I talked several times about what to do next. We could give our two widows some kind of bullshit story that the Coleman case got dismissed for some legal or factual reason that was not our fault. We would not have to send the widows the actual dismissal order, and not being very legally sophisticated, they probably would not question us. This would avoid a possible legal malpractice case against Jerry and me. But after discussing this and other possibilities, I told Jerry that we had to meet with the two widows and openly disclose our failure to start the Coleman lawsuit in time. This would probably mean a malpractice claim against both of us. Even though it was Jerry who really goofed, I was lead counsel for the plaintiffs, and arguably I could have called Jerry before the thirty days ran out to ensure he had followed the correct procedure. Both Jerry and I had malpractice insurance, and we both alerted our carriers of this possible or, more correctly, probable claim. Both my policy and Jerry's policy had one million dollars in coverage, which might not have been enough to cover the high potential damages for the two widows.

We scheduled a meeting with the widows in Jerry's office.

From the time of the Coleman dismissal I agonized through many sleepless nights over how explaining our screw-up would go with these two very nice ladies. At the meeting I was embarrassed to receive hugs from both widows. Small talk was quickly shut down, and we got down to the serious explanation. I remember saying in the discussion that we had "simply goofed." At least one, if not both of the ladies, cried. We openly told them that they should consult with another attorney about the malpractice claim against us. I recommended that the lady from Salt Lake City go back to the local lawyer who had originally brought me into the case. We told them that we would continue the case against the tent manufacturer and would process an appeal of the Coleman dismissal to the appellate court. We admitted that there was little chance of success on the appeal. After the ladies departed, I recall collapsing in a chair in Jerry's office and saying that it was one of the hardest things I had ever done.

This story is far from over. Jerry processed the circuit court appeal, which would not be decided for a year or more. Sometime during that next year we did reach a small settlement with the tent manufacturer. The claim was so weak that I think we only got $75,000 for each widow. Jerry and I did divide a $25,000 fee in each case, with the ladies each receiving $50,000. The big event was news we received from Coleman. At some time we had sent the camping lantern to Coleman for their inspection. They reported that the lantern had been assembled incorrectly, and that was the reason it produced the high amount of carbon monoxide. They sent the lantern back to me with the assembly diagram that had been in the hands of the two decedents when they bought the lantern and assembled it. My engineer and I compared the diagram with the lantern and quickly saw the problem. There were four small metal tabs that supported the screw-on top, leaving an air space at the top of the glass globe. Whichever of the two men had assembled it thought the tabs should be bent down and did so, eliminating the air space. We photographed it, re-bent the tabs back up, and again tested it for carbon monoxide. Just as Coleman suggested, bending the tabs had disrupted the propane and air mixture, resulting in the production of the deadly amounts of carbon monoxide. Plain and simple, our two experienced campers had killed themselves. The claim against Coleman, even if timely started, really wasn't worth anything.

The Salt Lake City lawyer contacted us with the malpractice claim. I put him in touch with my malpractice carrier. I had told this lawyer about the new finding about the incorrectly assembled lantern and that the men had accidentally killed themselves. This did not deter him, and he continued to pursue the claim with our insurers. I talked with my insurance claims man and told him as strongly as possible that he should not pay one dime on the malpractice claim as the underlying lawsuit was not winnable. Since I had a $10,000 deductible on the policy, meaning that the first $10,000 came out of my pocket, I insisted that they pay nothing. He followed my directions, and eventually the lawyer gave up on pursing the claim. No lawsuit against me was ever started.

As the circuit-court appeal was still progressing, the Coleman lawyers were concerned enough that they offered us a settlement to avoid the result on the appeal. It was not much, but it was something more for the ladies. We took no fee from that and handed it over just to be done with it. On this case my time probably came out to about ten dollars per hour, but I had done the ethical thing and had also avoided being sued. The two ladies should not have felt too badly about the experience. In this unfortunate case, where one or both of the men was the cause of their own deaths, the wives at least received some compensation from our legal efforts.

CHAPTER 56

THE FIRST COLEMAN CASE

The vast majority of my legal time in the last years of my career was directed against the Coleman Company, Inc., for the wrongful deaths caused by Coleman-manufactured camping heaters. When I got involved in the first case I never thought that so much of my last fifteen years in practice would be spent in aggressively pursuing the same kind of lawsuit. It all started with the *Wilson/Pointer* case in 1996. Two young men named Wilson and Pointer decided to build themselves a first-class ice fishing house. Being both handyman types, they built a well-insulated, nearly airtight, six-by-ten-foot fishing house. They did put two 4-inch vents in opposite sides of the structure. Wilson's girlfriend supported the ice fishing effort by buying a portable heater for her boyfriend. While shopping in the camping section at a large discount store she had asked a clerk what type of heater would be appropriate for the fish house. The helpful clerk showed her a Coleman-manufactured Focus 15 propane-fueled radiant heater. She would later testify that she was impressed by the Coleman name on the heater, as Coleman was the leader in camping equipment. At Christmas her boyfriend happily received the Focus 15 and was anxious to try it out in the fish house.

Within days of Christmas, Wilson and Pointer moved the fish house onto a lake a few miles north of St. Paul and set it up for an overnight of fishing. Of course the Focus 15 heater was there to provide the heat necessary for a long night of fishing, drinking, and companionship. When they did not return the next morning, Pointer's father went to the fish house to investigate. Inside he found Wilson dead and Pointer just barely alive. Autopsies showed that Wilson's death and Pointer's injury were caused by carbon monoxide poisoning. The only item in the fish house capable of producing carbon monoxide was the Focus 15 heater. Pointer survived, but was left with some fairly significant brain damage. He could not return to work because of his disability.

I was called into the case by a fellow lawyer who was then representing Pointer and his wife. He felt there would be a conflict in representing Wilson's family in the same case. After spending some time looking at the case and visiting with Wilson's mother and sister, I agreed to get involved. From the start it looked like a tough product liability case, but Pointer's lawyer was very good and fun to work with as a co-plaintiff. I first consulted a great source of information on deaths and injuries from consumer products, the Consumer Product Safety Commission (CPSC) in Washington, and made a Freedom of Information request for documents on all propane heater deaths from carbon monoxide poisoning. This produced documents of about fifteen past carbon monoxide deaths and injuries caused by Coleman heaters. With that encouragement we commenced the lawsuit against Coleman and the discount store that sold the heater. As in any product liability case, we anticipated a thorough and expensive defense effort from Coleman. That's exactly what we got, with a large law firm from Wichita, Coleman's home base, leading the defense team along with competent Minneapolis counsel.

We first obtained in discovery all the historical documents of Coleman's design and development of several Focus heater models. We also received many files that Coleman had gathered about customers' complaints, many involving deaths and injuries related to the use of the Focus heaters. Poring over the several boxes of records turned up some most interesting documents to use against Coleman. The first designs for the heaters appeared in 1984 with the initial model, the Focus 5 (a 5,000 maximum BTU heater), first being sold in 1985. Coleman engineers had test chambers equipped with various gauges to check emissions while the heaters operated inside. When we learned how to read these graphs and printouts, we could see a consistent pattern. The heaters, when operated inside these airtight enclosures, had two major effects: They used oxygen, reducing it from the normal level of 20.9 percent (in the air we breathe) to a percentage in the teens or lower, and at the same time produced poisonous carbon monoxide. From other sources, including OSHA standards, we learned that safe levels of carbon monoxide are 50 parts per million (of molecules in the air) or less. On the Coleman tests we would see CO levels rising to 500 ppm or higher as oxygen was depleted to 15 or 16 percent. This was a deadly combination, and Coleman's engineers knew it from the get-go. Testing of other Focus models in subsequent cases confirmed the same dangers.

What you really need for any successful product liability case is an alternative design for the product that, if used, would have led to a different result—in this case, not killing and injuring campers by CO poisoning. Further searching in the Coleman documents revealed two safety features that could have been added to the heaters' design. In 1984 and 1985 Coleman engineers had tested the propane heaters of a competing company, Primus, which had already been selling similar camping heaters.

These tests showed that the Primus models would shut down or, as the test sheets called it, "flame out" before CO reached dangerous levels. A second large comparative study was done in February of 1990, when Coleman engineers tested a Primus heater and two different models of Mr. Heater, another leading manufacturer of propane heaters. Alongside these three heaters Coleman tested one of its own Focus 5 heaters. Again, just as in the early comparisons, in every test the Primus and Mr. Heater models flamed out before dangerous levels of CO were produced. By contrast, the Focus 5 continued to operate at dangerous CO levels without any flameout. This led to the obvious question: Why did the competitors' heaters flame out and Coleman's did not?

The second key discovery in the Coleman test documents was testing done in 1982 of an unvented room heater called Valor. This heater was equipped with a safety shutdown device called an oxygen depletion sensor (ODS). As we later learned, an ODS is a thermocouple-like sensing device with a small flame to keep the thermocouple warm as long as there is plenty of oxygen available around the flame. But when oxygen levels decline, the flame separates from the thermocouple, allowing it to cool and shut down the heater. Coleman ran three tests of the Valor heater in its test chambers, and it functioned perfectly each time to shut down the heater when oxygen levels declined to 18 or 18.5 percent, which was well before CO levels reached 50 ppm.

With those two possible different designs in hand, we went to hired engineers for help. Bob Engberg, a mechanical engineer specializing in gas and propane, was my first choice. Bob had been a great help several years before in one of my million-dollar verdicts. Bob first wanted to test our Focus 15 heater in the ice fishing house. Armed with the Focus 15 and oxygen, carbon monoxide, and other gauges, Bob ran the heater in the ice house for several hours. To our surprise he could not generate high levels of CO inside. After puzzling over how different variables such as wind, humidity, and temperature affect oxygen consumption and CO output, the results were still hard to explain. It was several years later that Bob found a source book describing how much oxygen two human beings could consume; inside the fish house, the two humans were competing with the heater for oxygen, which significantly affected the CO output from the heater.

Even though Coleman knew from its own testing that its heaters produced deadly amounts of CO, the warnings on the heaters did not mention the hazard. Instead, Coleman thought it sufficient to say on a warning decal that the heater was "for outdoor use only" and not for use in tents, campers, or other unventilated or enclosed areas. Our warning expert was highly critical of the warning, primarily because of the lack of a CO warning, but also because of the confusing language. For instance, how much ventilation would be enough? Also, if the heater was used in a fish house or a tent, isn't that "outdoor use"?

Thus, when we started our first Coleman product liability lawsuit in 1996, we had two design defect liability theories relating to safer designs used by competitors as well as a solid inadequate warning theory. As could be expected, Coleman did not roll over easily. Coleman's home-state counsel, led by attorney Ken Lang (with whom I would battle for the next fifteen years), strongly denied the defective nature of the Coleman heater and immediately blamed the two product users for their negligent use of the Focus 15.

In big firm defenses of lawsuits, way too much time and energy is spent in battling minor discovery issues long before getting to trial. Big firm defense lawyers feel compelled to take full-day depositions of all witnesses and every expert hired by the plaintiff's attorney. In this case Coleman's high-priced experts aggressively challenged the defect opinions of our experts. We also had the right to take depositions of their experts. We were alerted that their primary expert on warnings was a PhD from upstate New York who was going to charge $600 per hour for his deposition. With a limited budget on our side of this case, I agreed to take a two-hour telephone deposition from this high-priced expert for a $1,200 fee. The arrogance of this fellow in the comfort of his university office was appalling, but it came back to haunt him in later Coleman cases.

The case was moving towards trial in Minneapolis. We reached a settlement with the retailer because of the solid argument that there was negligence in selling an "inside" heater to the young, uninformed girlfriend of my deceased client. With some expense money in the bank, the case continued towards trial against Coleman. As sometimes happens, events derailed our good lawsuit before trial. About six weeks before the scheduled trial date, Coleman added to its local defense attorneys one of the most prominent insurance defense firms in Minneapolis. This smart defense attorney sent one of his legal assistants to the St. Paul crime lab to retrieve vials of autopsy blood that had been taken from my deceased ice fisherman. The blood sample was then sent to the University of Wisconsin where it was tested for drugs, which had not been done as part of the initial St. Paul autopsy. What was revealed to us was shocking. We had known from day one that our two fishermen had consumed alcohol in their fish house, and it was rumored but not confirmed that they had been using drugs. The Wisconsin drug results on my deceased client's blood sample showed high levels of marijuana. With that finding, the new defense attorney presented a prominent toxicologist with an opinion that under the influence of that level of drugs, my deceased fellow could not have read, let alone understood, the warning on the heater about safe use.

Every now and then in this business you must back up and reevaluate your case and take a different position towards resolution. This revelation a month before trial was a real kick in the head. Just telling my deceased client's mother and sister of the drug level finding was hard to do and even more difficult for them to accept. But, with some level of background experience on how this drug issue would affect a Minnesota conservative jury, I convinced these family members that winning a lawsuit was now an unrealistic possibility and that we should settle for what we could get.

Negotiation continued on with Coleman's attorneys and some more money was offered, which together with what had already been received from the retailer made for a decent settlement for the families and even made some money for the lawyers. The great benefit of this case for me was that this was the first of my many lawsuits against Coleman for these camping heater deaths. The knowledge I gained from the documents disclosed in this first case set the background for all of the later lawsuits and some great recoveries from Coleman.

The first Coleman case did not end with the settlement. I personally got sued by Coleman. Big manufacturers always want a protective order prior to release of their so-called confidential and secret documents during the discovery process of a lawsuit. The manufacturer's motives are twofold: First to protect against disclosure of vital information to competitors (a legitimate reason for protection), and second to prevent plaintiffs' attorneys from spreading the word to other attorneys about how to sue the manufacturer. This latter reason for a protective order is totally inappropriate, and better-informed judges have refused to restrict the dissemination of information to other attorneys. At the conclusion of this first case, Coleman demanded all of its documents back pursuant to the protective order entered into during the case. By that time I was already involved in the next Coleman carbon monoxide death case, that one in Oregon, so I had no desire to start all over with demanding and recovering from

Coleman all of the same documents already in my possession. So I refused to return the documents disclosed after the Minnesota lawsuit closed, and Coleman sued me for breach of contract.

Needless to say, this was the first time I had ever been personally sued. As there was no major downside to this lawsuit, such as a threat to my license to practice, I chose to defend it and have some fun with the Coleman lawyers. Before this document issue was resolved in the Minnesota court, the next Coleman case in Oregon would reach trial. As it turned out, the Coleman documents produced in the Minnesota lawsuit, which I had kept in my office, were critical to the success of the Oregon trial.

The critical issue in *Coleman vs. Stageberg* was a single missing signature. Early in the Minnesota lawsuit Coleman's attorneys had sent me a stipulation to sign agreeing that a protective order could be signed by a judge. I had signed the stipulation and returned it to Coleman's lawyers. They, however, had failed to follow through and get the trial judge's signature on the actual order protecting their documents—a major boo-boo for an attorney. I contended that they had no right to get their documents back because there was no valid protective order signed by a judge. After lengthy briefing and argument the Minnesota trial judge ruled against me, concluding that even if no judge had signed the order, I had agreed by signing the stipulation to return the Coleman documents. Since I still tried to remain a law-abiding citizen and follow court orders, I felt obligated to return Coleman's several boxes of documents. Lest they get the final word, I called the defense lawyer's office and left a message that I would be dropping off the boxes outside their office—on the sidewalk in downtown Minneapolis—at one o'clock the next day, and they had better have someone their to retrieve their documents. I did just as promised. Several young lawyers and clerks were waiting on the sidewalk to gather their documents.

Even though battling Coleman on their documents was fun,

it had a much broader benefit. From this first Coleman case I now had full knowledge of the background and development of all of the Coleman propane heaters and the company's vulnerability in these product liability death cases. I had to return the Coleman documents, but it was impossible for Coleman and its attorneys to erase from my mind the contents of those documents and their support for product liability cases against Coleman. I further knew that I could require Coleman to produce the same several boxes of documents in every subsequent lawsuit. This was the start of something big in my career.

CHAPTER 57

THE COLEMAN EXPERTISE SPREADS

Unbeknownst to most folks, there is a great network through which trial lawyers share information. The national organization of trial lawyers, originally called the Association of Trial Lawyers of America, or ATLA, and more recently called the American Association for Justice, or AAJ, is a wonderful resource for member lawyers. You can request all available information on a subject matter relating to your case from the records and database of the AAJ. Once you make this request, the AAJ database lists you as a called-for-information person on the subject matter of your request. The next attorney looking for help from AAJ on the same subject matter will be put in touch with you as a source of pertinent knowledge. My earliest request to the AAJ for information on carbon monoxide and propane heaters causes my name to pop up, and frequently I converse by phone with a lot of lawyers with similar cases. Sometimes these calls are so parallel that they lead to my becoming an associate attorney on the case. At other times I have given a lot of free telephone advice to lawyers around the country with carbon monoxide death or injury cases. Oftentimes I have supplied contacts with my group of experts. In August of 2006 I wrote a lengthy how-to article entitled "Carbon Monoxide Deaths from Propane Heaters" for the AAJ magazine *Trial.*

Then again, there are some calls that are most unusual. One that I will not forget came out of the blue from Uriel, a sole practicing lawyer from Long Island in New York. The callers always start out buttering me up because of my past experience, which the caller has no doubt researched. Not being bashful, I have never held back from elaborating on my experience and expertise. Starting out as the expert with an attentive student can be enjoyable. After the preliminaries, Uriel told me about his case. He represented a widow in her early fifties whose husband had died from carbon monoxide poisoning while working in a separate shop building behind their house. Uriel blamed a kerosene heater manufactured by a large Japanese company. The heater was found in front of the deceased, out of fuel and with the switch on: A pretty good set of facts indicting the heater as the source of the deadly CO. I explained to Uriel that this was quite different from my Coleman cases, which involved CO produced by propane burning heaters. Uriel had already sued it out against the Japanese company and was embroiled in lots of discovery battles with a mighty defense firm for the defendant. The case had been removed by the defendant from New York state court, so it now slowly progressed in the U.S. District Court for the Southern District of New York. During our conversation Uriel admitted he had little experience with product liability suits and battling in federal court. I ended the conversation with some general advice and wished him well with his case.

Perhaps three months later there was a call: "Mark, do you remember me? This is Uriel." I listened halfheartedly as Uriel brought me up to date on his case. Not much progress had been made on discovery with the defense lawyers, who were apparently sandbagging this sole practitioner, recognizing him as an apparent novice in federal court. Uriel had now retained three expert witnesses: A mechanical engineer who had done nothing on the case, a medical examiner type who had confirmed the obvious, that the deceased died from carbon monoxide, and a most interesting third expert. Somehow, Uriel found an engineer who formerly worked for the Japanese manufacturer and who had written some professional papers critical of the carbon monoxide hazards of the kerosene heaters. Uriel had interviewed this fellow, and he was for real and willing to cooperate to testify against his former employer. Uriel thought this was so good as to justify a claim for punitive damages. (He had no idea how to make the punitive claim in the pending federal court action.) But now, with the potential for large punitives, Uriel had my interest. Again, this call ended with my suggestions for overcoming the stalling tactics of the defense lawyers.

Two months passed before Uriel's next call. Now he unabashedly admitted he needed help in handling this case in federal court. He had contacted a few New York lawyers, none of whom were interested in associating with him. Even though he had already invested many thousands into the case, he was willing to split fifty-fifty any fees, including any punitive damages recovered, with a new helping lawyer. Without even being too subtle, he was clearly fishing for my agreement to help on his case. He almost gasped with relief when I suggested that he package up and send to me all the key documents and let me review them to see if I wanted to help him out on the case. Two days later a package from Uriel arrived by overnight mail.

I now had the opportunity to review everything that Uriel had done on the case and digest the police and coroner's reports describing how they found the decedent in his work shed. Copies of photographs were provided. In the workshop there was not only the kerosene heater, but also a gas-operated snowblower, recently used by the decedent, and a large Harley Davidson motorcycle. Apparently no one had checked to see whether either the Harley or the snowblower had been running when the man was found. In addition, the documents contained interviews with Uriel's client, the deceased's wife, and with other family members, as well as a medical history on the decedent. It seemed that only a few days before his death the decedent had received some negative medical news that he had a serious, life-threatening heart condition.

Remembering a few cases from my past where I had leaped into something without all of the facts, I did some due diligence on Uriel's case. The Internet is a wonderful source for information even for a computer klutz like me. In two hours of searching I found very little information to support that any model of kerosene heater had a track record of producing deadly amounts of CO. If fact, I did not find one successful lawsuit against a manufacturer of kerosene heaters for a CO death. Kerosene heaters were not like propane heaters. Now very skeptical, I relayed to Uriel that I had read his whole file and had some questions. The big one was this: "Uriel, how do you know that the Japanese kerosene heater in the work shed would produce enough carbon monoxide to kill someone?" His response was a mumble-jumble amounting to "That's the only thing in there that would do it." I countered by asking whether maybe this guy who knew he had major medical problems just decided to turn on his Harley or the snowblower and sit down in front of the warm heater and kill himself with the CO. My suggestion shocked Uriel, who vouched for the integrity of this family. My next inquiry was, "Uriel, how do you know that this heater would produce deadly amounts of CO, in excess of 400 parts per million, sufficient to kill someone? Has the heater ever been tested as to its CO output?" Uriel's answer to this was "No, but we lawyers have talked about doing that." Apparently this had been discussed for months but never completed, even though the federal court discovery deadline was three months away. In my nice, fatherly way I said that finding out whether this kerosene heater was even capable of producing deadly amounts of CO was the very first thing that should have been done on the case. Uriel agreed and said he would call the defense lawyer the next day to set up the testing.

This conversation ended with my agreeing to help him as co-counsel on a fifty-fifty fee deal if his testing of the heater produced the anticipated high level of CO. If the testing was a negative, I said I could not help him.

A month later I had a very sad Uriel on the phone. I could tell instantly from his tone that the testing had been a failure, and an impressive one to boot. As expensive engineers stood around with CO test equipment, the kerosene heater was started and allowed to run inside the shed. As I had predicted, the heater produced only negligible levels of CO no matter how long it was operated, at any setting. Uriel had already spent thousands of his money in preparing many parts of the case, but he had never determined the one vital fact as to whether the heater *could* have killed his client's husband. It was a foregone conclusion that I wanted nothing more to do with his case. I bade him farewell and encouraged him to get whatever money he could in any settlement offered by the defendant.

Reflecting back on my many Coleman heater cases, I can state with confidence that as a first step we always had our engineers test the heaters involved to verify that they could produce deadly amounts of CO. Once we had that vital fact secured, with the engineers supplying supporting opinions, we could then start the case in court. In every case the Coleman lawyers would make a big fuss that they should have been involved in the heater testing with our experts. On every one of their protests we prevailed. Our testing was always nondestructive, so the heaters could be later transferred to Coleman to be tested to their hearts' delight. Maybe I am a better lawyer than Uriel, but it seems pretty basic to me that if you are going to blame a product, you'd better be darn sure you can prove that it did the dirty deed.

CHAPTER 58

EXPERT WITNESSES

The more complex the lawsuit, the more need there is for the specialized assistance of expert witnesses. The use of experts is governed in both state and federal courts by rules and case law defining the level of qualifications an expert needs, what type of disclosures and reports are required, and the extent to which the expert can go in expressing opinions in court. The basic rule is that lay witnesses must only testify to facts—that is, what they did, saw, or heard. But if an expert has the requisite qualifications and the subject matter he or she addresses will be of assistance to the jury, the expert can render opinions on the issue at hand. The rule even allows a qualified expert to render opinions on the ultimate issue, such as whether a product is defective or whether a defendant physician committed medical negligence and caused harm to a patient. What I, as both a defense attorney and even more so on the plaintiff's side, found most appealing about involving expert witnesses was the creativity that it brought to developing your side of the case.

A simple example is about an expert that I used when I was the defense attorney in facial scar cases. Plaintiffs' lawyers love cases involving facial scars to women, especially young girls. Most often these are caused by dog bites or car accidents. For a plaintiff's lawyer the cases are easy and usually result in a lucrative settlement without a trial. To help reduce the impact of the facial scars, I found and hired as an expert a professional makeup artist who daily applied makeup to actors and actresses in TV commercials. I would supply her with some of the graphic photos of the plaintiff's scars, and she would render an expert opinion that she, or any other makeup person, could create a personalized makeup program for approximately $50 that would practically make the facial scars disappear. The projected cost of the plaintiff's makeup was not much more than what the average woman would regularly spend. This expert never had to testify at trial, but her opinions greatly reduced the settlement value of several cases.

If one looks far enough, there are people in almost all walks of life who are willing to serve as expert witnesses in litigation. Many nationwide organizations offer a roster of experts in exchange for a finder's fee. In the medical malpractice area, where local doctors seldom agree to assist a claimant against a local defendant doctor, finding an out-of-state expert through an outside organization for a $500 fee is the only option. Often the best experts are those who have many years of practical experience, rather than an advanced degree. For instance, who could be a better witness in a failed automobile brake case than a mechanic who has serviced brakes for twenty years and has seen every possible defect and brake problem? In other cases, university professors are great expert witnesses. Usually, a PhD with teaching duties at the local university has credentials well received by a jury. At the University of Minnesota, professors are encouraged to spend up to one-third of their time doing outside consulting. This allows them to assist as expert witnesses and supplement their teaching salaries with expert fees at a much higher hourly rate. Most experts find it flattering to be consulted for their expertise, and they like to be paid handsomely for talking about their specialty. In my view, the use of expert witnesses is only limited by the lack of creativity of the lawyer.

A major change in expert witness testimony happened in 1993, when the U.S. Supreme Court rendered its decision in *Daubert v. Merrell Dow Pharmaceuticals, Inc.*, 509 U.S. 579 (1993). Apparently believing that expert testimony had been too liberally allowed in the federal courts, the Supreme Court set out a procedure for federal trial judges to determine in a preliminary ruling whether an offered expert was qualified in his or her field, had done appropriate supporting work or methodology, and could put forth reliable opinions. The trial judge was to become the gatekeeper, deciding whether an expert could testify and render all or some of his or her opinions. No longer was the jury, after even broad cross-examination of an expert, to decide the believability of an expert's opinions. That duty was now a pretrial issue solely in the hands of a single federal judge, who would view the facts and the experts' credentials and opinions with all of his or her built-in biases, prejudices, and even political leanings. Hardly was this an improvement over a jury of six or twelve scrutinizing the expert's background and opinions!

Two Supreme Court decisions followed the *Daubert* case and made matters worse. The next case expanded the *Daubert* case to all types of expert witnesses, including medical witnesses. The third case addressed the duty of the judges of the eleven federal circuit courts of appeal in reviewing the decisions of the trial judges on *Daubert* motions. The standard of review the appellate court could apply to overturn a trial judge's expert ruling was if there was an "abuse of discretion." This left the trial judge's decision almost inviolate, reversible only on appeal if the ruling on an expert was really far off base. Seldom have the eleven circuit courts reversed a judge's *Daubert* rulings. Our local Eighth Circuit court is considered the worst, and its decisions on *Daubert* issues have filtered down to the trial judges resulting in many good cases being perfunctorily thrown out on *Daubert* motions. A number of states have also adopted the *Daubert* case, requiring state court judges to similarly become gatekeepers on expert issues. Minnesota did not, however, and there still remains a lesser standard on judging expert testimony.

Needless to say, plaintiffs' attorneys hate the *Daubert* requirement, and defense lawyers love it. In every serious product liability or technical case, defense lawyers will spend many billable hours challenging plaintiffs' experts on *Daubert* motions. If you start a product liability case, it is now routine for the defendant to challenge the plaintiff's engineering experts on *Daubert* motions to dismiss. Plaintiffs' lawyers have spent many thousands of their dollars fighting such challenges just to keep their cases alive until trial. Reports indicate lawyers spending $20,000 to $30,000 to hire a second expert witness to review the methodology and opinion support of the first expert witness, the better to convince the trial judge at a *Daubert* hearing of the reliability of the first expert.

I have personally encountered the effects of *Daubert* on several occasions. The first involved a helicopter crash in South Dakota. An emergency airlift helicopter ferrying a sick patient back to a Sioux Falls hospital lost power, necessitating an emergency landing in an Iowa cornfield. No one died, but the helicopter was destroyed and its fifty-year-old pilot seriously injured. Because I had tried two similar helicopter crash cases, I was asked to assist the South Dakota lawyer. Aviation testing showed that the speed governor on the engine was malfunctioning and not allowing sufficient RPMs to keep the helicopter afloat. We had a well-respected aviation expert who gave us opinions that the governor manufacturer was at fault and liable because of an inadequate overhaul of the governor. In my preparation of this case, I attended and completed depositions in Dallas, Los Angeles, and Biloxi, Mississippi, as well as Denver twice, Sioux Falls twice, and South Bend, Indiana, twice. The defense made its *Daubert* motion in Sioux Falls a month before trial. It was apparent that our federal trial judge was overworked and facing perhaps three weeks of trial on our case. Extensive briefs and arguments were presented to the judge on the validity of our expert's opinion. Two weeks later our case was wiped from the map as the judge granted the defense's *Daubert* motion. He made a determination, which logically should have been left for jury decision, that the amount of decrease in RPMs on the governor could not have caused the loss of power, and our expert's opinions to the contrary were not reliable. Since this was within the Eighth Circuit and appeal of this decision was considered hopeless, several months of legal work and $30,000 of my money went down the drain.

In my Coleman heater cases, every one of the lawsuits against Coleman has resulted in a flood of *Daubert* motions against every one of my experts. Even my CO expert, Dr. David Penny, with unimpeachable CO research credentials, has repeatedly been challenged by Coleman's *Daubert* motions. The worst abuse was Coleman's *Daubert* motion against my extremely well-qualified engineering expert, Dr. Gary Hutter, in the *Covas* case in Miami, Florida. Dr. Hutter's résumé was most impressive, his opinions well founded, and he had given a full day of testimony in a deposition elaborating on his preparation and opinions. In addition, I had prepared with Dr. Hutter a supplemental affidavit that added significant supporting background for his credentials and trial preparation. Miami Federal Judge Joan Lenard decided to call a *Daubert* hearing right before the start of trial and required me to present all of Dr. Hutter's anticipated direct testimony. She then allowed a full cross-examination by the defense attorney. As this three-day pretrial hearing extended over a weekend, I had to fly Dr. Hutter down twice from Chicago to Miami (then, to complete his testimony in the following trial, I paid for two more airline tickets for him from Chicago to Miami).

Fortunately, Dr. Hutter was the best, most polished engineering expert I have ever had on the witness stand. On cross-examination he could twist the defense attorney every which way but loose. After listening to Dr. Hutter's full testimony, Judge Lenard ruled from the bench that the majority of his testimony and opinions would be allowed. She followed with a well-written twenty-four-page opinion on why she denied the *Daubert* motion. In this case the *Daubert* motion really backfired on Coleman. Until hearing Dr. Hutter's testimony at the hearing, Judge Lenard had been very hard on us plaintiff attorneys, often expressing dissatisfaction with the whole *Covas* case and our presentation. It was quite apparent that after listening to the solid testimony of Dr. Hutter for three days, Judge Lenard had changed her view, now believing that our plaintiff's case and liability theories had significant merit. Thereafter, the judge's attitude toward us improved and her rulings were almost consistently in our favor.

A fascinating part of expert witness testimony is my right as a trial lawyer to cross-examine opposing experts. My mentor, law partner, and good friend, John Lommen, used to say that his greatest pleasure was cross-examining the opposition's experts. He used to smile with anticipation at the possibility. I took that advice to heart and similarly developed the same excitement in crossing experts. For many years that challenge has lit my fire in a big way. Facing the opponent's expert is playing in the enemy's ballfield. One thing you quickly learn is that you will never get the expert to come about-face through your questioning and admit that his or her opinion is unfounded or wrong. You must attack more subtly, showing the faults or inappropriate assumptions in the expert's foundation. At one of the best seminars I ever attended, the Wyoming cowboy trial lawyer Gerry Spence maintained that you can never convince the opposing expert to abandon his or her opinions, but you can use the questioning time to reinforce your own case and your expert's theory and position. Over my career I took this advice to heart and put it to good use. No matter what level of lawsuit, my preparation for the cross of an expert was thorough and often left me sleepless at night as I planned my attack on the next day's expert.

My expert cross-examination stories are many. A favorite episode was the cross of Coleman's engineering expert Peter Susey in the Florida *Covas* case. Our theory, as supported by our experts, was that the Focus 5 heater had become contaminated through an unprotected opening in the propane flow tube, resulting in the production of the deadly amounts of CO. Susey's expert report for Coleman suggested other possible causes for the high production of CO by the Focus 5. My pretrial deposition of him was fun. I referred his report and inquired about the possible causes other than contamination. After dancing around with his bullshit answers, I pinned him down to admit that there were just two realistic causes. Upon exploring further these two causes, he had to acknowledge that both were tied to contamination of the heater, exactly our theory. Now, when you get someone committed on a favorable answer like that, you want to lock him into cement so he can never wiggle out of it. My follow-up questions did just that. A week later, after Coleman's lawyers realized Susey's deposition actually supported our theory, they filed a supplemental affidavit, supposedly prepared by Susey, suggesting that he had been confused by my questions and then identifying six other possible causes. Well, a deposition transcript "ain't gonna lie," and Susey found out about that at trial.

Trial: *Covas v. Coleman*, Miami, Florida, June 2005. Our plaintiff's case had been concluded, and Coleman called to the witness stand their chief engineering expert, Peter Susey. After an excessive amount of time spent establishing Susey's supposed credentials as an expert, Susey rendered opinions that the Focus 5 heater was not defective and not a cause of the two carbon monoxide deaths. He didn't touch his six alternative causes. The following cross may have been as fun as anything in my career. During Susey's direct examination, the Coleman lawyer had stressed in great detail Susey's past employment with the Atomic Energy Commission working on jet-propulsion issues. Impressive before a jury, right? Well, I had carefully reviewed Susey's printed résumé. Nowhere did it mention in his past employment any such work for the AEC. Once again, before using the résumé I repeated many of the prior defense lawyer's questions, allowing Susey to proudly boast of his AEC work. Then, boom! Exhibit 49 was marked and laid in front of the witness. After I got done crossing on his claimed credentials, the jury didn't know if Susey, the defense lawyer, or both were lying.

Then Mr. Susey and I talked about the possible causes of the heater emitting the excess carbon monoxide. Having locked himself into cement in his deposition, he was easy pickings. He had to acknowledge that the only realistic causes he could find were exactly those of our theory of contamination. He even totally forgot the six alternative causes the lawyers had prepared for him in the affidavit. Susey finished the session stammering and sweating profusely, knowing that he had not helped Coleman one bit. My Florida co-counsel said after I finished my cross, "That guy was just pitiful." No one knows how much the failure of the defense's chief expert played in the resulting verdict. But the jury deliberated only about two hours and awarded $8 million to the plaintiff.

CHAPTER 59

RESPECTING OUR ELDERS

When I entered the world of big and small law firms, there was a hierarchy that rivaled the caste system in India. If you were a partner in a law firm, whether because of your legal acumen and business-getting prowess or for a multitude of other reasons, you had it made. Whether or not it was justified, the senior partners demanded respect, deference, and near-worship from their young peons in the law firm hierarchy. To gain this status in any sizeable, respectable law firm, you traditionally had to climb up through the ranks of associate, senior associate, and junior partner before reaching the elevated status of senior partner.

I have a broad spectrum of opinions on senior partners. Some I respected; others landed at the other end of the spectrum. John Lommen was my ideal of how a skilled lawyer and senior law firm president should conduct himself. In every respect he was my hero. No one I have encountered in the profession has ever matched his acumen in administering people. At age sixty, he died too soon to ever enjoy his senior status.

In two of my Coleman cases I joined forces with outstanding senior lawyers. Bill Trine of Boulder, Colorado, was seventy-five years old when we tried a winning case together. Jackson Howard, of Provo, Utah, was eighty years old when we worked together, and he was sharp and energetic. I have great respect for both of these great lawyers.

However, there are a lot of old-timers who should have given up the practice long before their skills started slipping. I remember early on, about a year or two into the practice, when I was assigned to assist a partner in the case of a large warehouse fire allegedly caused by our client's repairman performing welding near a loading dock. Our firm was associating with another prominent defense firm, and I had been assigned to attend several depositions of critical witnesses. My colleague on the same side was named Nate and was probably then in excess of seventy years of age. He was a named senior partner in his firm. I was instructed by my senior colleague to follow Nate and keep my mouth shut. As I listened to a competent plaintiff's attorney ream out the critical witnesses, I frequently thought the questioning was objectionable, but since Nate was not objecting to the questions, how could I object? After some significant and uncomfortable period of time, I looked over at Nate and found him sound asleep. Obviously, he was well over the hill and should have been put out to pasture by his firm long ago. But for me this was a good lesson that I never thereafter forgot: If you don't like what is happening, raise an objection no matter how dumb it may seem at the moment.

My experience in the Coleman cases provided further examples of lawyers well past their prime. Coleman's lead lawyers from Wichita somehow felt they needed to associate with the largest local law firm in whatever city hosted the trial, designating a well-respected senior partner in that firm as co-defense counsel. Usually my local plaintiff's counsel would try to impress me that Mr. Big Name was one of the really experienced and prominent defense attorneys in the local area. But the Wichita attorneys controlled the litigation during all of the preparation stages, and never did Big Name appear at any depositions or most pretrial proceedings. In the second Washington case, Mr. Big Name did appear at a pretrial oral argument before the federal judge on several critical motions. When he was introduced to me, my first impression was that the guy was really past his prime. Thereafter, on several occasions, Big Name rose to address the court and fumbled through an oral argument indicating that he really knew nothing about the case. To the federal judge and everyone in the courtroom, this performance was embarrassing. This fellow was not only worn out, but actively sliding down to the bottom of legal competence.

Another example occurred in my Montana Coleman case. Coleman had selected the largest insurance defense firm in Missoula to associate with as local counsel. A forty-five-year-old partner was involved in most aspects of the trial preparation. He was a nice guy, competent and easy to work with. As we got near trial, the name of the firm's senior partner began to appear on documents. Once again, my local counsel sang the praises of this esteemed member of the Montana bar, well respected in the defense community and even past president of the Montana State Bar Association. On only a single pretrial occasion did I meet this supposed giant of the profession, at a conference among attorneys. He was well-coiffed, tanned, wearing an expensive suit, and totally cordial in his greeting to me. Though he had not done a diddly-damn in the preparation of the case for trial, come day one of trial there he sat at the end of the defense counsel table. After I gave an hour-and-half-long extemporaneous opening statement without a single note, the judge turned to defense counsel and asked if they wished to make an opening statement. To our surprise, the gray-haired senior partner sauntered up to the podium and provided a twenty-minute reading of his prepared notes. His delivery throughout was that of a senior scholar whose every word the jury should believe as God's chosen pronouncements. When he finished, I looked at local counsel and said, "Was that impressive? What did he say that was worthwhile? He didn't know anything about the case."

That Montana case proceeded into the third day of trial before it was settled shortly before noon. Except for the opening statement, the gray-haired wizard had not participated in the trial at all. After the judge announced the settlement to the jury, they were discharged and free to visit with the lawyers. In my co-counsel's discussion with the jurors, he asked what they thought of the lawyers. The response was, that they liked all of the lawyers except that old guy at the end of the table who was sleeping during the trial. A great laugh for us. So much for impressive senior attorneys!

The lesson I learned from these old-duffer encounters was that there is definitely a time to give up the courtroom battles and take down the shingle. Trying lawsuits is a very strenuous, high-pressure occupation. Working thirteen or fourteen hour days for the duration of a trial is, needless to say, very hard work. John Lommen used to say that every time you try a case you leave some of yourself in the courtroom. The alternative to continuing to do battle in the courtroom is to settle more cases. Too often I have seen senior lawyers give away a good case with a nominal settlement when the client deserved a hard-fought trial. Taking the easy settlement road is no way to end a career. For many trial lawyers, giving up the fight is hard to do, but when your skills start failing you must recognize that it is time to quit. In my case, I have had mixed emotions about giving up the courtroom. My hearing was going, and I refused to wear a hearing aid. My stamina was waning, so a ten-hour courtroom battle left me quite exhausted. As the next chapter relates, I went out battling the Coleman Company. The death cases were going to keep coming, of course, and for many more years I could have kept on pursuing Coleman. For some time now I have been looking for an aggressive attorney to carry on the Coleman fight. As of this writing, however, that trial lawyer has not been found.

CHAPTER 60

ENDING A CAREER AGAINST COLEMAN

Even before the first case against the Coleman Company ended in Minnesota, a call came in for help on the next one thanks to my listing with the national information bank for plaintiffs' lawyers. Two young lawyers in Eugene, Oregon, had sued out a death case involving a thirty-nine-year old carpenter who had taken a Coleman Focus 15 heater into a tent and was found dead in the morning. The young Oregon lawyers had no idea how to put the case together, let alone try it. I agreed to help and share fees with them.

Oregon trial procedure is antiquated, requiring trials to proceed as they did a hundred years ago, with no pretrial discovery and a surprise a minute in the courtroom. In contrast to the procedures of every other state, there is no need there to disclose expert witnesses or their opinions. On the morning of trial I received a list of fifteen Coleman proposed witnesses with no identification of which were expert witnesses. I had no idea what expert testimony was coming from Coleman. But what the heck,

I had my good experts from Minnesota and the product liability theories were solid, so off we went to trial.

Coleman's Wichita defense lawyers associated with a senior partner from the largest defense firm in Portland. Their chosen trial lawyer turned out to be a real buffoon. He thought he had a great sense of humor, and during the course of the trial he would laugh at the most inappropriate times. I really appreciated this guy's willingness to continue making an ass out of himself in front of the jury. Sometime in midtrial this guy came up to me and laughingly said, "Tough case, huh, Mark?" In response I turned away and said, "Let's wait and see what the jury says." Before trial the Coleman representative, later known to be Marc Clements, offered $25,000 to settle the case. It was pleasant to tell him where to shove his pittance offer. This guy turned out to be the person who controlled the purse-strings in all of Coleman's later cases. He had absolutely no compassion for the many victims his company had killed, and he was a hard negotiator on settlements.

The case went to trial in Eugene for two weeks, starting in early December 1999. I got my first taste of Oregon winter weather. Every day it was either raining or about to rain. I eventually decided that the depressing atmosphere was conducive to trying a wrongful death case. Another matter of image seemed to be in our favor as well. Picture the plaintiff's lawyer team—myself (at about five-foot-nine) and the five-foot-five Middle Eastern referral lawyer—compared to the mighty defense-lawyers team consisting of two six-foot-tall senior partners, one six-foot-tall associate attorney, one six-foot-tall female legal assistant, and a six-foot-two engineer from Coleman. This five-person defense team felt obligated to dress alike in dark, mortician-type suits, and they huddled together and entered and left the courthouse en masse, usually within easy view of the jury. It looked like the Mafia was defending this trial. I really enjoyed the contrast, and

I thought the jury would be in our favor. Our jury investigation disclosed that Eugene had decades earlier become the getaway place for the California hippie generation, obviously a very liberal group. At least on paper, this looked like a perfect place for a sympathetic plaintiff's case.

Oregon procedure for jury selection was again something else. Forty-five prospective jurors were brought into the courtroom, and the lawyers were given brief bios of all of them. After the judge gave a short summary of the case, each lawyer was allowed to give a five-minute summary of his side's position before questioning began of all forty-five. I fumbled through a logical summary of the product liability theories and why Coleman was at fault. The defense lawyer stood up with a large exhibit that said "Never use in a tent." He then explained that the deceased carpenter had ignored this warning on the heater and, after becoming very intoxicated, took the heater into his tent and killed himself. After that intro the judge asked some general questions of all forty-five prospective jurors. The following five minutes may have been one of the lowest points of my trial work. The judge's first question was something like, "From what you have heard from the lawyers, does anyone believe they could not be a fair juror in this case?" Immediately several hands went up. The first to speak was a forty-year-old gentleman whose response was something like, "If this is about a drunk who killed himself by taking a heater into his tent, what are we doing here?" At least ten of the other prospective jurors either nodded agreement or repeated the same negative opinion. Some of this group of obviously biased jurors were dismissed, but the remaining large group had heard all about the others' dislike of my lawsuit. Now the judge turned it over to me to begin questioning this group. I felt like I was starting to push a rock up an insurmountable hill.

In looking back at this whole jury selection process, I do have fond memories. After stumbling around with various inquiries and not getting any favorable responses or body language, I asked if anyone had ever had owned a product that they thought was defective and became involved with a recall by the manufacturer. An older gentleman raised his hand and began telling me about the bad tires on his retirement RV and that the tire manufacturer had done a recall and given him a brand-new set of tires. This fellow opened the door, and several other jurors began describing for me the dangers they felt about their defective products. This was exactly the type of fear I hoped to instill in my jury about the hidden dangers in the use of the Coleman heaters. When I talked with them about propane camping heaters, a forest ranger on the panel described seeing loggers taking heaters of this type into their tents many times. Because Coleman's lawyers had to use their two preemptory strikes to eliminate other jurors, they had to leave the forest ranger on the jury. I could not have asked for a better juror on this case. Also, there remained a law-and-order deputy sheriff who turned out to be the foreman of the jury. After a very traumatic jury selection process, I was quite pleased with our group of final jurors.

The trial judge was quite helpful to our side. She allowed me to disclose to the jury all of the prior documented deaths caused by these Coleman heaters. As the days progressed I could feel the jurors warming to our claims. After several days of trial, my young Oregon colleague wanted to get more involved and, after a long prep session, I let him cross-examine one of the Coleman witnesses. After he floundered around for fifteen minutes without accomplishing anything, I tugged at his coat to get him to quit and sit down.

After nine days of trial and final arguments concluded, the jury began deliberating. I left and caught a plane to visit my daughter in San Francisco. When I arrived, there was a phone call from Eugene explaining that not only had we won, but the jury was very generous. The jury excused the intoxication of the decedent and found Coleman totally at fault for its defective heater. The verdict amount was $796,000, which was more than I had asked that the jury award to the plaintiff. This had never happened before in any of my trials.

Coleman appealed, and after two more years the verdict was totally affirmed and Coleman paid up. The appellate decision is found at *Benjamin v. Wal-Mart Stores,* 185 Or. App. 444, 61 P.3d 257 (2002). A few days after the trial concluded, my co-counsel met one of the jurors in a grocery store. The juror was wondering why they could not have awarded punitive damages against Coleman. This jury definitely liked our case and really disliked Coleman and its heaters. It is quite surprising that in none of the subsequent cases could we get the jury quite as mad at Coleman as this Oregon jury had been. Clearly, Coleman's lawyers learned a lot from this first trial and used it to improve their trial performance.

After the Oregon trial I prepared a consumer awareness website called Carbonmonxidedeaths.com to warn consumers of the risks of using the Coleman heaters and also discussing the Oregon result and my product liability experience. Soon new Coleman cases came knocking at my door. I had suddenly become the national expert on suing Coleman for the deaths caused by its propane heaters. In cases throughout the country I associated with local lawyers to supply the expertise to sue Coleman in wrongful death cases. Every case had remarkable issues and battles, each of which deserves a chapter of memories. Here is a more limited chronological summary.

Arizona: Two hunters died in a tent while using a Focus 30 heater. Although I was not directly involved in this one, my help behind the scenes resulted in a nice settlement just before trial commenced.

Montana: Two fifty-five-year-old fishermen died in a tent by a lake while using a Powermate 5012 heater. One widow settled before trial, and during the third day of our trial in Missoula's federal court, Coleman settled the second case for a nice sum.

Wisconsin: Two men died in a hunting shack while using a Powermate 5012 heater. Even though named as a co-counsel for the plaintiff, I only provided advice to the young plaintiff's lawyer, leading to a pretrial settlement.

Michigan: Two deputy sheriffs died in a hunting shack while using a Powermate 5014 heater. This case settled with only behind-the-scenes help from me. I later learned that Coleman told the Michigan lawyer that if Stageberg got involved they would not settle but would take it to trial. Coleman was going to make me work in any of my cases.

Utah: Two prominent twenty-nine-year-old men from Cedar City, Utah, died in a tent from carbon monoxide from a Focus 15 heater while on an elk hunting trip. A stupid (and I emphasize stupid) female judge, whose background was as a criminal prosecutor, interpreted Utah product liability law so as to totally eliminate our defective design claim about the heater. This left for trial only the claim that there was a defective warning on the heater. I knew going in that trying only a warning claim is tough, especially when the trial took place in a Mormon religious stronghold in central Utah. After four weeks of trial in this town of four thousand residents, the jury came in against us, finding the two decedents more at fault than Coleman. Even though there was a solid appeal issue on the trial judge's eliminating the defective design claim, the two widows, who had by that time remarried, refused to go further for the appeal.

Washington: I was lead counsel in three Coleman cases. A Native American couple died in a tent while using a Powermate 5012 heater, leaving a young daughter surviving. After all of the Coleman pretrial efforts, this case was settled. The second case involved the death of three people using a Coleman Powermate 5045 heater. A Southeast Asian couple had been providing ethnic food in a portable booth at flea markets and similar events. Both husband and wife died, together with their fourteen-year-old daughter, while sleeping in their truck at such an event. They left behind a five-year-old boy. After a tremendous amount of pretrial battling with Coleman, this case settled for a nice amount three days before trial.

That was the first of the three Powermate 5045 cases. It was a larger heater than other models (45,000 BTU output) and looked more like a commercial heater. The third Washington case involved a double death from a Powermate 5045 heater. A woman lost both her father and husband when they died of CO poisoning while sleeping in a camping trailer on a hunting trip in the mountains. Coleman refused to settle this one, and it went to trial in Tacoma federal court. Local counsel recommended a woman magistrate rather than one of the federal judges. On their recommendation I agreed. That was a mistake, as many significant rulings in trial went against us. The jury returned a finding of no fault on Coleman. This was a big loss after we had invested a lot of money in the case. But you win some and lose some. Wait until we get to Florida.

Florida: This was a good one! A Hispanic woman had lost her electrician husband and her sixteen-year-old son from a previous marriage. Both men had gone up to a northern Florida hunting camp and were found dead in their tent after using a small Focus 5 Coleman heater. Before contacting me, a local Florida lawyer had screwed up the case almost beyond redemption. He had taken the heater to an engineer at Florida University and without any guidance let the guy dismantle it, test it, and give an opinion of what had happened. There is a severe judicial concept called "spoliation" that provides in a product liability case an absolute defense if the allegedly defective product is destroyed or changed before the manufacturer has an opportunity to inspect it. The Florida professor had done a classic spoliation job of destroying evidence without adequately recording by photograph the steps taken in dismantling and testing the heater. At this stage, with Coleman already claiming spoliation, I got involved. Believing that my other experts could do independent testing of similar Focus 5 heaters, I felt we did not need the Florida expert and we could get around the spoliation defense.

For some reason the federal judge in Miami initially did not like this case. On Coleman's spoliation motion, she ruled out not only the Florida professor as an expert, but also my three new experts. Her reasoning was that my three guys, despite having done their own testing and analysis, had been advised of the Florida guy's blunders and were thus tainted as well. There went $60,000 of expert witness expense. The judge gave me thirty days to come up with a brand-new expert. In a scramble to find someone, I was led to Dr. Gary Hutter from Glenview, Illinois. As I mentioned in an earlier chapter, this PhD in engineering proved to be the best engineering expert witness I ever placed on the witness stand.

As in prior cases, Coleman's Wichita lawyers worked with the largest defense firm in Miami. There were swarms of defense lawyers involved. In the later appeal by Coleman, eight different lawyers were identified as participating in the appellate brief. We estimated that Coleman spent in excess of $3 million in defending this one case. Before it got to trial we were ordered into settlement mediations four different times. In all of these settlement efforts Coleman's maximum offer for both death cases was $375,000. Our lowest demand was $1 million, but we would have taken $750,000 if it had been offered. With no resolution, the case went to trial in Miami federal court in June of 2005.

As in the other Coleman trials, I carried the ball. It was hot and humid in Miami. After walking the two blocks from the parking lot to the courthouse each morning, I found my dress shirt to be totally soaked with sweat. It was tough to freshen up and look ready to go under those conditions. One rather humorous part of the trial occurred during opening statements. We had paid over $4,000 for some nice blowups on tagboard for my opening. Our side thought the opening went very well. Coleman's lawyers had spent many thousands on a PowerPoint presentation to use during their opening. It totally malfunctioned, and after a half hour of attempted repairs, the defense lawyer proceeded with a flat and unpersuasive opening.

I still find it amazing that Coleman and its team of lawyers could not see this disaster coming. This was Miami-Dade County, with a population that is about 75 percent Latino and black. Our client was Hispanic, as was her deceased husband, as well as five out of the eight people selected for the jury. With the favorable rulings from the judge, our evidence went in without a major hitch. Coleman's chief expert looked like a fool on the witness stand. In closing argument I felt I could really lay into Coleman for once. My argument theme was corporate responsibility, and I emphasized Coleman's corporate irresponsibility and corporate arrogance in its denials and refusal to compensate for this tremendous loss. The jury was out less than three hours. They found Coleman 70 percent at fault and the campers 30 percent at fault. The total damage award was $10.1 million dollars, leading to a net recovery of $8.1 million. Coleman processed an appeal to the Eleventh Circuit Federal Court of Appeals, but the appeal was quickly rejected in a three-page opinion from the appellate court. Coleman then paid the entire $8.1 million.

There was one sorry ending to this great victory. My local Florida lawyer, whom I had rescued from his disastrous spoliation, tried to screw me out of some of the contingent attorney fee. Without getting into the ugly details, I ended up hiring another lawyer to represent me against this guy and eventually agreed to settle the dispute by giving up about $40,000 of my hard-earned fee.

New Mexico: A father and his thirteen-year-old son died in a small shack near Santa Fe while using a Powermate 5045 heater. The setting of this case was interesting. Just outside of Santa Fe was a huge ranch that had been used for the filming of several cowboy movies. On this occasion Turner Films was filming a multipart television western onsite. The father was a security guard at the entrance to the ranch. The evening that his son came along, he unfortunately used the Coleman heater in the guard shack. Two cases were started in New Mexico state court with two Albuquerque law firms involved. I supplied the expertise and the liability experts and planned again to be lead counsel. I got along very well with the state court judge at the first hearing.

Then the New Mexico lawyers began spending outrageous amounts of money on the case. As the case approached trial, they also decided that they could try the case better than I could and that I would sit in the back as a consultant. This proved to be a tedious experience. During the two-week trial, seldom did the trial lawyers take and utilize my advice and suggestions. They thought they could do it better. Many times during the trial I cringed at the trial performance, especially from an older, supposedly very experienced trial lawyer. I could tell the jury was turned off by this guy. The jury returned its verdict totally for Coleman. I really don't know if my active trial work could have turned this case around, but it certainly could not have been any worse.

Colorado: A lovely lady named Gale in Denver had read my Carbonmonoxidedeaths.com site and sent me an e-mail stating that in September of 2006, her fifty-one-year-old husband and twenty-six-year-old son had died from CO from a Focus 15 heater while hunting in the Colorado mountains. After I visited with her in Denver, she became my client and I co-counseled with a very experienced trial lawyer in Boulder. Coleman put up its usual expensive and tedious defense and refused to pay any reasonable amount in settlement. As with the others, this product liability case was challenging and expensive. Since this one is fairly fresh in my mind, I can recall that we lawyers spent $145,000 of our money (most of it mine) in preparing and presenting this case. Our Denver federal judge was a crusty seventy-eight-year-old senior member of the bench. By injecting some timely humor I managed to hit it off well with him. It helped that my co-counsel was himself seventy-five years old and trying his last case. Throughout the trial the judge was far less friendly with the Coleman lawyers and their witnesses.

After eight tough trial days the jury gave an unusual verdict. They found for Coleman that the heater was not defective and the warnings were adequate, but found Coleman negligent. They also found the father and son negligent and 66 percent at fault. The total damage award was over $2 million, but under Colorado's pure comparative-fault law this amount had to be reduced by 66 percent, leaving an eventual recovery of $850,000. Coleman processed an appeal, and we counter-appealed to the Tenth Circuit Court of Appeals. After six months of negotiation, Coleman paid the full verdict amount.

What follows may be an incredible disclosure, and if Coleman's lawyers read it they might succumb to depression. (I rather hope they do.) In fact, Coleman should sue its lawyers for malpractice. During the six months of post-trial negotiation, my Boulder co-counsel did some legal research and discovered three Tenth Circuit product liability cases with jury findings identical to ours of no defect in the product but negligence by the manufacturer. In each case, the jury result favoring the plaintiff was reversed because the finding of no defect in the product precluded any other finding of negligence by the manufacturer. Had Coleman's lawyers discovered these three cases, winning their appeal and reversing our $850,000 verdict would have been a slam dunk. Had they continued on with their appeal, we would not have had any defense to the reversal.

There was a tragic footnote to the Colorado case. Gale had lost her husband and son. Her only other child was a twenty-four-year-old daughter who had a two-year-old baby with her fiancé. About three months after the final settlement of the Coleman case, the fiancé lost control of his car, striking a tree head-on and resulting in the child's death and permanent brain injury to himself. Thus, in a three-year period this wonderful client had lost her husband, her son, and her granddaughter, and had nearly lost her son-in-law-to-be.

Utah: In June of 2009, a family group from Grand Junction, Colorado, attended a paintball event in northern Utah. On a cold, rainy evening, a twenty-eight-year-old fellow and his ten-year-old niece died from CO while using a Powermate 5017 heater in a tent. As this goes to print, this case, with me as lead counsel, is pending in federal court in Salt Lake City.

Illinois: In April of 2010, a fifty-year old man died and his twenty-five-year old son was injured from CO while sleeping with a Powermate 5045 heater in a pop-up camper in southern Illinois. Efforts by co-counsel to settle with Coleman have not been successful. As this goes to print, the case has yet to be sued out.

The history of carbon monoxide deaths and injuries from Coleman heaters is not over. Between the Coleman Focus and Powermate lines, more than 1.7 million units were sold in the United States and Canada. The last Focus heater was sold in 1996, when the sale of Powermates started. Powermates were sold up through 2006. Although promoted as industrial heaters, the Powermates have been killing people at a faster rate than the Focus heaters. As the heaters get older they actually become more dangerous due to contamination and physical abuse. As we have done, Coleman kept track of the reported deaths and injuries and prepared its own list of the tragedies. Although the deaths and injuries have continued to mount, and no doubt will continue in the future, Coleman has refused to make any type of a recall. The Coleman website fails to mention anything about the CO hazard. There has never been any type of publicity campaign through the Consumer Product Safety Commission or elsewhere to warn of the real dangers of these Coleman heaters. The frustrating part of these cases has been my inability to obtain a punitive damage award against Coleman. Often a large punitive award against a manufacturer will promote a recall of a dangerous product. Over the years I have personally contacted the CPSC on three occasions to urge a full investigation and recall of the heaters. In 1992, and again in 1999, the CPSC did initiate some investigation of the Coleman heaters, but correspondence reviewed from these efforts shows the Coleman lawyers smothering the overworked CPSC investigators with denials, objections, and outright fabrications. In both instances, the investigations soon fizzled with no action taken.

I will close with a description of one of the most enjoyable parts of the Coleman cases. In 2002, Coleman hired Dr. Goldhaber, an expensive PhD from upstate New York, to conduct a consumer study of the effectiveness of its heater warnings and to determine public awareness of the dangers in the use of the heaters. At two outdoor camping shows, a booth was set up with a Focus 15 heater to be handled and inspected by persons attending the shows. Then a sheet of questions about the heater warning and the safe use of this type of heater was presented to attendees. The results were printed for Coleman in what was called the Goldhaber Report. A total of 1,005 responses were considered statistically valid. Dr. Goldhaber then massaged the responses into some conclusions he felt were favorable to Coleman. My careful reading of the report showed that it backfired for Coleman and actually disclosed just how dangerous these heaters were to the users. The responses further showed that the heater warnings were ineffective. Towards the end of the report, three of the statistical conclusions were that 45 percent of respondents felt it would be safe to use this heater in a plywood fish house; 28 percent felt it would be safe to use in a tent; and 38 percent felt it would be safe to use in a camper. My cross-examination questions to Dr. Goldhaber went something like this: "From your own study, if a thousand campers took this Focus 15 heater into their plywood fish houses to stay warm, then 450 of them would be dead in the morning, isn't that correct, sir?" Then, after his stumbling response, I followed with, "Isn't it also correct from your study that if a thousand experienced campers took this heater into their tents, 280 of them would be dead in the morning?" The next question asked about 380 dead people in campers. Even when Coleman chose to leave Dr. Goldhaber at home, my own experts at trial really enjoyed using his report and its statistics.

ABOUT THE AUTHOR

Mark Stageberg is a Minnesota attorney who has spent his career as a civil trial lawyer. He has been repeatedly recognized since its inception in the national directory, *Best Lawyers in America*. In 2002, his peers in the Minnesota bar voted him to be in the top 100 Super Lawyers. He has completed over 175 jury trials with million-dollar jury awards in seven cases including an eight-million dollar wrongful death verdict in Florida federal court. He continues to represent injury and wrongful death clients. Mark Stageberg resides in Minnetonka, Minnesota, and is an avid outdoorsman.